GRIER OF SAN FRANCISCO

William Milton Grier, Sr., 1927

GRIER
OF
SAN FRANCISCO

BUILDER IN THE WEST
AND HIS FAMILY
1878-1988

WILLIAM M. GRIER, JR.

DENVER

GRIER & COMPANY

Copyright © 1989 by William M. Grier, Jr.
All rights reserved. Published
by Grier & Company, Denver, Colorado

Library of Congress Cataloging-in-Publication Data

Grier, William M. (William Milton), 1928–
    Grier of San Francisco.

    Bibliography: p.
    Includes index.
    1. Grier, William Milton, Sr., 1878–1935. 2. Construction
industry--West (U.S.)--Biography. 3. Construction
industry--West (U.S.)--History. 4. Businessmen--
California-- San Francisco--Biography. 5. San Francisco
(Calif.)--History. I. Title.
HD9715.U52G734 1989   338.7'624'0924 [B]   89–5498

ISBN 0-9623268-0-1

Printed in the United States of America

To

my wife

JOAN GRAFMUELLER GRIER

and

the memory of my parents

WILLIAM MILTON GRIER, SR.

and

ELO LANNON GRIER

whose love and humor,

sorrows and triumphs,

verve and fortitude

enriched my life.

ABOUT THE AUTHOR

Born in Oakland, California, Bill was raised in nearby
Piedmont and San Francisco and educated at the
University of California at Berkeley and Columbia
University Business School. He also studied at the
University of Oslo and the Sorbonne. Bill is married,
with a son by his first wife, and lives with his second
wife in Denver, Colorado. He is president of Grier &
Company, management consultants and publishers,
and founder in 1976 of *Real Estate West*, a newspaper
serving the commercial real estate industry from the
Midwest to the Pacific Coast.

...for historians ought to be precise, faithful, and unprejudiced, and neither interest nor fear, hatred nor affection, should make them swerve from the way of truth, whose mother is history, the rival of time, the depository of great actions, the witness of the past, example to the present, and monitor to the future.

—CERVANTES
Don Quixote
(Part I, Chapter 9)

CONTENTS

PART TWO

ELO GRIER AND HER SONS

PART THREE

THE NEXT GENERATION

PART FOUR

ALLIED FAMILIES

ILLUSTRATIONS

xvi

xvii

PREFACE

From his early years in a youthful San Francisco to his service in the Spanish-American War and his major accomplishments in construction and engineering during the first four decades of the twentieth century, my father William Milton Grier, Sr. was an active participant in the development of the American West.

An independent thinker, his talents and entrepreneurial spirit had been nurtured outside the strictures of any establishment. They were expressed early in his career through his work in real estate development, oil exploration, and gold mining and, later, in his extensive railroad and civil construction across the West, where Grier met the challenges of his time and made his most lasting contributions.

Grier's life and career were undoubtedly shaped by the colorful, vibrant era in which he lived—an age in which the United States emerged as the world's industrial leader and the new frontiers to be conquered were no longer geographic, but scientific and technological instead.

Only a small boy when my father died at age fifty-seven in 1935, I, of course, never knew him well. Yet, from our few short years together, I cherish several vivid images of him—teaching me, in his precise hand, to write the alphabet as we sit in the garden of our home in Piedmont, California; chiseling toy locomotives and cars for my brother Eloyd and me; giving us vials of gold—samples from his mining project in the Sierra Nevada.

While growing up in San Francisco, my aunt May Grier Borman told me many stories of her brother and their parents, William John and Georgie Grier; of their illustrious uncle, Thomas Johnston Grier; and of their postmaster-grandfather, James Grier. My mother Elo Lannon Grier also shared her memories and gave me my father's papers, including a brief yet invaluable autobiographical sketch.

In 1972, recognizing that my father's eventful life deserved to be documented and published, I began to compile his biography, hoping to fix this history with the clarity of old photographs and assure that it not be lost to posterity. Later, I also added material on several allied families. My research, conducted while founding and developing my own company and newspaper, took me across two continents—the American West, eastern Canada, and East Africa.

A rewarding labor, this history has evoked the many sides of my father's life through the turbulent decades of the late nineteenth and early twentieth centuries. Moreover, I have "met" such pivotal figures as George and Phoebe Hearst, William Randolph Hearst, Warren Bechtel, Henry J. Kaiser, A.P. Giannini, Judge John Twohy, Bernard Maybeck, Julia Morgan, Templeton Crocker, Herbert Fleishhacker, Frank C. Havens, and James D.

Phelan. I have also "lived" through epoch-making events—the discovery of gold and railroad expansion, the Spanish-American War and Philippine Insurrection, the 1906 San Francisco earthquake and the Panama-Pacific International Exhibition, the '29 Crash and Great Depression.

Lastly, I hope that this book, published 111 years after my father's birth, not only captures the essence of his life and accomplishments, but preserves and illuminates this history for new and future generations.

Denver, Colorado   William M. Grier, Jr.
October 1989

ACKNOWLEDGMENTS

For documents, photos, and advice which were crucial to this volume, I thank Elo Lannon Grier, my mother; Eloyd John Grier, my brother; cousins David D.E. Grier, George Ann Palmer, Victoria ("Muddie") Grier Nelsen, and Dorothy Withycomb Miller (Mrs. A. Pirie Miller); Kathleen Zwicker Grier (Mrs. Charles Denham Grier); Raymond Fell Lillie, grandson of Anne M. Grier (Mrs. A. Gilbert Fell); Donald H. McLaughlin, late president of Homestake Mining Company; Mildred Fielder, author of *The Treasure of Homestake Gold*; Madge Ferrie Christie; Virginia Havens Gowing; John H. Nopel, historian of Butte County, California; and Donald D. Toms, co-director of the Black Hills Mining Museum in Lead, South Dakota.

In addition, I thank William P. Banning, Jr. (Muddie Grier's son by her first husband); Joan Taylor Grier Bird (adopted daughter of Ormonde Palethorpe Grier); and John S. Mead (son of Winfield Scott Mead, partner in Grier and Mead).

Allied family papers and photographs were graciously provided by Joan Grafmueller Grier, my wife; by my cousins Wilma Henn Tamblyn, James Morrison Knapp, Margaret Wright Gallaway, Deirdrellen Dickson Peterson, Maureen Connolly Merritt, and Edwin Wallace Flanagan; and by Eleanor Grant (Mrs. Will Brewer Grant), Albert M. Grafmueller, and Adelaide Brownlee Bolton Meister.

My gratitude, too, to the librarians at the following institutions: *in the United States*—California State Library (California Section) in Sacramento; Sutro Library, a branch of the C.S.L. in San Francisco; California Historical Society Library in San Francisco; Bancroft Library at University of California, Berkeley; Natural History Museum of Los Angeles County; Meriam Library Special Collection, California State University at Chico; Oregon State Historical Society Library in Portland; Genealogical Library of the Church of Jesus Christ of Latter-Day Saints in Salt Lake City, Utah; and New York Genealogical and Biographical Society in New York City; *in Canada*—Anglican Church of Canada, Dioceses of Ottawa, Montreal, and Ontario; Public Archives Canada in Ottawa; the Archives of Ontario in Toronto; National Postal Museum in Ottawa; Iroquois Public Library in Iroquois, Ontario; National Library of Canada in Ottawa; Stormont, Dundas and Glengarry Historical Society in Ontario; and Glengarry Genealogical Society in Ontario.

I am grateful to the staffs at the main public libraries in San Francisco, Oakland, Sacramento, and Oroville, California; Portland, Oregon; Ogden and Salt Lake City, Utah; Helena, Montana; Lead and Deadwood, South Dakota; Denver, Colorado; and New York City, New York.

Special thanks are due to the staff of the *Lead Daily Call* in Lead, South Dakota, who provided me with editorials regarding T.J. Grier and the Homestake Mining Company; to John D. Russell, director emeritus of Menlo College, for his thoughtful reading and helpful suggestions on a portion of the manuscript; to Eleanor Keats and Dena R. Savin, editors of the first draft of this biography; to Joy Townsend, who entered the text in the computer and organized the mass of files; and to Laura E. Vance, my indispensable assistant, who patiently incorporated the many revisions.

Finally, Joan W. Sherman has rendered invaluable assistance in editing and shaping the final draft; the book in its present form would never have seen the light of day but for her.

GRIER COAT OF ARMS

The Grier coat of arms illustrated above was drawn by a heraldic artist from information officially recorded in ancient heraldic archives and documented in Burke's General Armory. Heraldic artists of old developed their own unique language to describe an individual coat of arms. In their language, the arms (shield) is as follows:

> Az. a lion ramp. or, armed and langued gu. betw. three antique crowns of the second, on a canton ar. an oak tree eradicated, surmounted by a sword in bend cinister, ensigned on the point with a royal crown all ppr.

Above the shield and helmet is the crest which is described as:

> An eagle displayed ppr. charged on the breast with a quadrangular lock ar.

When translated, the blazon also describes the original colors of the Grier arms and crest as they appeared centuries ago.

Family mottos are believed to have originated as battle cries in medieval times. The motto recorded with this Grier coat of arms was: *Memor Esto.*

THE GRIER FAMILY

Genealogical Tree of William Milton Grier, Sr.

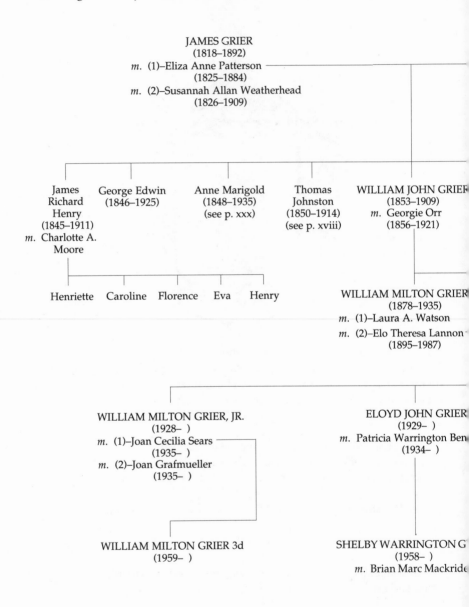

JAMES GRIER
(1818–1892)
m. (1)–Eliza Anne Patterson
(1825–1884)
m. (2)–Susannah Allan Weatherhead
(1826–1909)

James Richard Henry (1845–1911) *m.* Charlotte A. Moore

George Edwin (1846–1925)

Anne Marigold (1848–1935) (see p. xxx)

Thomas Johnston (1850–1914) (see p. xviii)

WILLIAM JOHN GRIER (1853–1909) *m.* Georgie Orr (1856–1921)

Henriette   Caroline   Florence   Eva   Henry

WILLIAM MILTON GRIER (1878–1935)
m. (1)–Laura A. Watson
m. (2)–Elo Theresa Lannon (1895–1987)

WILLIAM MILTON GRIER, JR.
(1928–)
m. (1)–Joan Cecilia Sears (1935–)
m. (2)–Joan Grafmueller (1935–)

ELOYD JOHN GRIER
(1929–)
m. Patricia Warrington Ben (1934–)

WILLIAM MILTON GRIER 3d
(1959–)

SHELBY WARRINGTON G
(1958–)
m. Brian Marc Mackride

* *Name changed to Marigold in next generation.*
** *Daughter died in infancy.*

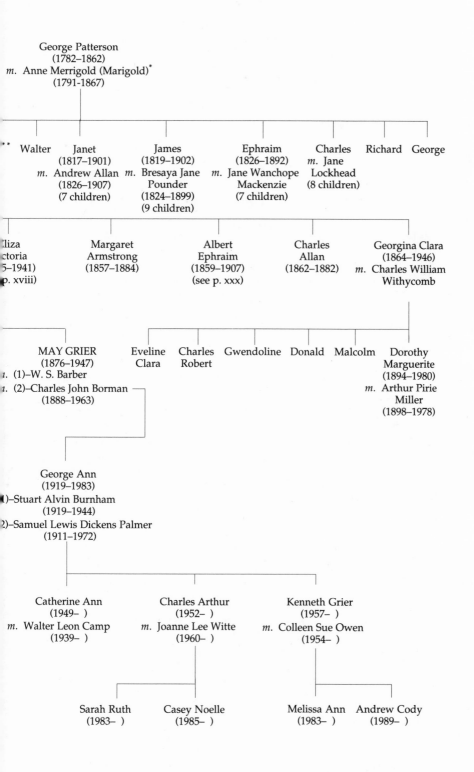

George Patterson
(1782–1862)
m. Anne Merrigold (Marigold)*
(1791-1867)

** Walter   Janet   James   Ephraim   Charles   Richard   George
           (1817–1901)   (1819–1902)   (1826–1892)   *m.* Jane
           m. Andrew Allan   *m.* Bresaya Jane   *m.* Jane Wanchope   Lockhead
             (1826–1907)   Pounder   Mackenzie   (8 children)
             (7 children)   (1824–1899)   (7 children)
                         (9 children)

liza   Margaret   Albert   Charles   Georgina Clara
ctoria   Armstrong   Ephraim   Allan   (1864–1946)
5–1941)   (1857–1884)   (1859–1907)   (1862–1882)   *m.* Charles William
p. xviii)   (see p. xxx)   Withycomb

      MAY GRIER   Eveline   Charles   Gwendoline   Donald   Malcolm   Dorothy
      (1876–1947)   Clara   Robert   Marguerite
1. (1)–W. S. Barber   (1894–1980)
1. (2)–Charles John Borman ——   *m.* Arthur Pirie
     (1888–1963)   Miller
                                           (1898–1978)

     George Ann
     (1919–1983)
4)–Stuart Alvin Burnham
   (1919–1944)
2)–Samuel Lewis Dickens Palmer
   (1911–1972)

     Catherine Ann   Charles Arthur   Kenneth Grier
       (1949–)   (1952–)   (1957–)
m. Walter Leon Camp   *m.* Joanne Lee Witte   *m.* Colleen Sue Owen
      (1939–)   (1960–)   (1954–)

         Sarah Ruth   Casey Noelle   Melissa Ann   Andrew Cody
          (1983–)   (1985–)   (1983–)   (1989–)

THE GRIER FAMILY

Genealogical Trees of Thomas Johnston Grier, Sr. and
Eliza V. Grier (Mrs. Arthur J. Williams)

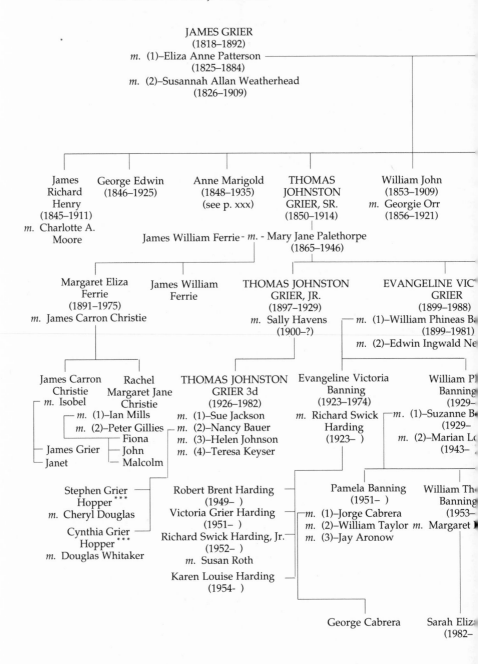

JAMES GRIER
(1818–1892)
m. (1)–Eliza Anne Patterson
(1825–1884)
m. (2)–Susannah Allan Weatherhead
(1826–1909)

James Richard Henry (1845–1911) *m.* Charlotte A. Moore

George Edwin (1846–1925)

Anne Marigold (1848–1935) (see p. xxx)

THOMAS JOHNSTON GRIER, SR. (1850–1914)

William John (1853–1909) *m.* Georgie Orr (1856–1921)

James William Ferrie - *m.* - Mary Jane Palethorpe (1865–1946)

Margaret Eliza Ferrie (1891–1975) *m.* James Carron Christie

James William Ferrie

THOMAS JOHNSTON GRIER, JR. (1897–1929) *m.* Sally Havens (1900–?)

EVANGELINE VIC' GRIER (1899–1988) *m.* (1)–William Phineas B. (1899–1981) *m.* (2)–Edwin Ingwald Ne

James Carron Christie *m.* Isobel *m.* (1)–Ian Mills *m.* (2)–Peter Gillies Fiona James Grier John Janet Malcolm

Rachel Margaret Jane Christie

THOMAS JOHNSTON GRIER 3d (1926–1982) *m.* (1)–Sue Jackson *m.* (2)–Nancy Bauer *m.* (3)–Helen Johnson *m.* (4)–Teresa Keyser

Evangeline Victoria Banning (1923–1974) *m.* Richard Swick Harding (1923–)

William Pl Banning (1929– *m.* (1)–Suzanne B (1929– *m.* (2)–Marian L (1943–

Stephen Grier Hopper*** *m.* Cheryl Douglas Cynthia Grier Hopper*** *m.* Douglas Whitaker

Robert Brent Harding (1949–) Victoria Grier Harding (1951–) Richard Swick Harding, Jr. (1952–) *m.* Susan Roth Karen Louise Harding (1954–)

Pamela Banning (1951–) *m.* (1)–Jorge Cabrera *m.* (2)–William Taylor *m.* (3)–Jay Aronow

William Th Banning (1953– *m.* Margaret M

George Cabrera

Sarah Eliz (1982–

---

* *Name changed to Marigold in next generation.*
** *Daughter died in infancy.*
*** *Adopted by Jack Hopper (Nancy B. Grier's second husband).*
**** *Adopted by Ormande P. Grier.*

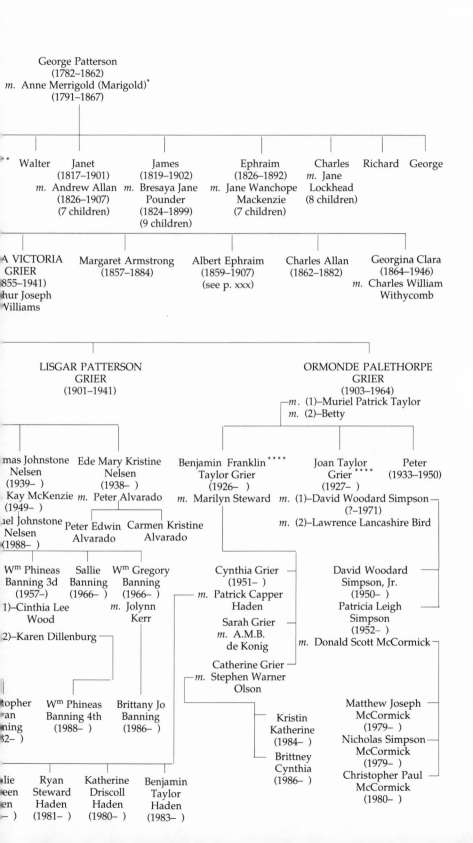

George Patterson
(1782–1862)
m. Anne Merrigold (Marigold)*
(1791–1867)

Walter
(1817–1901)
m. Andrew Allan
(1826–1907)
(7 children)

Janet
(1819–1902)
m. Bresaya Jane
Pounder
(1824–1899)
(9 children)

James

Ephraim
(1826–1892)
m. Jane Wanchope
Mackenzie
(7 children)

Charles
m. Jane
Lockhead
(8 children)

Richard   George

A VICTORIA
GRIER
855–1941)
hur Joseph
Williams

Margaret Armstrong
(1857–1884)

Albert Ephraim
(1859–1907)
(see p. xxx)

Charles Allan
(1862–1882)

Georgina Clara
(1864–1946)
m. Charles William
Withycomb

LISGAR PATTERSON
GRIER
(1901–1941)

ORMONDE PALETHORPE
GRIER
(1903–1964)
m. (1)–Muriel Patrick Taylor
m. (2)–Betty

mas Johnstone
Nelsen
(1939–)
Kay McKenzie
(1949–)
uel Johnstone
Nelsen
(1988–)

Ede Mary Kristine
Nelsen
(1938–)
m. Peter Alvarado

Peter Edwin
Alvarado

Carmen Kristine
Alvarado

Benjamin Franklin****
Taylor Grier
(1926–)
m. Marilyn Steward

Joan Taylor
Grier****
(1927–)
m. (1)–David Woodard Simpson
(?–1971)
m. (2)–Lawrence Lancashire Bird

Peter
(1933–1950)

Wᵐ Phineas
Banning 3d
(1957–)
1)–Cinthia Lee
Wood
2)–Karen Dillenburg

Sallie
Banning
(1966–)

Wᵐ Gregory
Banning
(1966–)
m. Jolynn
Kerr

Cynthia Grier
(1951–)
m. Patrick Capper
Haden

Sarah Grier
m. A.M.B.
de Konig

Catherine Grier
m. Stephen Warner
Olson

David Woodard
Simpson, Jr.
(1950–)
Patricia Leigh
Simpson
(1952–)
m. Donald Scott McCormick

topher
van
ning
2–)

Wᵐ Phineas
Banning 4th
(1988–)

Brittany Jo
Banning
(1986–)

Kristin
Katherine
(1984–)
Brittney
Cynthia
(1986–)

Matthew Joseph
McCormick
(1979–)
Nicholas Simpson
McCormick
(1979–)
Christopher Paul
McCormick
(1980–)

lie
een
en
–)

Ryan
Steward
Haden
(1981–)

Katherine
Driscoll
Haden
(1980–)

Benjamin
Taylor
Haden
(1983–)

THE GRIER FAMILY

Genealogical Trees of Anne M. Grier
(Mrs. A. Gilbert Fell) and C. Denham Grier

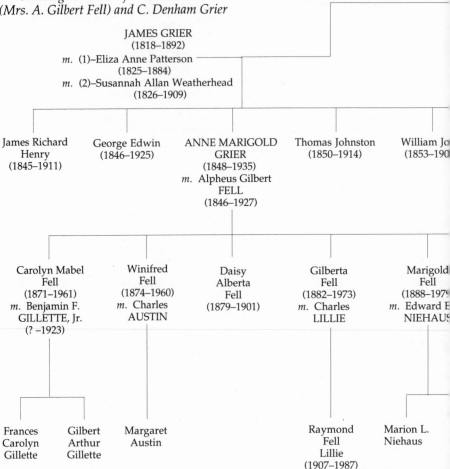

JAMES GRIER
(1818–1892)
m. (1)–Eliza Anne Patterson
(1825–1884)
m. (2)–Susannah Allan Weatherhead
(1826–1909)

| James Richard Henry (1845–1911) | George Edwin (1846–1925) | ANNE MARIGOLD GRIER (1848–1935) m. Alpheus Gilbert FELL (1846–1927) | Thomas Johnston (1850–1914) | William Jo (1853–190 |

| Carolyn Mabel Fell (1871–1961) m. Benjamin F. GILLETTE, Jr. (? –1923) | Winifred Fell (1874–1960) m. Charles AUSTIN | Daisy Alberta Fell (1879–1901) | Gilberta Fell (1882–1973) m. Charles LILLIE | Marigold Fell (1888–197! m. Edward E NIEHAUS |

| Frances Carolyn Gillette | Gilbert Arthur Gillette | Margaret Austin | | Raymond Fell Lillie (1907–1987) | Marion L. Niehaus |

* *Name changed to Marigold in next generation.*
** *Daughter died in infancy.*
*** *Couple has chosen to remain unmarried.*

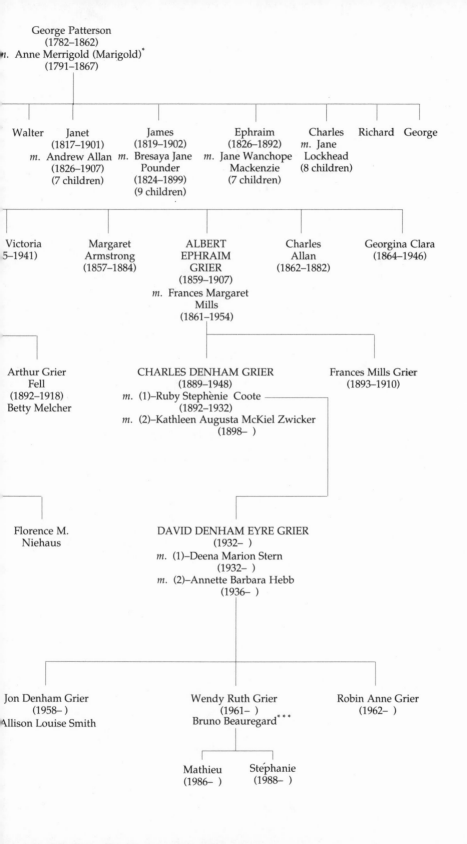

George Patterson
(1782–1862)
m. Anne Merrigold (Marigold)*
(1791–1867)

Walter | Janet | James | Ephraim | Charles | Richard | George
(1817–1901)	(1819–1902)	(1826–1892)	*m.* Jane	
m. Andrew Allan	*m.* Bresaya Jane	*m.* Jane Wanchope	Lockhead	
(1826–1907)	Pounder	Mackenzie	(8 children)	
(7 children)	(1824–1899)	(7 children)		
	(9 children)			

Victoria | Margaret | ALBERT | Charles | Georgina Clara
5–1941) | Armstrong | EPHRAIM | Allan | (1864–1946)
(1857–1884)	GRIER	(1862–1882)
	(1859–1907)	
	m. Frances Margaret	
	Mills	
	(1861–1954)	

Arthur Grier | CHARLES DENHAM GRIER | Frances Mills Grier
Fell | (1889–1948) | (1893–1910)
(1892–1918) | *m.* (1)–Ruby Stephènie Coote
Betty Melcher | (1892–1932)
| *m.* (2)–Kathleen Augusta McKiel Zwicker
| (1898–)

Florence M. | DAVID DENHAM EYRE GRIER
Niehaus | (1932–)
| *m.* (1)–Deena Marion Stern
| (1932–)
| *m.* (2)–Annette Barbara Hebb
| (1936–)

Jon Denham Grier | Wendy Ruth Grier | Robin Anne Grier
(1958–) | (1961–) | (1962–)
Allison Louise Smith | Bruno Beauregard***

Mathieu | Stéphanie
(1986–) | (1988–)

PART ONE

WILLIAM MILTON GRIER, SR.
1878–1935

CHRONOLOGY OF WILLIAM M. GRIER, SR.

1878   Born in San Francisco, California on September 24

1883–1888   Attends Lincoln School in San Francisco

1888   Moves with family to Palermo, California

1895   Graduates from high school at age sixteen in June;
            joins Bills & Putnam's general merchandise store in
            Oroville, California

1896   Opens own general merchandise store in Palermo

1898   Sells business; enlists in First Regiment California
            U.S. Volunteers (Spanish-American War and Philippine
            Insurrection) on July 20; trains at the Presidio in San
            Francisco from July to October

1898–1899   Serves in Philippines from December 11 to July 23

1899   Visits Japan during summer; returns to San Francisco on
            August 24; mustered out of service on September 21;
            hired by Phoebe Hearst to work with Hearst Real Estate
            and Development Company in San Francisco, embark-
            ing on career in construction, in November

1901   Promoted to position with Hearst Oil Company

1902–1903   Tutored by University of California-Berkeley professor
            in metallurgy and mining engineering (arranged by
            Phoebe Hearst)

1903   Works for Phoebe Hearst at Homestake Mining Com-
            pany in Lead, South Dakota; returns to California in
            December, supervising Hearst gold mining projects in
            Palermo

1904   Marries Laura A. Watson on June 20; joins Twohy
            Brothers Company in San Francisco in October

1904–1907	With Twohy Brothers, works on Southern Pacific Railroad's Bayshore Cutoff project in San Francisco
1906	San Francisco earthquake on April 18
1906–1909	Made partner in Twohy Brothers Company; supervises North Bank project in Washington State
1909	Father, William John Grier, dies in Oakland, California on June 25
1909–1919	Continues with Twohy Brothers, working on Deschutes project and various contracts in Montana, Washington State, Oregon, and western Canada
1914	Uncle, T.J. Grier, Sr., dies in Los Angeles, California on September 22
1915	Visits Panama Pacific International Exhibition in San Francisco; visits cousin, Charles Denham Grier, in Treadwell, Alaska
1919	Forms General Construction Company in Oregon on January 29; forms Boschke Miller Grier Company in Oregon in May
1921	Mother, Georgie Orr Grier, dies in Oakland on October 23; divorces Laura Watson Grier; purchases partners' interest in Boschke Miller Grier Company and relocates to San Francisco in December; acquires 40% interest in Erickson Petterson Company in San Francisco and changes its name to Erickson Petterson Grier Company
1923	Erickson Petterson Grier awarded contract for Southern Pacific Railroad's Blue Canyon-Emigrant Gap project in January
1925	Erickson Petterson Grier dissolved on November 2; forms Grier and Mead in San Francisco with partner Winfield Scott Mead (offices move to Oakland in 1927)
1926	Grier and Mead awarded contract for construction of Claremont water tunnel in Orinda and Oakland, California in July

1927	Marries Elo Theresa Lannon in Reno, Nevada on November 9; moves into Piedmont, California home on November 19
1928	Son, William Milton Grier, Jr., born in Oakland on September 23
1929	Son, Eloyd John Grier, born in San Francisco on July 4; private yacht, *ELOGRIER*, completed; stock market crashes on October 29
1930	Suffers first heart attack
1933	Suffers second heart attack
1934	Kidnapped in Sacramento, California; forms Grier and Fontaine, gold mining firm; moves family to Sacramento in fall; leases out Piedmont home
1935	Dies in Sacramento on December 8, after third heart attack, at age fifty-seven

1

HERITAGE

"Oh, here's a warning
San Francisco has only one drawback
'Tis hard to leave."
—Rudyard Kipling

William Milton Grier was the embodiment of the self-made man. With modest beginnings as the son of a San Francisco bookkeeper, he completed his high school education by sixteen and opened his first business just two years later. Gifted and industrious, he built a remarkable career over the next two decades and was, by the age of forty, one of the leading entrepreneurs in the West.

Born in the last quarter of the nineteenth century, Grier came of age during a period of vast expansionism in the West. Through his subsequent work in engineering and construction, he became a contributor to the growth of the American frontier—growth which brought him both professional acclaim and wealth.

The forces acting upon William Milton Grier's life were multiple: the urban—birth and early years in San Francisco; the bucolic—adolescence in a small northern California town in the Sierra foothills; the patriotic—service in the Spanish-American War; the altruistic—the beneficence of Phoebe Hearst; the eruptive—the 1906 San Francisco earthquake; and the expansive—the feverish growth of the western states, which opened opportunities and stirred prospective entrepreneurs to action.

His friends and competitors in the construction industry included Henry J. Kaiser and Warren A. Bechtel. Another friend, Amadeo P. Giannini, founder of the Bank of Italy (later known as Bank of America), financed many of Grier's railroad and civil construction projects.

Grier's professional life touched on gold mining, railroads, construction, real estate, and oil. It led him to the Pacific Northwest, the Rocky Mountain West, and western Canada; to Lead, South Dakota and Palermo, California; to Japan and the Philippines; and repeatedly it brought him back to his native city, San Francisco.

SCOT FOREBEARS

Grier's family can be traced back to the Middle Ages, that period in western Europe preceding the formation of nation-states. The surname Grier (also spelled Greer) is an abbreviation of Grierson, both names having been a "sept," or division, of the Scottish Macgregor clan, whose members were direct descendants of the Albanich or Alpinian aboriginal inhabitants of Scotland.

It is believed that Grier's Scot forebears first settled in Dumfries-shire, coming from the Highlands of Scotland at the beginning of the 1400s. Two centuries later, when the persecution of the Macgregors was at its worst, many Griers emigrated to Northern Ireland and, eventually, to Canada and the United States.

The Scottish estate of Straharlie was owned by one line of the Grier family. The original owner's eldest son became a Knight Banneret and was granted the title of Sir James Grier, Knight. In time, James's son Henry migrated to Ireland, where he lived in County Tyrone at Radford near Grange and became the ancestral head of the family of Greer of Grange MacGregor.

Other Griers settled in Ireland's County Antrim, where the 1669 Hearth Money Roll includes: Ffranc Greer, Dreen Townland, Parish of Craigs; Thomas Greer, Ballee Townland, Parish of Connor; and William Greer, Craigfaddock Townland, Parish of Dunghy.

EASTERN CANADA, 1800s

William Milton Grier's paternal grandfather James was born in Northern Ireland in 1818. In the late 1830s, he emigrated to Upper Canada (now Ontario) and settled in Pakenham. In the early years, he worked as a carriage- and sleigh-maker, and it was in Perth, Upper Canada that he met and married Eliza Anne Patterson on July 4, 1844 in the Episcopal Church of St. James.

Born in 1825, Eliza Anne, a Perth native, was the second daughter of George Patterson and Anne Merrigold (later changed to Marigold). (See Allied Families: Patterson)

James and Eliza Grier first lived in Perth, where their son James Richard Henry (1845–1911) was born. In 1846, they moved to Pakenham, thirty-two miles to the northeast, where three more children followed: George Edwin (1846–1925), Anne Marigold (1848–1935), and Thomas Johnston ("T.J.") (1850–1914).

In 1851, the family moved to Matilda Township (later renamed Iroquois), fifty-five miles southeast of Pakenham on the St. Lawrence River. Six years later, James was elected to the first Iroquois town council. He was appointed postmaster of Iroquois in 1860.

The Griers' fifth child, William John— who would become William

8

Milton Grier's father—was born in Iroquois on June 19, 1853. Following him came five other children: Eliza Victoria (1855–1941), Margaret ("Maggie") Armstrong (1857–1884), Albert Ephraim (1859–1907), Charles Allan (1862–1882), and Georgina Clara (1864–1946). All the children were baptized at St. John's Episcopal Church in Iroquois.

While growing up in Iroquois, William John and his brothers and sisters clerked in their father's post office. They helped sort and deliver mail, learned bookkeeping, and became telegraph operators. These skills later proved invaluable to William John and T.J. when they emigrated to the American West.

AMERICAN WEST, 1870s

In 1872, nineteen-year-old William John moved to the American West from Montreal, where he had joined brother T.J., three years his senior, to work as a telegrapher at Montreal Telegraph Company. (Their sister Anne and her Canadian husband A. Gilbert Fell had preceded them, moving to Ogden, Utah two years earlier.) He and T.J. then became telegraphers in Denver, Colorado and, later, in Corrine and Salt Lake City, Utah.

While working in Salt Lake City, William John met and married Georgie Orr in 1875; T.J. was his best man. His bride, born in Kansas City, Missouri on August 5, 1856, was the daughter of Joseph Milton Orr and Martha H. Whitney. [1]

William John and Georgie's first child, May, was born in Salt Lake City in 1876, the year the nation celebrated its centennial birthday. At that time, the United States had a population of only forty million, and just thirty-eight stars flew on its flag.

Two years later, the brothers parted. T.J. headed east to the Black Hills of the Dakota Territory, joining Homestake Mining Company as a bookkeeper and telegrapher in Lead. William John moved west: he, Georgie, daughter May, and in-laws Joseph and Martha Orr traveled by train from Salt Lake City on the transcontinental railroad (which joined the Union Pacific and Central Pacific lines), arriving in Oakland, California in the spring of 1878. Sea gulls wheeled about the deck as they boarded the ferry for the short trip across San Francisco Bay, where three-masted schooners dotted the harbor about them.

---

1. Joseph Milton Orr was born in Ohio in 1829. His father was born in Kentucky, his mother in New York. Martha H. Whitney, Georgie Grier's mother, was born in Illinois in 1837. Martha's father was a Vermont native and her mother, from Kentucky. Georgie had one sister, Mattie Orr.

In San Francisco, William John continued as bookkeeper and telegrapher with Western Union Telegraph Company, and it was there that his son William Milton was born on September 24, 1878. Two years later, William John was reassigned by his firm, and the young family lived less than a year in Napa, California from 1880 to 1881. They returned to San Francisco in 1881 when he accepted a position as bookkeeper and supervisor of telegraphers with the Central Pacific Railroad (later named Southern Pacific Railroad Company).

A. Gilbert Fell, the husband of William John's sister Anne, had been superintendent of the Central Pacific in Ogden, Utah. His tenure there coincided with the completion of the transcontinental railroad on May 10, 1869 in nearby Promontory Point—and produced an amusing anecdote as well.

To celebrate the historic connection of the nation's first coast-to-coast railroad, officials had decided to "broadcast" via telegraph the exact moment when the east- and west-bound tracks were joined. To do this, one telegraph line was attached to the project's last spike and another to a silver sledgehammer. Leland Stanford, one of the "Big Four" of the Central Pacific Railroad in California and the firm's president, was given the honor of hammering in that last spike. Amidst great fanfare, he stood by the track, raised his silver sledgehammer, swung down, and completely missed his mark.

Fortunately, a quick-witted Gilbert Fell was on hand to save the day by immediately simulating the blow with his telegraph key, thereby flashing the message to President Ulysses S. Grant in the White House.

Like Anne Grier and her brothers, Gilbert had learned to operate the telegraph in James Grier's Iroquois post office. In later years, Fell pursued a successful political career, serving two terms as mayor of Ogden, Utah from 1911 to 1915.

10

Top, Georgie Orr Grier
in San Francisco, c.
1880s

Middle, Georgie Orr in Salt
Lake City, c. 1870

Bottom, William John Grier, c.
1890s

11

Anne Marigold Grier Fell,
c. 1900

Martha H. Whitney
(Mrs. Joseph Milton Orr),
c. 1872

2

EARLY YEARS IN SAN FRANCISCO
1878–1888

When William Milton Grier was born in San Francisco on September 24, 1878, his native town was a vibrant city of 230,000 people, with another 50,000 residents living in the towns around the Bay. Robert Louis Stevenson described its magnetic qualities in an 1882 article, "San Francisco—A Modern Cosmopolis":

> A great city covers the sand hills on the west, a growing town lies along the muddy shallows of the east; steamboats pass continually between them from before sunrise til the small hours of the morning; lines of great seagoing ships lie at anchor; colors fly upon the islands; and from all around the hum of corporate life, of beaten bells, and steam, and running carriages, goes cheerily abroad in the sunshine....The town is essentially not Anglo-Saxon; still more not American. The Yankee and the Englishman find themselves alike in a strange country.[1]

CITY'S HISTORY

At the time of Grier's birth, San Francisco was the financial capital of the West. Just a small Mexican village in the 1840s, by 1878 it had become one of the major cities in the United States. Unlike the typical frontier city, which developed gradually from an agricultural base, San Francisco was almost immediately a center of commerce, transportation, communication, and finance.

But some 100 years before Grier's birth, San Francisco was itself being born. Although Gaspar De Portola's expeditionary forces had discovered San Francisco Bay in 1769, the city's official birthday was celebrated on June 29, 1776, the date of the first mass at Mission San Francisco de Asis (Mission Dolores), the sixth religious center in Father Junipero Serra's chain of Spanish missions. In 1821, the area was transferred from Spanish to Mexican possession.

In the mid-1830s, a sleepy village named Yerba Buena (after a sweet-smelling local herb) grew up around a cove where ships anchored.

---

1. Cited in Katharine D. Osbourne, *Robert Louis Stevenson in California* (Chicago: A.C. McClurg & Co., 1911), pp. 53-55.

English-speaking Californians launched and won a short-lived revolt against Mexican rule—The Bear-Flag Rebellion—in June 1846. Several weeks later, the area was absorbed by the United States, and in the following year, the village of Yerba Buena was renamed San Francisco.

Shortly thereafter, in 1848, gold was discovered in the foothills of the Sierra Nevada, 150 miles to the east at Sutter's Mill in Coloma, California. As a result, the population of San Francisco soared from less than 1,000 in 1849 to over 50,000 by 1855. By the time of William Milton Grier's birth some twenty-three years later, the city's population had increased nearly five-fold.

With the unbridled growth came wild times, fast fortunes, and an explosively alive city. San Francisco in 1878 was a lawless, roaring, exciting town, a city of courage and luck. Violence was still a part of life there, and many men routinely carried guns.

LIFE IN THE CITY, 1870s–1880s

Grier spent the first nine years of his life in this stimulating San Francisco environment.[2] At the time, the city consisted of long blocks of narrow, two-story houses, their bay windows protruding. (In this city of frequent fog and chill winds, bay windows in the front parlor and the master bedroom were a necessity.) The streets were paved with cobblestones or planking and edged by board sidewalks.

William Milton (called "Milt" or "Billy" by his family) and his sister May attended Lincoln Grammar School on Fifth Street just south of Market Street—a four-story brick structure where 1,386 pupils were enrolled; Milt completed the first five years of his schooling there.[3] His family worshipped at Trinity Church, on Post and Powell Streets, and at Grace Church, on California and Stockton Streets, where the children attended Sunday school.

---

2. From 1878 to 1880, the Griers lived at 417 Mason Street; in 1880, they moved to 1719 Jessie Street, which runs between Market and Mission Streets. Milt's father was then transferred to Western Union's office in Napa, California. In 1881, however, he returned to San Francisco after joining the Central Pacific Railroad Company. From 1881 to 1884, the Griers lived at 22 1/2 Langton Street; from 1885 to 1888, at 11 Langton Street between 7th and 8th and Howard and Folsom Streets. (The two-story structure at 22 and 22 1/2 Langton still stands there today.)

3. First named in honor of the martyred president, the school burned on Washington's birthday in 1871. Reconstructed that same year, it was totally destroyed in the fire of 1906. David Belasco, the theatrical producer, was a member of the first graduating class and organized the Lincoln School Alumni Association.

Young Milt and May loved to climb the city's many steep hills with their mother and father. Together they walked to the top of Telegraph Hill or Russian Hill or Nob Hill, the three highest points in the northeast section. From that vantage point, William John and Georgie could show the children that San Francisco was almost an island, with the Pacific Ocean on the west, San Francisco Bay on the east, and the Golden Gate Straits on the north.

From Telegraph Hill, they could also see the many schooners sailing off to far-away places and the tall clipper ships bringing goods from the East Coast and the Orient. They watched the steam schooners that brought lumber for local building and took other cargo north to Puget Sound and Alaska, and the ferryboats making their twenty-minute run from Oakland to San Francisco.

In fair weather on Sundays and holidays during the 1880s, the Griers and the Orrs (Georgie Grier's parents) often went on picnics and promenades to Golden Gate Park, to Pacific beaches, and to Cliff House, overlooking the ocean. For these trips, they boarded horse-drawn streetcars or horse-and-buggies on Market Street in downtown San Francisco.

William John and Georgie also took Milt and May on outings around the city by horse trolley or the newer cable car. Public transportation was expanding rapidly during the 1880s and featured horse-drawn street-cars running between the business center of the city and the outlying industrial and residential areas. Five years before Milt's birth, Andrew Hallidie's plan to bury a moving cable in a slot beneath the trolley tracks, to which the cars could be attached by a device called a "gripping clamp," had also been put into operation, and in October 1873, the first cable car began its climb up Clay Street. (Sixty-six years later, in 1939, when Milt's widow Elo and his two sons lived in a third-floor walk-up apartment on Clay off Hyde Street, the cable car continued to run past their building.)

Out in the city at dusk, Milt and May watched as the lamplighter came around with his torch, placed his ladder against lampposts on the street corners, then climbed up to ignite the gas jets whose flames glowed softly up and down the streets.

During the summers in San Francisco when Milt was eight and nine years old, his family and friends crossed San Francisco Bay to camp on the beach near beautiful Sausalito in Marin County. At such times, William John would commute to work on the ferry from Sausalito to San Francisco every morning and return to the little tent colony each night.

The Griers sometimes lunched in the Cliff House at Point Lobos Avenue and Great Highway. Through its glass walls, they could look beyond Seal Rocks for miles across the Pacific, and the setting on a cliff was a perfect departure point for strolls along the beach. (The Cliff House had been purchased by Adolph Sutro in 1879, but fifteen years later, on Christmas Day, it burned to the ground. A second Cliff House was erected in 1896;

ten years later, during the earthquake of 1906, it was thrown from its foundation and fell into the ocean.)

JAMES AND ELIZA GRIER IN RETIREMENT

William John and Georgie also enjoyed dining and entertaining out-of-town family and friends at San Francisco's Palace Hotel. Among their special guests in the fall of 1883 were William John's parents James and Eliza and his sister Maggie. After more than twenty-three years in the Canadian Postal Service as postmaster of Iroquois, Ontario, James Grier had retired on June 11, 1883. Soon after, he and Eliza and their ailing daughter Maggie visited their four children in the American West. In Lead, South Dakota, they saw their thirty-three-year-old son Thomas Johnston, a bachelor who was working as a bookkeeper for Homestake Mining Company. They then stopped in Denver to visit with son Albert Ephraim, a young, unmarried attorney. On their way to the West Coast, they visited with their daughter Annie, her husband A. Gilbert Fell, and their children in Ogden, Utah.[4] Arriving at last in California, the Griers were reunited with their son William John, his wife Georgie, children Milt and May, and Georgie's parents Joseph Milton and Martha Orr.

James, Eliza, and Maggie soon settled in Anaheim, California, but despite the favorable climate, Maggie, who suffered from tuberculosis, was never able to regain her health. She died and was buried there in the spring of 1884.

Missing Canada and mourning their daughter's death, James and Eliza returned to Montreal that spring. En route, they revisited William John and his family in San Francisco and attended the wedding of their lawyer son, Albert Ephraim, in Denver. Albert married his Iroquois, On-

---

4. Anne ("Annie") Marigold Grier (May 27, 1848–October 28, 1935) had married Alpheus Gilbert Fell (March 13, 1846–December 28, 1927) at St. John's Church in Iroquois on October 13, 1870. The ceremony was performed by J.A. Anderson.

The Fells had six children: 1). Carolyn ("Carrie") Mabel Fell (September 2, 1871–November 17, 1961) who married Benjamin F. Gillette, Jr. (b.?–1923) and had two children—Frances Carolyn Gillette and Gilbert Arthur ("Bud") Gillette; 2). Winifred ("Winnie") Fell (April 20, 1874–December 13, 1960) who married Charles Austin and had one child, Margaret Austin; 3). Daisy Alberta Fell (1879–November 18, 1901) who never married before dying in her early twenties at William John and Georgie Grier's home in Palermo; 4). Gilberta Fell (1882–1973) who married Charles Lillie and had one son, Raymond Fell Lillie; 5). Marigold ("Goldie") Fell (1888–September 12, 1979) who married Edward E. Niehaus in 1910 and had two children — Marion Niehaus Wiggins and Florence ("Billie") Niehaus Glaser; and 6). Arthur Grier Fell (June 14, 1892–March 31, 1918) who married Betty Melcher and had no children.

Annie Grier Fell died on October 28, 1935 at the home of her daughter Gilberta Fell Lillie in San Francisco.

tario girlfriend, Frances Margaret Mills, on April 28, 1884 in St. John's Episcopal Cathedral in the Wilderness. The bride's father, an Iroquois merchant named Cephas Mills, also attended.

Shortly after the Griers re-settled in Montreal, Eliza died suddenly while visiting her daughter Georgina Clara, on October 14, 1884. Two days later, she was buried next to her youngest son, Charles Allan (1862–1882), in St. John's Episcopal Cemetery in Iroquois.

On June 17, 1886, at the age of sixty-eight, James Grier married Susannah Allan Weatherhead, a fifty-nine-year-old widow, in St. Andrew's Presbyterian Church in Perth, Ontario. The couple then took up residence on Drummond Street in Perth. (Ironically, Susannah's brother Andrew Allan was married to Eliza's oldest sister, Janet Patterson.)

Nearly six years after his marriage to Susannah, James Grier died of a heart attack in Toronto on May 11, 1892. He was buried beside his first wife, Eliza, and his son Charles Allan, who had died of tuberculosis at twenty, while he and brother Albert Ephraim were studying law at Osgoode Hall in Toronto. Surviving James by seventeen years, Susannah died on April 11, 1909 and was buried in Elmwood Cemetery in Montreal.

San Francisco, c. 1852 (from a Currier and Ives lithograph)

San Francisco, c. 1878 (from a Currier and Ives lithograph)

19

Cliff House, c. 1898 *(Courtesy of the California Historical Society Library)*

Palace Hotel, c. 1900 *(Courtesy of the California Historical Society Library)*

20

St. John's Episcopal Church in the Wilderness, Denver, Colorado, c. 1880s
(*Courtesy of the Denver Public Library Western History Department*)

21

3

PALERMO YEARS
1888–1898

In 1888, William John Grier left his post at Central Pacific to accept a bookkeeping and land management position with Palermo Land and Water Company (PL&W) in Palermo, Butte County, California, located some 160 miles northeast of San Francisco in the foothills of the Sierra Nevada.

First surveyed in 1865, Palermo had long been an agricultural area, where cattle raising was the principal industry and farmers experimented in growing cotton. Sheepherding was introduced in 1870 and became the dominant activity until the fall of 1887, when PL&W was formed. Within five years, cattle, sheep, and grain productivity declined dramatically, while 1,600 acres were planted with oranges, olives, figs, prunes, pears, peaches, apricots, and grapes.

The large northern California citrus fairs of that day were concentrated in the Palermo area. The 1877 fair, for example, was held in Oroville, the old gold mining town five miles north of Palermo that is the county seat of Butte County. When it became clear that oranges and olives could be successfully grown in northern California, this land, which was cheaper than that in southern California, was in great demand.

PALERMO LAND AND WATER COMPANY

The PL&W was formed by the firm of Perkins and Wise, which, in late 1887, acquired the Palermo Ditch from J.B. Hewitt and former California governor F.F. Low. Twenty-five miles long, this ditch conveyed water from the South Fork of the Feather River to Ophir (later named Oroville), making this city the most important mining town in California.

Perkins and Wise owned another 5,000 Palermo acres and needed additional funding to develop a town and orchards on their vast land holding; to that end, they associated themselves with McAfee Brothers, real estate brokers in San Francisco, and began marketing parcels of their property.

Palermo Colony was incorporated on January 7, 1888. By the time Milt Grier's family moved there the following summer, PL&W had already drawn a detailed map of the area, dividing the land into house lots, orchards, and streets and designating sites for a school, park, hotel, railroad depot, and businesses. The even-numbered blocks were sold in San Francisco through McAfee Brothers; odd-numbered ones were offered by T.B. Ludlum and Company in Oroville. Palermo's first land sale occurred after advertising appeared in newspapers in San Francisco and elsewhere on January 19, 1888 in which Palermo was billed as "The Riverside of the North."

In an article published in the October 17, 1890 edition of Palermo's frontier newspaper, the *Progress*, Frank Rutherford described the dramatic metamorphosis of this California town:

> Could one of our citizens of Palermo have stood in this place forty-one years ago, he would have seen in the north the same mountain ranges, in the south and west the same open plains, with the blue Coast Range and the rugged Buttes in the background....He would have seen a band of startled antelope galloping across the prairie or have been greeted by the howl of a coyote, announcing the friendly shades of evening had once more arrived and his predatory raid on his long-eared neighbor was ready to begin, or perhaps he might have seen a red man with his long pole threshing, from the oaks, acorns which he hulled, dried, and placed away for winter store, while his dusky squaw swept the grass with her willow basket, greeting with a glad heart, what is today painful to the ear of the farmer and fruit grower, the snap of the grass-hoppers wing....[By mid-year of 1888] all at once a transformation began and surveyors with their assistants began to wander about and drive down little white stakes seemingly without order....The winter and spring of 1889 developed livelier times than this district ever saw, and clearing, grading avenues, building fences and ditches furnished occupation for upwards of 300 men. Improvements of a permanent character grew rapidly and constantly and many small dwellings were scattered over the colony in all directions.[1]

Palermo's five- and ten-acre house lots sold rapidly at $75 and $100 per acre, attracting many wealthy investors. Among them was Milt's uncle T.J. Grier, then superintendent of the Homestake Mining Company in Lead, South Dakota. On March 22, 1888, he purchased 20.17 acres in Palermo's subdivision one, block 76, consisting of ten lots—1,000 feet on Lloyd Avenue and 1,040 feet on Messina. When completed in early 1889, T.J.'s magnificent home was the most costly structure in Palermo. California's U.S. Senator George Hearst, one of the three owners of the Homestake Mining Company and a good friend of T.J. Grier, acquired 700 acres of Palermo land through McAfee Brothers.

A total of four subdivisions were constructed, thus attracting

---

1. Frank Rutherford, "Palermo Chronicles," from the *Palermo Progress*, 17 October 1890, reprinted in *Diggin's*, Butte County Historical Society, Inc., Oroville, California, Vol. 18, No. 3, Fall Edition, 1974, pp. 4-8.

businesses to Palermo, and a school, hotels, and homes were soon built. On May 30, 1888, McAfee Brothers began promoting this citrus resort community and auctioning five- to ten-acre parcels of the Palermo Colony via a special first-class excursion train, which made a round trip between San Francisco and Palermo for a cost of three dollars; the Griers were among the passengers on the May 30 excursion. This unique promotion continued through the following year.

All of this activity soon created a boom and greatly changed the character of the town by the time the Grier family moved there in the summer of 1888. In addition to Palermo's commercial attraction, the town was also becoming a health and pleasure resort, and within twelve months, twenty-three buildings were constructed, including the school where May and Milt would enroll.

The Grier children first attended Palermo's one-story frame school and, later, its replacement, a two-story brick building with tower. May received her diploma from Oroville Union High School in 1893; Milt, who had worked as a clerk for PL&W while in high school, received his diploma in June 1895, at age sixteen.

During the Palermo years, Milt's father not only managed his own land but assisted in the management of PL&W's land sales and the Hearst estate's citrus ranch in Palermo after George Hearst's death on February 28, 1891.

YOUNG ENTREPRENEUR, 1895–1898

After Milt's graduation from high school at age sixteen, his parents urged him to study metallurgy and mining engineering at the University of California at Berkeley, but, eager to enter the business world, Milt instead took a job with Bills & Putnam's, wholesalers and retailers of hardware and general merchandise (steel, coal, barbwire, crockery, tin, glassware, paints, and oils). The firm, which was also an agent for John Deere plows and Deering mowers, was located on Montgomery Street in Oroville, on the south bank of the Feather River.

In 1896, he resigned due to ill health and spent the next three months convalescing and traveling in the West. He visited his uncle T.J. in Lead, South Dakota; his uncle Albert, an attorney, and his cousins Denham and Frances ("Franny") Grier in Denver; and his aunt Anne Grier Fell and her family in Odgen, Utah.

On his return, Milt was offered his former position at Bills & Putnam's for twice his previous salary, but, intent on establishing his own business, he declined. He then opened a general merchandise firm in Palermo, which he ran successfully for over a year and sold at a profit in

24

1898, after the outbreak of the Spanish-American War and the Philippine Insurrection. The war, stirring his patriotism, had proved even more enticing than entrepreneurship.

Palermo Colony, c. 1888

THE PROGRESS.

Vol. 4.   PALERMO, BUTTE CO., CAL., WEDNESDAY, JUNE 28, 1893.   No. 25.

A MIDWINTER FAIR

THE PROPOSITION TO HOLD ONE IN CALIFORNIA FINDS FAVOR.

A Meeting Held in San Francisco Tuesday Evening of Last Week to Consider the Matter—Leading Citizens Express Themselves as Favorable to the Idea and Believe it Will Result in General Good to the State.

We are to have the midwinter World's Columbian Fair. It is a decided fact. The motion has been put and carried in a most enthusiastic manner. Even the conservatives, those who doubted to go slowly and see whether we really want the fair or not, were carried off in the general tumult at the moment and declared themselves most roundly for the fair, first, last and all the time. The meeting, which it seemed to start slowly and with a slight degree of distrust, assumed in a few moments to a situation so extremely favorable to the trying to out—the rest in enthusiasm, and the whole affair ended in the manliest good feeling, with congratulations and hearty shakings on every side.

This is the way the Chronicle put it in that more consistent

make a call for the meeting. We began canvassing for opinions on this affair several days ago. We met with objections and encouragement almost everywhere, but invariably, upon explanation, the cold was gave way to enthusiasm. We explained that we would to attempt to duplicate the great fair at Chicago, but many people said at once that nothing of the sort could be done in six months. They were right. We told them that our object was more for a big winter fair, to show the world our climate and possibilities than anything else—that it should be a gigantic advertisement of California. We told them that it was an opportunity, an excuse for inviting friends and acquaintances from all over the United States and Europe to come to California. This board did good work in its big advertisement of "California on wheels," and this is a chance that eclipses that until it effort. I wish to emphasize the remark that we have met absolutely with no opposition. We were met simply with doubt, and were so liable to dispel that. With everybody it has been simply a question of expediency. People said that it would be better not to hold one at all than to California to have a poor one. When they saw what we could do and what is promised they invariably thought it the one chance of a lifetime. It is the biggest, awful chance we have ever had to let the world get acquainted with us. Of course the opening, important thing; there is difficulty, in fact that was a condensed

AN IMPORTANT DECISION

RECLAMATION DISTRICT NO. 542 LOSES ITS SUIT AGAINST R. M. TURNER.

Judge Gray Decides That Any Assessment Levied For the Purpose of Purchasing Levees Built On Private Property is Void—Waite and James Knocked Out of An Opportunity to Reimburse Themselves.

Superior Court, County of Butte, State of California.

Reclamation District No. 542, plaintiff vs. R. M. Turner, defendant.

This action was brought to foreclose an alleged lien of a delinquent assessment upon the lands of defendant, situate within the plaintiff in Butte county. The defendant presents many reasons why this action should not be maintained, and they will be considered in the order presented, so far as it is convenient to do so.

The first point attention is called to is that the point if has not been legally levied into a reclamation district, and

to wrap it from the 23d day of December, 1892, to January 28th, 1892, both days inclusive, and the Board of Supervisors met on the second day of February following to hear it. The law requires that it shall be published once a week for four weeks next, preceding the hearing thereof. The fact that it was published oftener than required by law will not invalidate it. A week did not intervene between the first publication and the date fixed for its hearing.

A part of the tax sought to be raised was for the purpose of purchasing levees already constructed at the time of the formation of the district. They were obliged to have built long before the reclamation district was contemplated but they were along the line where the new levees would have to be built had not been there. Defendant cannot contain that while the district had the power to levy a tax to build new levees, it had no right to levy a tax to buy the old one, and cites the case of Dean vs. Frisk, 30 Cal. 407, in support of this position.

It is sufficient to say that since that decision was rendered, section 3464, Pol. Code, has been amended, and as amended there now have the power to acquire by purchase, among other things therein named, & etc. And, having the power to purchase, the power to raise money by taxation for that purpose follows.

The evidence disclosed the fact that of the three trustees of the district, Ho's, James and White, two of them, with

The June 28, 1893 edition of the *Progress*, Palermo's frontier newspaper

The Northern California Railroad, which ran through Palermo in the 1800s

Palermo Depot, c. 1890

Top, The Hearsts' residence in Palermo, 1897
(Courtesy of John H. Nopel)

Middle, Palermo's first schoolhouse, 1889

Bottom, and its replacement, 1904

William Milton Grier, c. 1894

Milt and May Grier in
an amateur theatrical
production, 1890s

29

William John Grier in Palermo, c. 1900

William John and Georgie Grier outside their Palermo home, c. 1900

4

SPANISH-AMERICAN WAR
AND PHILIPPINE INSURRECTION
1898–1899

Perhaps seeking new horizons, eighteen-year-old Milt Grier responded to President William McKinley's call for volunteers and enlisted as a private on July 20, 1898. With his parents' permission, he joined the California U.S. Volunteers—the "Boys in Blue"—and was attached to Battery A of the First Battalion Regiment of Heavy Artillery. He was given 90 days of training at the Presidio in San Francisco—and thirteen dollars per month.

THE "SPLENDID LITTLE WAR"

Called a "splendid little war" by Theodore Roosevelt, then Secretary of the Navy, the Spanish-American War was short-lived (April 1898–August 1899) and resulted in only 379 combat deaths.

The conflict grew out of America's sympathy for the oppressed people of Cuba and the desire to expand U.S. power in the world. In the Treaty of Paris, signed on December 10, 1898, the United States won the spoils of victory, including sovereignty over the Philippine Islands. Ten million Filipinos, however, were unwilling to become part of a U.S. protectorate. The ensuing Philippine Insurrection forced the United States to call upon its armed forces to secure that which U.S. officials had intended to acquire by diplomacy.

The First Regiment of the U.S. Volunteers of California was one of the original National Guard regiments to heed McKinley's call for volunteers in this war that was meant to end the rule of Spain in North America. California was also the first state to fill its national quota, and its soldiers were the first to depart from American soil. When the *City of Peking* steamed through the Golden Gate on May 25, 1898, bearing the initial wave of Volunteers to embark for Manila, it was a history-making voyage.

If the United States were to win the Spanish-American War, the strength of Spain as a colonial power would be shattered forever, and the ultimate acquisition of desirable territory, affecting the commerce of the world, would be secured. The high stakes in this war stirred an immense amount of patriotism, and the embarkation of the First Regiment was

31

treated with enormous fervor, surpassed only by the incredibly joyous celebrations at the Regiment's return more than a year later on August 23, 1899.

CALIFORNIA VOLUNTEERS

In almost Whitmanesque language, the Patriotic Publishing Company extolled the virtues of the troops and the war in December 1898:

> In the ranks of that body of men [the First Regiment] can be found, either through birth or parentage, a representative of every great nation on earth. From out of the great human crucible of early California, has come the most thoroughly cosmopolitan body of military men that ever marched under a single banner. Here is found the American, the Frenchman, the German, the Irishman, the Englishman, the Scotchman, the Welshman, the Austrian, the Italian, the Hungarian, the Russian, the Swede, the Norwegian, the Greek, and in fact a representative of every distinct type on earth. In the matter of religious opinions the diversity is as great as it is in the matter of ancestry. Jew and Gentile have been made one by the cohesive bonds of patriotism. All the branches of science and all of the various callings of a great commercial commonwealth were represented within its ranks. The doctor, the lawyer, the merchant, the mechanic, and the laborer became one homogeneous body for the sake of country. The college student and the city clerk shared the same bed and the same board without a feeling of sacrifice or sycophancy. The sons of the rich and the sons of the poor stood upon the same social plane that their fathers stood upon in the days of the Argonauts. They were fighting for a cause; that cause was dear to all. With them a war for humanity knew neither tongue nor creed....[1]

The sinking of the battleship *Maine* near Cuba led to the First Regiment's sailing to assist Admiral Dewey in Manila in the far-off Philippines. Shortly after, this regiment "was the first to offer a life sacrifice upon the alter [sic] of its country...in the person of brave Maurice Justh, Sergeant of Company A, who sleeps in a soldiers [sic] grave 6,500 miles from home and friends."[2]

The battle cry became the famous "Remember the Maine!" and perhaps stimulated the fervid patriotism that helped America come through the war a victor, having won from Spain the independence of Cuba and possession of Puerto Rico, Guam, and the Philippine Islands.

---

1. *California's Tribute to the Nation* (San Francisco: Patriotic Publishing Co., 1898), p. 1.

2. Ibid., p. 2.

GRIER AND BATTERY A

Private Grier's First Battalion Regiment of Heavy Artillery, California U.S. Volunteers consisted of Batteries A, B, C, and D. The government's original intention in calling the First Battalion into existence was to man the coast fortifications which protected California from attack by sea. However, due to the successes of the American fleet beyond the seas, the prospective siege by Spanish vessels never materialized.

The call, however, was for Volunteer artillerymen of above-average intelligence and education to man these guns. Two hundred soldiers were to be recruited for each of the four batteries. While many hundreds presented themselves in an endeavor to enlist and don the blue and brown, only 800 were sworn in, making the full strength of the battalion equivalent to two full battalions of infantry.

Private Grier and his fellow Volunteers in Battery A were first quartered at the run-down Fontana Warehouse, located at the end of Van Ness Avenue in San Francisco. The men slept on its hard floor, and the wind and fog rushed through its broken windows. After ten days, the structure was declared unsafe, and the Volunteers were sent to the Presidio for training.[3]

There were several sailings to the Philippines over the next few months. Private Grier and most of Battery A, under the command of First Lieutenant J.B. Morse and accompanied by Second Lieutenant John F. Lucey of Battery D, sailed from San Francisco on October 18, 1898 on the transport *Valencia*.

Batteries A and D were reunited in the Philippines on December 11, 1898 in the historic town of Cavite, the former site of the Spanish navy yard and the point at which the first American flag was unfurled in the Philippine Islands. At that time, Battery A consisted of three officers and 182 men; Battery D had four officers and 184 men.

---

3. The Presidio began as a diminutive fort within adobe walls, built in 1776 by a group of Spanish soldiers. It was not until 1846 that the American flag flew over the post, following a raid by Kit Carson and eleven fellow soldiers.

In its illustrious history, this post—the oldest continuously operating one in America — served as a refuge for 70,000 San Franciscans after the devastating 1906 earthquake and was also the home of General "Black Jack" Pershing.

Today, the Presidio is the administrative headquarters for many commands and employs nearly 6,000 people. With a parklike setting on 1,500 acres in northern San Francisco, the Presidio is also home to some 10,000 military personnel.

PHILIPPINE COMBAT

At Admiral Dewey's request, the battalion was assigned as his special support to protect the old Spanish navy yard and its environs. After its capture by American forces on May 1, the navy yard had been made the supply base for all the ships of the Asiatic Squadron, and valuable property was stored in the arsenal. The surroundings at Cavite were extremely pleasant, with various *palacios* used as barracks by the different organizations located there.

Cavite was also the first headquarters of the Filipino insurrectionists. After the fall of Manila on August 13, the insurgent troops withdrew from the city of Cavite and took up a position at San Roque, a town of equal size (5,000 people) separated from Cavite only by a narrow artificial causeway 600 yards in length.

Under the command of General Estrella, governor of the province of Cavite, the insurgents began massing their forces at San Roque on February 1, 1899. One week later, Admiral Dewey came ashore from the *Olympia*, and, after consultations with the district commander, issued a demand for the insurgents to evacuate the town of San Roque. An ultimatum accompanied the demand: if the evacuation were not completed by nine o'clock the following morning, the town would be bombarded.

As the deadline approached, the insurgents requested further time, but Dewey refused. Shortly thereafter, flames burst out all over San Roque, and the town was soon ablaze.

The entire garrison of Cavite was promptly called to arms. In addition to Batteries A and D of the California Heavy Artillery (in charge of two sections of Gatling guns), two battalions of the Fifty-first Iowa Infantry, U.S. Volunteers, the Wyoming Light Battery, and the Nevada Cavalry were dispatched across the causeway.

Every passage through San Roque was in flames. To gain entrance to the town, Grier and the Volunteers had to flank it by moving along the seashore, at times wading waist-high in water. Grier and the men fought through the flames of the burning city in pursuit of the retreating enemy, dragging their heavy guns by hand and skirmishing at every opportunity.

Together with the cavalry troop and the infantry, Grier and his artillery battalion took the town of Caridad, several miles away, and passed Dalhican, beyond which lay the causeway leading to the mainland. (It was here that insurgents in former rebellions had massacred hundreds of Spaniards by luring them onto the narrow causeway, then mowing them down.) Grier went ahead with scouting parties to assure that the woods were free of insurgents. Details were sent to bury the dead, and battalion, infantry, and cavalry went into camp.

On February 15, Grier's battery was on the firing line. The Filipinos had advanced to within 300 yards when the battalion opened fire, and the insurgents beat a hasty retreat. Firing continued all night between the outposts, and numerous exchanges would take place in the following weeks. On March 2, Grier and three other Volunteers were sent to reconnoiter. Their party advanced to within fifty yards of the insurgents' lines before being discovered; when the enemy opened fire, Grier and the scouting party fell back, their retreat covered by a portion of the battalion outpost guard.

At ten o'clock in the morning of June 14, white flags were seen on the beach near Rosario and Salinas. The next day, Grier and eighty Volunteers from Batteries A and D, under command of Captain Dennis Geary, started for Novaleta at 7:00 a.m. and routed the insurgents in time to return to camp for supper. A day later, the battalion scouted the roads leading to San Francisco de Malabon, Cavite Viejo, Salinas, and Novaleta, and on June 17, the battalion left camp at 5:00 a.m., marching to Caridad. They received the surrender of the town of Rosario on June 19. Grier and the scouting parties then moved in the direction of San Francisco de Malabon and Cavite Viejo and engaged the enemy in crossfire.

For sixty-nine consecutive days, the First Battalion was under fire, guarding a critical point to the advance on the navy yard. Although Grier and his fellow Volunteers were "subjected to all the rigors of a campaign, depleted by sickness, and hounded and shot at by the natives in their immediate front, with orders that they must grin and bear it; with attacks on their outposts every night...the men of this organization kept at bay 6,000 insurgents." [4] Before defeating the insurrectionists, Private Grier and his California Volunteers endured four months of battle in the Philippine swamps and jungles.

TUMULTUOUS WELCOME IN SAN FRANCISCO

With hostilities ended, the troops prepared to leave the Philippines, and on July 23, 1899, Private Grier and the California Volunteers embarked on the U.S. Army transport *Sherman* for their return to San Francisco. En route, the ship passed through the Inland Sea of Japan, where Grier and his shipmates went ashore to visit Nagasaki, Yokohama, and Tokyo. The *Sherman* then sailed for San Francisco, arriving off its coast on August 23, 1899 at 5:46 p.m. They were greeted by the rosy glare of bonfires burning along the city's hilltops.

---

4. *A Brief Historical Sketch of the California Heavy Artillery, U.S.V., and the Operations of Batteries A and D in the Philippine Islands* (San Francisco: Patriotic Publishing Co., 1898), p. 101.

As the *Sherman* waited four miles off shore near the Farallone Islands, San Francisco's Mayor James D. Phelan sent a message to Lieutenant Colonel Duboce aboard the S.S. *Sherman*:

Colonel Victor Duboce: Greetings to the First California. Come in tomorrow and we will welcome you as soldiers have never been greeted before.

On the morning of August 24, 1899, the scarred white hull of the *Sherman* was ushered into port by a flotilla of colorful boats. The noise was deafening. Every tug had a band, and rapid-fire guns on the *Sherman* returned their salutes. Over 100,000 San Franciscans turned out to view the incoming ship. On her starboard decks facing the city, 1,800 "Boys in Blue," the heroes from San Francisco, stood at the rails. When the *Sherman* docked at Folsom Street Wharf at noon on that bright August day, Grier's joyous parents William John and Georgie, his sister May, and his aunt Mattie Orr were waiting to embrace him.

The reaction of San Franciscans and the press to the return of the troops aboard the *Sherman* was ecstatic. The *San Francisco Chronicle* wrote:

An hour after yesterday's noon the Golden Gate swung wide open and revealed, standing just within its portals, San Francisco waiting, arms outstretched, to greet her own—no longer a weary, anxious, heavy-hearted San Francisco, but a city feverish with gladness, trembling 'twixt joy, tears and loving laughter....All last night the tremulous echo of those cheers beat on the eardrums of troubled sleepers, while there remained on their eyeballs the picture of a fair white ship, all a-flutter with bunting, and on her decks and in her rigging a swarm of noble fellows, all soberly garbed in blue and yellow. There have been other transports, but none like this one; other soldiers have come home, but not such as these. Other regiments did fine things in the Philippines, but these are household heroes, the proof that San Francisco can breed blood of her blood and bone of her bone....Rockets rushed high up into the veil of thin fog and then drowsily popped and loosened all the beauties of variegated colors in fantastic sprays of slowly dropping fire....More awful than blazing hulk and belching red fire on the water and myriads of electric lights in artistic designs ashore were the wailing, quivering, tremulous, thundering voices of the sirens on the *Sherman*....The *Sherman*, from which all the glories of the night radiated, loomed up like a great house illuminated for a festivity....Perhaps the most remarkable sight along the front was Telegraph Hill, where human beings were packed together like bunched cattle at the close of a day's round-up and formed for the promontory a vast cap as complete and dense as the earth on which they stood....[5]

---

5. *San Francisco Chronicle*, 25 August 1899.

The next morning, the soldiers appeared newly outfitted in khaki uniforms, wide-brimmed campaign hats, and red four-in-hand ties. A continuous shout kept pace with the men as they marched from the wharf to the Ferry Building, accompanied by beating drums and songs, including "When Johnny Comes Marching Home Again" and "Hail, the Conquering Hero Comes." In the Ferry Building's grand nave, Private Grier and the Volunteers were reunited with their loved ones and were later served breakfast in the east nave at tables covered with white cloths.

The men were greeted by James Phelan, the patrician mayor of San Francisco—an orator, art patron, and uncommon public servant who was much esteemed by the Grier family for his reforms and his vision of San Francisco as a city of art and progressive government...the Florence of the Pacific. Private Grier, along with many other Volunteers, met the mayor during breakfast, exchanging a few words with him as he introduced himself around the tables.

As members of the Relatives' Association, Grier's mother, sister, and aunt—each dressed in white with red-white-and-blue sashes—had helped arrange the welcoming breakfast with other mothers, wives, and sisters of the First California Volunteers. Instead of trying to conduct the breakfast personally, the relatives secured a good caterer. After months of a monotonous diet, Grier and the men were served a sumptuous menu:

Eastern Oysters
Relishes
Olives   Pickles   Tomatoes   Lettuce
Entree
Chicken Fricassee
Vegetables
Green Peas   Mashed Potatoes
Roast
Turkey en Gelee   Filet de Boeuf
Eastern Ham   Smoked Tongue
Dessert
Chocolate Cakes   Coconut Cakes
Jelly Cakes
Coffee   Fruit in Season   Cheese
Mineral Waters

A feast for anyone, it was especially so for Private Grier and the other Volunteers who had endured a very different kind of breakfast for months: beans and slabs of fat bacon and hardtack, washed down by bitter coffee.

During the meal, there were cheers for the mothers, sisters, wives, and sweethearts, and the great hall rang with hearty expressions of love and approval.

As Grier and the Volunteers rose to leave, a band played patriotic airs, from "The Stars and Stripes Forever" and "The Star-Spangled Banner" to "Marching Through Georgia" and "Dixie."

After breakfast, Grier and the Volunteers marched up Market Street, past jubilant throngs of people crowding the sidewalks and peering out of office and hotel windows. By then, the men wore laurel wreaths on their brown campaign hats, and their gun barrels were filled with flowers and flags. The parade turned north on Van Ness Avenue, then continued west on Lombard Street and on to the Presidio.

An article on the front page of the *San Francisco Chronicle* described the scene:

> As the men turned in at the Presidio gates the band was playing in a reminiscent sort of way, "We shall meet, but we shall miss him, There will be one vacant chair." Over the hill, the refrain went, "One vacant chair." To each hearer the vacant chair stood for a different name. Some thought of Justh and some of Dunmore, some of Richter, some of Dewar and Maher, and all the other brave fellows whose graves are down there.[6]

San Francisco's welcome had just begun. Private Grier and his fellow Volunteers marched once again, in a second parade on Saturday evening, August 26 that was watched by over 150,000 people. A newspaper reporter captured the evening's magic:

> It was...the most beautiful pageant the city ever saw....The illumination made the city more beautiful than fairyland...the lines of light zig-zagging across the street, here parallel, there oblique, with an irregularity that enchanted the eye....The tall, slender tower of the Ferry Building showed all its noble proportions....At the other end of the bridge of light...[the City Hall dome] gleamed and sparkled and twinkled....The late twilight had hardly died before the fireworks commenced. More beautiful rockets never soared aloft to a California sky. [7]

Still a minor at age twenty, Private Grier was mustered out on September 21, 1899, having served fourteen months and one day. His twenty-first birthday would be celebrated three days later with family and friends at home, in Palermo, California.

Young Grier had felt the fire of combat and the loss of friends; he had endured war and survived. Now, he was again eager to test his mettle in the world of business.

6. *San Francisco Chronicle*, 26 August 1899.
7. *San Francisco Chronicle*, 27 August 1899.

The Griers' house in Palermo, c. 1898 (William John, Georgie, and Milt in U.S. Volunteer's blue uniform)

The S.S. *Puebla* leaves San Francisco Bay, en route to Manila, 1898
(Courtesy of the California State Library)

California U.S. Volunteers' encampment at the Presidio
(Courtesy of the California State Library)

Entrance to the Presidio
(Courtesy of the California State Library)

40

The burning of San Roque
(Courtesy of the California State Library)

The S.S. *Sherman* steams into San Francisco Bay, August 24, 1899
(Courtesy of the California State Library)

San Francisco welcomes its returning heroes

5

PHOEBE HEARST
Friend, Patron

After Grier's discharge and triumphant return from the Philippines, Phoebe Hearst hired him to work in San Francisco for the Hearst estate, which controlled business interests and philanthropies across the country—from saving George Washington's Mount Vernon home and building the Washington Cathedral in the East to supporting free kindergartens, libraries, and the University of California at Berkeley in the West.

Phoebe Apperson Hearst, widow of U.S. Senator George Hearst, directed these wide-ranging activities. The daughter of a Missouri farmer, Phoebe had married forty-one-year-old Hearst when she was nineteen. Her husband, also a Missouri native, was a successful mine owner in the West and a prominent San Franciscan at the time of their marriage in Missouri in 1862. After their honeymoon, the couple returned to San Francisco in September, aboard a ship traveling via Panama.

After her husband's death in 1891, Mrs. Hearst was named the first female regent of the University of California at Berkeley. Over the years, she would become one of its major benefactors; among her projects were the International Competition (an architectural design for the university's site) and construction of the Hearst Memorial Mining Building.[1]

In the 1880s, Phoebe Hearst became a close friend of William John and T.J. Grier (superintendent of the Hearst-owned Homestake Mining Company in Lead, South Dakota). Their families were often guests at her estates "Wyntoon," in northern California, and "Hacienda," in Pleasanton, east of San Francisco in the hills of southern Alameda County.[2]

She also took a personal interest in Milt Grier, recognizing in him

---

1. Her son William Randolph Hearst gave the Hearst Gymnasium for Women to the university in her memory. Designed by Bernard Maybeck and Julia Morgan, the building was dedicated on April 8, 1927, with Mr. Hearst in attendance. He also gave Berkeley the Hearst Greek Theater, built in 1903.

2. "Hacienda" was completed in 1896 after a large addition designed by Julia Morgan was finished. Elaborate gardens surrounding the home were ablaze with color. Pergolas were overhung with wisteria, cloisters shaded with climbing roses and jasmine. The music room was crowded with art, statues, and rare tapestries. Mrs. Hearst died at "Hacienda" on April 13, 1919. William Milton Grier, then involved in civil and railroad construction in the Pacific Northwest, attended her funeral on April 16, 1919 at Grace Church (later Grace Cathedral) in San Francisco.

a young man of ability.[3] Through the years, she provided him with opportunities, first in her family's real estate development company and then with Hearst Oil. She also had him tutored by a professor from the University of California at Berkeley and later sent him to Lead, South Dakota to gain experience in the Homestake Mining Company.

HEARST ENTERPRISES, 1899–1903

In November 1899, young Grier began as a laborer with the Hearst Real Estate and Development Company, whose office was in the Mills Building, Room 926, at 220 Montgomery Street in San Francisco. The office was a short walk from his apartment at 526 Post Street, near Union Square and the St. Francis Hotel, where he would live until 1903.

Starting on Hearst's Potrero district project on the southwest hill of San Francisco, young Grier became a project foreman within six months. Later, he was promoted to supervisor of a 150-man crew, directing the construction of streets, sidewalks, utility lines, and twelve retail, residential, and office buildings.

In 1901, Mrs. Hearst promoted him to a position under her cousin's son Edward Clark, who managed Hearst Oil Company, also located in the Mills Building. While Grier was at Hearst Oil, she arranged for him to receive instruction in metallurgy and mining engineering two afternoons a week with a Berkeley professor. With this experience, Grier established a successful mine assaying laboratory while continuing with Hearst Oil.

HOMESTAKE MINING AND T.J. GRIER, 1903

For six months in 1903, Mrs. Hearst had Grier work and study at the Homestake Mining Company in Lead, South Dakota, where the superintendent was his uncle T.J. While en route by train, Grier stopped to visit his aunt Anne (Mrs. A. Gilbert Fell) and her four daughters and son in Ogden, Utah. (Anne's fifth daughter had died while visiting Milt's family in Palermo a few years earlier.) He also visited his uncle Albert E. Grier and cousins Franny (age ten) and Denham (age fourteen) during a stopover in Denver. (Albert, who was admitted to the Colorado Bar in 1888, was counsel

---

3. In 1886 at age eight, Milt had met the Hearsts' only child, twenty-three-year-old William Randolph, whose father soon after gave him the *San Francisco Examiner*, his first newspaper. Grier renewed his relationship with William Randolph while working with Hearst enterprises in San Francisco, from 1899 to 1904. Hearst married Millicent Willson of New York in 1903.

for several Denver firms, including the early utility, predecessor of today's Public Service Company of Colorado.)

On reaching Lead, Grier settled in with his uncle T.J. and aunt Mary Jane. This was a challenging period for twenty-five-year-old Milt: in the next six months, he would work in all of Homestake's departments, toiling ten hours a day, six days a week as "the lowest paid man on the payroll," he wrote years later. His uncle saw to it that he learned all aspects of Homestake's operation which, under T.J.'s direction, was becoming the largest, deepest, and most productive gold mine in North America.

In the evenings, "Will" (as his uncle called him) studied or enjoyed the company of the Grier family, which included four young cousins: Thomas Johnston ("Tommy"), Jr. (1897–1929), Evangeline Victoria ("Muddie") (1899–1988), Lisgar (1901–1941), and Ormonde (1903–1964). T.J. frequently entertained Homestake officials and other guests from around the country, and their conversations were stimulating, as were the musical evenings organized by Mary Jane, an accomplished contralto and pianist who brought musicians from near and far to the superintendent's home.

RETURN TO CALIFORNIA, 1903–1904

Upon completing his unique apprenticeship at the Homestake Mining Company, Grier returned to San Francisco in December 1903. Phoebe Hearst then put his newly acquired skills to use in organizing and supervising gold prospecting activities on Hearst land in Palermo, California. Instead of utilizing the common prospecting method of drilling, Grier sank shafts to dredge for gold, a process which had been successful in the surrounding area. However, while some gold was recovered, the quantity was never economically significant, and the project was abandoned in the summer of 1904.

While working on the Hearst project, Grier married twenty-five-year-old Laura A. Watson, whom he had met in San Francisco after his return from the Philippines. The 4:40 p.m. ceremony took place on June 20, 1904 in the Superior Court of the County of Sacramento, with Judge Peter J. Shields presiding; Charles H. Holmes and Carolee W. Shields were witnesses.

Milt Grier, c. 1900

Phoebe Hearst at "Hacienda"
(Courtesy of Victoria Grier Nelsen)

The Hearsts' "Hacienda
del Pozo de Verona" in
Pleasanton, California
*(Courtesy of the Bancroft
Library, University of
California at Berkeley)*

47

Phoebe Apperson Hearst
(Courtesy of the Black Hills Mining Museum, Lead, South Dakota)

George Hearst
(Courtesy of the Black Hills Mining Museum, Lead, South Dakota)

The Hearsts' medieval castle
"Wyntoon" in northern
California
(Courtesy of Victoria Grier Nelsen)

Milt Grier at
Homestake Mining Company,
October 1903

The Fell family, c. 1898: seated—Annie, Arthur, A. Gilbert, and Goldie; standing— Daisy, Carrie, Winifred, and Gilberta

Mary Jane
Palethorpe Grier
in 1901
*(Courtesy of Victoria
Grier Nelsen)*

T.J. Grier, Sr. in
1898, with
photographs of
Phoebe
Hearst (upper)
and his mother
Eliza
Anne Patterson
Grier
(lower)
*(Courtesy of Victoria
Grier Nelsen)*

51

T.J. and Mary Jane at
Phoebe Hearst's
"Hacienda," c. 1908

T.J.'s home and office in Lead, South Dakota, pre-1897
(Courtesy of the Black Hills Mining Museum)

The T.J. Grier family,
c. 1911: back row—
T.J., Jr., Evangeline
Victoria, T.J., Margaret
Eliza Ferrie, Mary Jane;
front row—Ormonde
Palethorpe, Lisgar
Patterson
*(Courtesy of Victoria
Grier Nelsen)*

T.J., Jr., Ormonde, Henderson (the chauffeur), Lisgar, Muddie, and T.J.
in Spearfish Canyon, South Dakota, c.1909
(Courtesy of Victoria Grier Nelsen)

T.J.'s sons, c. 1918: Lisgar, T.J., Jr., Ormonde, and James Ferrie

6

TWOHY BROTHERS
1904–1919

Grier's career continued to progress in the first decade of the new century. In October 1904, after five years of experience in real estate development, oil, mining, and supervisory posts, young Grier accepted an assistant foreman position in San Francisco with Twohy Brothers Company, an engineering and construction contractor with headquarters in Portland, Oregon.

BAYSHORE CUTOFF, 1904–1907

At that time, Twohy Brothers had a contract with the Southern Pacific Railroad Company to construct its Bayshore Cutoff in San Francisco—an assignment that would be the first of a series of major railroad and civil projects in the West in Grier's fifteen-year partnership with Judge John Twohy's firm.[1]

Begun in October of 1904, the Bayshore Cutoff involved laying 9.81 miles of double railroad track from the terminal station in San Francisco to San Bruno, California; constructing five tunnels totaling 9,938 feet in length; and building a 4,110-foot trestle over the Islais Creek Basin.[2] When completed in 1907, project costs would exceed $9 million.

---

1. Judge John Twohy (1854–1927) was born in Copper Harbor, Michigan. After graduating from business school in Detroit, he was admitted to the bar and elected prosecuting attorney of Keweenaw County, Michigan. He practiced law and served as judge of the municipal court in St. Paul, Minnesota from 1890 to 1896. Two years later, he moved to Spokane, joining his brothers James C. and D.W. Twohy in their railroad and civil contracting firm, Twohy Brothers. Following the deaths of his brothers in 1908 and 1909, the firm was incorporated as the Twohy Brothers Company and run by Judge Twohy until his death in 1927. His four sons—John, James, Philip, and Robert—were also associated with this company.

Twohy Brothers constructed portions of the Northern Pacific, Union Pacific, and Southern Pacific railroads and built ships for Great Northern Shipbuilding Company and the U.S. government during World War I.

2. Four of the tunnels were of bore construction; the fifth was built up with bricks, its top covered with earth.

1906 EARTHQUAKE

On April 18, 1906, however, the Bayshore Cutoff was damaged by San Francisco's earthquake and fire. The earthquake struck at 5:12 a.m., and for sixty-five seconds, the city was pulled in all directions, leaving a mass of rubble and a raging fire. More than 100,000 residents were left homeless, and food, medical, and other supplies were rushed to the city from across the country.

The *Western Railroader* describes the devastating quake:

> From everywhere rose a terrifying rumble. Steeples wobbled in all directions at once. Chimneys crashed; walls toppled....Although Southern Pacific was hard hit, calm leadership by Vice-President and General Manager Edgar E. Calvin prevented panic among the railroaders. He re-organized railroad operations to meet the emergency. Office headquarters were temporarily established at Oakland and Alameda Piers and the Ferry Building. Later the Southern Pacific rebuilt the interior of the Flood Building and used it as its headquarters. On Valencia Street hill the rails lay twisted by the quake. Many small fires soon united into one huge conflagration in the neighborhood of Third and Market. The battle against the fire seemed hopeless. By noon of the first day it had consumed nearly a square mile of the city — and it was to burn for two more days....Through the night, 3,000 miles to the East, President E.H. Harriman of the Southern Pacific was racing westward by special train, smashing all speed records across the continent, to direct the railroad's rescue work personally. On the second day, famine threatened the city, and still the flames raged on....Within twelve hours after the earthquake the Southern Pacific and Union Pacific, under the direction of President Harriman, were turned over to the work of relief. Everything else was sidetracked. The record of the runs of relief trains will show all transcontinental freight train records shattered....Up to the night of May 3rd the Southern Pacific handled free into San Francisco 1,409 cars of freight totaling about 35,000 tons for the benefit of the sufferers. Besides this, Southern Pacific hauled over 224,000 passengers out of the city free of charge, and contributed $200,000 to other relief. [3]

As efforts to rebuild the city began, Grier's construction crew from Twohy Brothers laid track on city streets so that flat cars could haul away the rubble. Later, Grier supervised repairs on the Bayshore Cutoff, which included replacing twisted track and reconstructing the twin brick bores in Tunnel Two that had completely collapsed. Despite the delays caused by the earthquake, the Cutoff project was completed on December 8, 1907.

---

3.   Fred A. Stindt, "Peninsular Service: The Story of the Southern Pacific Commuter Trains," *Western Railroader*, 20 (1957): 17-19.

Ironically, the historic quake was directly preceded by a momentous cultural event in San Francisco. On the night of April 17, 1906, Enrico Caruso opened the Metropolitan Opera's run of *Carmen*, singing the role of Don Jose to rave reviews. For many, the event gave the night before the earthquake an aura of feverish excitement; as the critic in the *San Francisco Call* wrote, "The thrill, the throb, the quiver...was in the air."[4]

PALACE HOTEL

Caruso was staying at San Francisco's Palace Hotel. Situated on Market Street, the Palace was more elegant than anything of its time. As described by Oscar Lewis and Carroll Hall in *Bonanza Inn*, it featured "three large courts [supplying] light and air to the interior rooms [as well as] a circular driveway opening on the street, thus arriving guests would be driven [by horse and carriage] inside the building and deposited on a marble-paved floor in the midst of a forest of potted trees and plants. Extending upward on all four sides was...a series of seven galleries and, surmounting it all, a great domed roof of opaque glass."[5] Another unusual visual effect was the "vertical banks of bay windows [which] completely covered the great facades, giving an effect that natives proudly described as 'typically San Franciscan'. For these angular projections, designed to catch a maximum of sunshine in a fog-ridden climate, had long been an almost universal feature of the local domestic architecture."[6] Within a few years of its completion, this enormous chamber was famous around the globe.

"The Palace ran not only to size but to massiveness. Its outer walls, of brick, averaged two feet in thickness....Five hydraulic elevators provided access to the acres of upstairs rooms....The upper floors contained 755 rooms, with accommodations for 1,200 guests....Most of them were twenty feet square....Ceilings were uniformly fifteen feet high....So great was the amount of marble used that contracts had to be made with fifteen different firms for 804 mantels, 900 wash-stands, 40,000 square feet of pavement. Finishing woods came from many parts of the world: mahogany, East India teak, primavera from Mexico, rosewood, ebony. Much of it was elaborately carved, all was highly polished....The exterior [was] a dazzling white, with gold trim, sparingly used. Some observers were reminded of a gigantic wedding-cake."[7]

---

4. *San Francisco Call*, 18 April 1906.
5. Oscar Lewis and Carroll D. Hall, *Bonanza Inn, America's First Luxury Hotel* (New York: Alfred A. Knopf, 1939), pp. 19-20.
6. Ibid., p. 20.
7. Ibid., pp. 20-27.

While Caruso and many other notables were able to escape from the Palace during the earthquake, thus avoiding injury, the grandiose hotel itself was less fortunate. It was engulfed by the flames racing up Market Street and was destroyed with a more dramatic climax than any opera in which the great Caruso had starred. The famous tenor never returned to perform in San Francisco again.

The hotel had been a favorite and familiar place of entertainment for the Grier family. Milt was born near the hotel just two years after its construction, and when his father was a supervisor of telegraphers for the Central Pacific Railroad Company, his office was just a few blocks away from the landmark hotel. For many years, it was the center of family gatherings, for both Canadian and American Griers, including a few Christmas Day dinners in the hotel's festively garlanded dining room.

NORTH BANK PROJECT, 1906–1909

For Grier, the Bayshore Cutoff initiated the longest employment tenure of his career, and during this time, Judge John Twohy, a lawyer and entrepreneur, became an important friend and mentor.

In the fall of 1906, before the Bayshore Cutoff was completed, Grier was made a partner in Twohy Brothers Company and invited by Judge Twohy to supervise track construction on the Great Northern Railroad Company's new line on the North Bank of the Columbia River in Washington State.

During the early period in Washington and Oregon, Milt and his wife Laura settled in The Dalles, a town just northeast of Portland along the south bank of the Columbia River. Later, they lived in Portland,[8] where Twohy Brothers had its main office in the Wells Fargo Building at southwest 6th and Oak Streets.[9]

The North Bank project at that time represented the largest and most complex of the contracts ever undertaken by Twohy Brothers. It involved laying double-track and constructing tunnels and bridges for one of the great railroad builders of the time, James J. Hill.

Hill had determined that the natural downslope of the Columbia River offered a logical railway route to the Pacific Coast. A substantial legal

---

8. From 1916 to 1918, the Griers lived at 268 14th Street; from 1919 to 1921, at 166 Saint Clair Street. During this period, they enjoyed yachting on the Willamette and Columbia Rivers with Judge Twohy and his family.

9. When the Northwestern Bank Building at 6th and Alder Streets in Portland, Oregon was completed in 1913, Twohy moved his offices there. Grier and his companies also had offices there until December 1921, when he moved them to San Francisco.

battle ensued over the plan, as Edward H. Harriman, who controlled the Southern Pacific Railroad Company and the route along the south bank of the Columbia River, sought to block the new railway.

In secrecy, Hill, his Northern Pacific Railroad Company, and officials of the Great Northern Railroad Company combined forces in 1905 to build the North Bank railroad. The Portland and Seattle Railway Company was then organized to build a line in Washington State from Pasco down the Columbia River's north bank to Vancouver, crossing the Columbia and Willamette Rivers to Portland, Oregon. In two-and-one-half years, 7,000 men laid 230 miles of track and built thirteen tunnels. The original estimate for the project was $8 million; at completion, however, costs for the North Bank had swelled to nearly $45 million.

When the North Bank's double-track construction was finished, a golden spike ceremony was celebrated on March 11, 1908 at Sheridan's Point on the Columbia River.[10] Local and national officials, including Judge Twohy, Grier, and their wives, attended, and a ten-car train—the first to cross the new tracks—brought some 500 Vancouver and Portland residents to the junction of the rails. Its engine was bedecked with flags and bunting and a banner proclaiming "Hurrah for the North Bank." Government officials, who had gathered to mark the historic occasion, envisioned a great future for the region which would be served by the new railway, and Charles H. Carey, Portland counsel for the Hill lines, predicted that "down this road will come the great commerce to the Pacific Coast....Great cities will be built here and the population will be increased until it will be as dense as that along the Atlantic Coast."[11]

After the speeches concluded, Richard B. Miller, chief engineer on the North Bank project, drove in the golden spike.[12] Twohy Brothers laid the remaining stretch of track from Pasco to Spokane under Grier's supervision, completing the project in 1909.

---

10. Sheridan's Point was the site of a military block house used as a refuge by forty-seven white settlers when they were attacked by more than 200 Klickitat and Yakima Indians in 1856.
    Lieutenant Philip Sheridan, who would later gain fame as a Union general in the Civil War, rescued the small band of settlers after several days of heated battle with the marauding Indians.

11. *Dope Bucket: The Spokane, Portland and Seattle's Golden Jubilee Issue,* March, 1958.

12. Chief Engineer R.B. Miller later became Grier's partner in Boschke Miller Grier Company (1919–1921) and in the Miller Grier Company (1921–1922).

PACIFIC NORTHWEST PROJECTS, 1909–1919

On June 25, 1909, Grier's father William John died of a heart attack in his home at 1414 21st Avenue, Oakland, California. Grier attended his father's service at Albert Brown Company, a funeral home located at 584 13th Street, and was present at the interment of his ashes in the Columbarium at 4401 Howe Street in Oakland. Milt's mother Georgie Orr Grier, his sister Mrs. May Grier Barber, and Georgie's younger sister Mrs. Mattie Orr Barber also attended both services.

Grier continued on Twohy Brothers' next contract, the Deschutes project (1910–1911), laying track for James Hill in central Oregon's Deschutes River Canyon, as both Hill and Edward Harriman continued to carve railway out of rock, but on opposite sides of the river.

The bitter rivalry between Hill and Harriman was reflected in an almost constant state of warfare between each man's construction crews in the Deschutes Canyon.

> As early as the summer of 1909, when the only work being done was by engineering and survey gangs, one of the...surveyors recorded in his diary that they were lobbing bullets at each other across the river. "Fortunately," he wrote, "no one seems to be much of a shot." Later, when the construction crews were working right across from each other, things got rougher. After the evening meal it was quite common for a bunch to row across the river and take on anyone they could find from the other team for a session of thumping and knuckle-dusting. Nothing was barred, and the scraps got pretty rough with pick handles and rocks being used to balance the odds. Almost every train back to the Columbia on both lines carried one or more battered construction hands, bound for the hospital in The Dalles.[13]

Most of the crews working on the Deschutes project were from the Portland and Spokane areas. Because of the rugged terrain along the Columbia's banks and the fact that there was a steady demand for laborers in other, less hostile settings, good men were hard to come by and even harder to keep. They were, however, attracted by the project's pay scale: roughly 20¢ to 30¢ per hour for common laborers, 35¢ to 40¢ per hour for concrete workers and carpenters, 50¢ per hour for steel workers, and up to $7 per day for well drillers and teamsters. Lodging in primitive camps was furnished without charge, while meals were offered at 25¢ or 30¢ each.

The railroad construction in the Deschutes Canyon was one of the

---

13. *Dope Bucket: The Spokane, Portland and Seattle's Gold Spike Issue*, 1961.

last major projects to use black powder extensively, supplementing the manual labor of crews equipped with picks, hand drills, shovels, and wheelbarrows. In short order, however, the crews found another use for the black powder: industrial sabotage. Men from each side were sent to the clifftops to spy on the crews working across the river and locate the enemy's dynamite storage sites. Later, under the cover of night, five or six men would cross the river silently, climb the far banks, and detonate the opposition's black powder stock pile. As a result, both Hill and Harriman's projects experienced repeated delays due to lack of explosives, until a "cease-fire" was signed on May 17, 1910.

From 1913 to 1915, Twohy Brothers projects took Grier to Montana, where he stayed in the Bright Hotel in Lewistown; to Idaho; to Washington State; and to western Canada. In 1916, Grier worked on a 500-foot dam; the following year, he supervised the Prineville station project in Oregon. Tent camps were built at each of these sites to house the thousands of workers needed to complete the projects, but Grier's accommodations were considerably less Spartan: on-site, he had a private railroad car, complete with bedroom, bath, kitchen, dining area, office, and lounge.

DEATH OF T.J. GRIER, 1914

In late September of 1914, Grier attended the funeral of his uncle Thomas Johnston Grier, superintendent of Homestake Mining Company, in Lead, South Dakota. T.J. had died on September 22, while vacationing in his Los Angeles home. Just three weeks earlier, he had left Lead after dedicating the Homestake Opera House and Recreation Building and addressing the opera's opening night audience, on August 31.

In Lead, Grier paid his last respects to his uncle T.J., first as he lay in state at the Homestake Recreation Building (while the Homestake orchestra played Grieg's "Funeral March") and then at his burial among the pines and firs in the Masonic Cemetery overlooking Lead and T.J.'s beloved Homestake Mining Company. Thirty-two years later, in 1946, T.J.'s Scottish-born wife, Mary Jane Grier, would be buried next to him.

Thomas Johnston had been with Homestake Mining Company for over thirty-six years, the last thirty as its superintendent. At his death, he was credited with having set the company on the successful course it would follow for the next half century.[14]

---

14. T.J. was an inventor, as well, and was awarded a patent on March 24, 1891 for an improved ore-screen, which could be easily disassembled for repairs. He also received a patent (No. 17581) in Germany on July 23, 1904.

PANAMA PACIFIC INTERNATIONAL EXHIBITION, 1915

During their years with Twohy Brothers in Oregon and the Pacific Northwest, Milt and Laura visited San Francisco, where they saw his mother Georgie, his sister May, and his aunt Mattie. In 1915, Grier, Laura, May, and Georgie enjoyed two visits to the Panama Pacific International Exhibition (the San Francisco World's Fair), which opened on February 20, 1915 as Mayor Rolph led a parade of 150,000 people down Van Ness Avenue to the exhibition's site by the Bay.

Joining them for their first visit, on the Fourth of July, were Milt and May's aunt and uncle, Anne Grier Fell and her husband Gilbert, together with their son Arthur Grier Fell of Ogden, Utah and their daughter Marigold ("Goldie") and her husband Edward Niehaus from Berkeley, California. The Griers returned for a second visit on closing day, December 5.

The Griers were enchanted by the fair's romantic skyline of domes and towers, arcaded and colonnaded courtyards, its walled thematic palaces and gardens. Many critics still consider the Panama Pacific International Exhibition the last, and possibly the most beautiful, of the great American world's fairs, which began with Chicago's phenomenal "Great White City" in 1893. Inspired by the precepts of the Ecole des Beaux-Arts in Paris and by European examples, ideal classical cities appeared in Buffalo in 1901, in St. Louis in 1904, and, finally, in San Francisco in 1915. The PPIE— considered the best planned, the most cohesive, and, by most accounts, the lovliest—was built less than a decade after the city's ruin by earthquake and fire.

The Griers toured the fair's 635 acres, extending from Fort Mason to the Presidio (now the city's Marina district). They admired Bernard Maybeck's Palace of Fine Arts, which was mirrored by the waters of a lagoon. This tan-stuccoed, semicircular building, with its fronting peristyle of terra-cotta Corinthian columns and its ornamental domed rotunda, was the fair's art museum and remains in San Francisco today. In Maybeck's booklet, *Palace of Fine Arts and Lagoon*, he wrote, "I find that the keynote of a Palace of Fine Arts should be that of sadness, modified by the feeling that beauty has a soothing influence."[15]

Coincidentally, some seventeen years earlier, Grier, as a private in the California Volunteers during the Spanish-American War and Philip-

---

15. Bernard R. Maybeck, *Palace of Fine Arts and Lagoon* (San Francisco: Paul Elder and Co., 1915), pp. 9-11.

Grier met architects Bernard Maybeck and Julia Morgan while working for Hearst Oil and Hearst Real Estate and Development in San Francisco (1899–1904) and became a lifelong admirer of their work.

Maybeck had designed Phoebe Hearst's medieval castle, "Wyntoon," in northern Cali-

pine Insurrection, had been trained on that part of the Presidio where the Palace was later erected.

T.J. GRIER'S STATUE UNVEILED, 1916

In September 1916, Milt returned to Lead, South Dakota to attend the dedication ceremonies for a monument in his uncle T.J.'s honor. As an expression of their deep affection for him, over 2,000 local miners, businessmen, and residents had contributed to a fund to construct this lasting memorial immediately after T.J.'s death in 1914. A commission led by the Homestake Veterans' Association chose New York sculptor Allan G. Newman to complete a statue of their late friend and leader. When completed two years later, the bronze and granite monument rose over seventeen feet in height and was placed near the Homestake Recreation Building that T.J. had had built for the people of his town shortly before his death.

When the statue was unveiled on September 28, 1916, several thousand friends and colleagues crowded together on Main Street to observe the ceremonies, as the American flags draping the monument were lifted to reveal the 7'4" bronze likeness of T.J. Grier on its granite pedestal. On a platform to the right of the statue sat T.J.'s widow Mary Jane and his successor at Homestake Mining Company, Richard Blackstone. To the left stood choirs from Lead's Christ Church and the local high school. Following a tribute by Mr. Blackstone, which recounted T.J.'s youth, career, and remarkable contributions to his community, Mary Jane held a reception in the Recreation Building. Milt Grier was among those who stood by her that afternoon.

The *Lead Daily Call's* evening edition described the ceremony:

> The monument which the prudent deeds of philanthropy performed by the late Thomas Johnston Grier, built for him in the hearts of the people of Lead, found outward expression today in the unveiling of a granite and bronze memorial which will endure for ages and will stand as an evidence of the admiration of a community for one whose devotion to duty built up

---

fornia; the Hearst Gymnasium for Women at the University of California at Berkeley; and Frank C. Havens's home, "Wildwood," in Piedmont. Between 1897 and 1899, Maybeck oversaw Mrs. Hearst's International Competition, an architectural plan for the University of California at Berkeley.

Julia Morgan, a student of Maybeck's at Berkeley, completed her studies at the Ecole des Beaux-Arts in Paris, where she was the first woman ever accepted. Morgan practiced in San Francisco for fifty years, designing some 800 buildings. For twenty years, she was a designer and consultant to William Randolph Hearst on his San Simeon estate.

a great industry and fostered the prosperity and happiness of those who worked with him.[16]

Of the statue itself, the *Daily Call* noted that "the sculptor chose one of T.J.'s characteristic poses...standing, left hand thrust into the pocket of his inside coat, overcoat thrown back, and right hand grasping his lapel. He is wearing his customary soft, wide-brimmed hat, and his face reflects the earnestness that was the dominating mark of his character."[17]

16.   *Lead Daily Call*, 28 September 1916.

17.   Ibid.

The T.J. Grier residence, Lead, South Dakota
(*Courtesy of the Black Hills Mining Museum*)

65

The interior court of the Palace Hotel, c. 1880s
(Courtesy of the California Historical Society Library)

Bayshore Cutoff project in San Francisco, 1904-1907
(*Courtesy of Southern Pacific Railroad*)

Milt Grier and John Twohy at the North Bank project site, 1908

Golden spike ceremony at Sheridan's Point, Washington on March 11, 1908
(Courtesy of the Oregon Historical Society)

Wells Fargo Building in Portland, Oregon, c. 1913
(Courtesy of the Oregon Historical Society and the Angelus Studio)

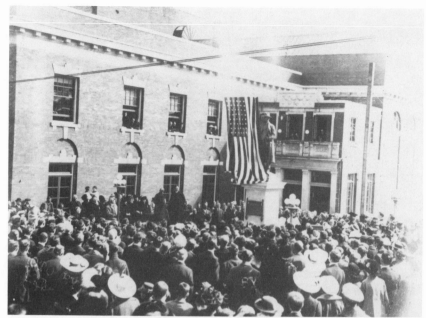

The unveiling of T.J. Grier's memorial statue, Lead, South Dakota, September 28, 1916 *(Courtesy of the Black Hills Mining Museum)*

Homestake's superintendent's residence in Lead, South Dakota, c. 1924
(Courtesy of the Homestake Mining Company)

70

T.J. Grier stands to the immediate right of President William Howard Taft during an underground tour of Homestake Mining operations on October 21, 1911

(Courtesy of Mildred Fielder; photographed by Ross & Gee)

71

Rare Homestake Mining Company stock certificate, issued in 1878, the year of Milt Grier's birth. This was also the year

Thomas Johnston Grier, Sr.
*(Courtesy of Homestake Mining Company,
Lead, South Dakota)*

UNITED STATES PATENT OFFICE.

THOMAS J. GRIER, OF LEAD CITY, (DAKOTA TERRITORY,) SOUTH DAKOTA.

ORE-SCREEN.

SPECIFICATION forming part of Letters Patent No. 448,762, dated March 24, 1891.

Application filed June 24, 1889. Serial No. 315,389. (No model.)

To all whom it may concern:

Be it known that I, THOMAS J. GRIER, a citizen of the United States, residing at Lead City, in the county of Lawrence, Territory of Dakota, have invented certain new and useful Improvements in Ore-Screens, of which the following is a specification, reference being had therein to the accompanying drawings.

This invention has relation to an improvement in screens, and more particularly to that class of screens used in ore-stamps, the main objects of the invention being to provide a screen which can be easily taken apart for repairs and to effect a saving in the screen material.

Other objects and advantages of the invention will appear in the following description, and the novel feature thereof will be particularly pointed out in the claim.

Referring to the drawings, Figure 1 is a side elevation of a portion of a stamp-mill, showing the screen in an operative position. Fig. 2 is a side elevation of the screen on a larger scale, and Fig. 3 is a vertical cross-section of the screen.

Like letters of reference indicate like parts in all the figures of the drawings.

The main frame of the screen, when intended for use in an ore-stamp, is made, as shown in the drawings, of the side pieces A and the top and bottom pieces A' and A², respectively, and the cross-bars A³. These parts may be made separately and then fastened in any suitable manner, or the whole frame may be cast in one piece. The inner sides of the side pieces A and the end pieces A' and A² and both sides of the cross-pieces A³ are formed with the shoulders A⁴, upon which and flush with the surface of the frame the small frames B are adapted to rest. The bolts C, screw-threaded on their ends, are adapted to receive the buttons D, which are held in place and adjusted by means of the nuts E.

The screening material F, which is generally perforated sheet metal, as in Fig. 3, but may be wire-cloth, is made in sizes to fit each small compartment formed by the side and end pieces A, A', and A². These sheets F are held firmly in place upon the shoulders A⁴ by means of the frames B, held by the bolts, buttons, and nuts C, D, and E, respectively. In a screen constructed in this manner one section of the cloth when worn out can be removed and a new one inserted without disturbing the main frame or any of the other sections. In this way a great saving is effected when repairs have to be made.

I do not limit myself to the form of screen shown and described. It is evident that the main frame may be divided up into smaller compartments of various shapes and sizes by varying the number and shape of the cross-pieces. Curvilinear compartments and compartments combining both curved and straight lines may be used, if desired.

What I claim is—

A stamp-mill screen or sieve comprising a main frame divided into vertical series of compartments, and independently-removable screens and screen-frames fitting said compartments, whereby any one section of the screening material may be removed independent of the others as it becomes worn, substantially as described.

In testimony whereof I affix my signature in presence of two witnesses.

THOMAS J. GRIER.

Witnesses:
WM. A. REMER,
FRED E. NELSON.

T.J. Grier's ore-screen patent, 1891

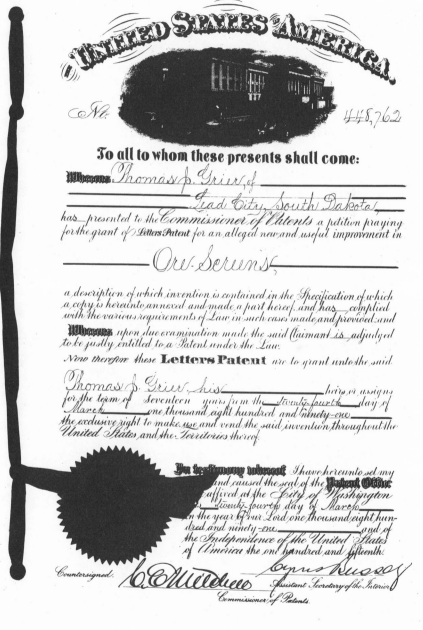

UNITED STATES OF AMERICA

N°. 448,762

To all to whom these presents shall come:

Whereas Thomas J. Grier, of _____ Lead City, South Dakota, has presented to the Commissioner of Patents a petition praying for the grant of Letters Patent for an alleged new and useful improvement in

_____ Ore-Screens, _____

a description of which invention is contained in the Specification of which a copy is hereunto annexed and made a part hereof, and has complied with the various requirements of Law in such cases made and provided: and Whereas upon due examination made the said Claimant is adjudged to be justly entitled to a Patent under the Law.

Now therefore these **Letters Patent** are to grant unto the said

Thomas J. Grier, his _____ heirs or assigns for the term of Seventeen years from the twenty-fourth day of March one thousand eight hundred and ninety-one the exclusive right to make, use and vend the said invention throughout the United States, and the Territories thereof.

In testimony whereof I have hereunto set my hand and caused the seal of the Patent Office to be affixed at the City of Washington this twenty-fourth day of March in the year of our Lord one thousand eight hundred and ninety-one and of the Independence of the United States of America the one hundred and fifteenth.

Cyrus Bussey
Assistant Secretary of the Interior

Countersigned.
C. E. Mitchell
Commissioner of Patents.

T.J. Grier's patent

75

Promenade of Palace of Fine Arts at the Panama Pacific International Exhibition, 1915 *(Courtesy of the California State Library)*

The statue of T.J. Grier, Lead, South Dakota, June 1972
(Photo by Bill Grier)

7

CHARLES DENHAM GRIER
An International Mining Career
1889–1948

During 1917 and '18, Milt visited his cousin Charles Denham Grier in Seattle several times while Denham was completing his Master of Science in metallurgy at the University of Washington.

The son of successful Denver attorney Albert Ephraim Grier (1859–1907) and Frances Margaret Mills Grier (1861–1954), Denham and his sister Franny (1893–1910) had attended Corona School with Mamie Doud, future wife of President Dwight D. Eisenhower. He graduated from Denver's Manual High School in 1907.

Several months later, on October 28, 1907, his father died of tuberculosis at the age of forty-eight. The family then moved from 1237 Corona Street—the home they had lived in since the 1880s—to 1283 Lafayette, a few blocks away.

Denham completed a five-year professional curriculum in engineering metallurgy at Colorado School of Mines and received a Bachelor of Arts degree in 1912.

EARLY CAREER, 1912–1921

Denham's first job was with the Homestake Mining Company in Lead, South Dakota. There, his uncle T.J., whom he had regularly visited while a student, hired him to do mill work in the firm's ore-processing plants. During this time, Denham stayed with T.J. and Mary Jane and their children, as his cousin Milt had done nine years earlier.[1]

In 1915, when Denham was working in Alaska as a chemical analyst for the Alaska Treadwell Gold Mining Company, Milt visited him at his home in Treadwell. Denham's subsequent promotion brought him in-

---

1. T.J. and Mary Jane Grier had four children together: Thomas Johnston, Jr. (1897–1929), Evangeline Victoria ("Muddie") (1899–1988), Lisgar Patterson (1901–1941), and Ormonde Palethorpe (1903–1964). Mary Jane's two children from her first marriage also lived with them: Margaret Eliza ("Madge") Ferrie (1893–1975) and James William Ferrie (dates unknown).

creased administrative, financial, and metallurgical responsibilities before he returned to "the lower forty-eight."

While working on his master's degree at the University of Washington in Seattle, Denham shared a home at 4552 Brooklyn Avenue with his mother Frances Mills Grier. After graduating in 1918, he served for six months as a second lieutenant in the U.S. Army Corps of Engineers, then returned to Seattle in 1919 to become a Fellow in Metallurgy under an agreement between the University of Washington's College of Mines and the U.S. Bureau of Mines.

SOUTH AFRICA, 1925

Between 1921 and 1922, Denham was a sales engineer for the New Jersey Zinc Company in New York City. The following year, he accepted a position with the American Cyanamid Company, the employer he was to serve until his death in 1948. He was transferred to Johannesburg, South Africa in 1925 and became director of South African operations for American Cyanamid Ltd., which began trading in South Africa through its agents Fraser and Chalmers (SA) Ltd.

In 1937, Denham became chairman of the board and managing director of the firm's newly created subsidiary, South African Cyanamid Company Ltd., which was formed to build a factory at Witbank, Transvaal to produce cyanide for the Witwatersrand gold mines.

FAMILY LIFE

During his long residence in South Africa, Denham took combined business and vacation trips to the United States and the New York headquarters of Cyanamid. In addition, he traveled widely in southern Africa, making sales and service calls to clients in mining and in citrus-growing. Along the way, he met Ruby Stephenie Coote, a young woman from Armagh in Northern Ireland, and they were married on February 26, 1927. A son, David Denham Eyre, was born April 12, 1932, in Johannesburg. Ruby, however, died in childbirth, and Denham's mother, seventy-one at the time, undertook the care of her newborn grandson.

In August of 1933, while on another trip, Denham met Kathleen Augusta McKiel Zwicker, a Canadian nurse who was to become his second wife. The shipboard romance started on the trip from England to North America (Kathleen was returning to Canada from a European vacation) and continued by correspondence.

Kathleen, a native of Lunenburg, Nova Scotia, was nine years younger than Denham, having been born on April 20, 1898.

Denham and Kathleen were married on April 3, 1937 in the Anglican St. George's Church in the Johannesburg suburb of Parktown, not far from the new home at 11 Pallinghurst Road which Denham had bought to accommodate his bride, mother, and young son.

Denham and Kathleen traveled widely in Africa (where she often accompanied him on business trips) and to Britain, Europe, the United States, and Canada.

An enthusiastic amateur photographer, Denham's work was exhibited is salon competitions, garnering a number of prizes. He was also active in the Johannesburg Camera Club and occasionally lectured on the art and science of photography. With his training in chemistry, he processed his own negatives and prints and was an early experimenter with the development of color photography.

During the last six months of his life, Denham suffered from nephritis, complicated later by liver failure and several mild strokes. He died in the family home on December 2, 1948 at the age of fifty-nine.

On February 10, 1949, South African Cyanamid Company recorded the following minute: "The chairman referred to the great loss the company had sustained in the death of Mr. Charles Denham Grier who had been Chairman of the Board and managing director of the company since its incorporation on March 10, 1937. Mr. Grier's wide experience had contributed materially to the successful progress of the company, and his loss would be one which would be very keenly felt by the company as well as by the members of the board personally."

Kathleen, her seventeen-year-old stepson David, and "Granny" Frances Grier returned to Canada in early 1949. Kathleen and David settled in Montreal, while Frances took up residence in Vancouver, where a nephew on the Mills side of her family resided. Outliving her two children, Frances died at ninety-three on May 31, 1954 in Vancouver, British Columbia. (See Part Three: David Denham Eyre Grier)

Albert Ephraim Grier (age 40) and son Charles Denham Grier (age 9) in 1899

Denham, choirboy at St.
John's Episcopal Church in
the Wilderness, Denver,
Colorado, 1899
(Courtesy David Grier)

Denham (age 29)
during service in the
U.S. Army Corps of
Engineers, 1918

Ruby Stephenie Coote
Grier

Kathleen Augusta McKiel Zwicker Grier

83

Kathleen and Denham on their wedding day in Parktown, South Africa, April 3, 1937

Denham Grier (age 46) in 1934

8

ENTREPRENEUR
1919–1925

William Milton Grier remained in the Pacific Northwest for fifteen years, thirteen of these with Twohy Brothers, where he had risen from construction supervisor to general manager and full partner.

In the course of these years, Grier's achievements had earned him both professional acclaim and wealth. He had built dams, tunnels, bridges, viaducts, and thousands of miles of track for the leading railroads and municipal governments in the Pacific Northwest, the Rocky Mountain West, and western Canada. In addition to his major contracts with James J. Hill's Northern Pacific, he had completed construction projects with seven other railroad companies: Oregon & Washington Railway & Navigation; Union Pacific; Southern Pacific; Great Northern; Spokane, Portland & Seattle; Milwaukee & Burlington; and Canadian Northern.

By the age of forty, Grier was ready to direct his own firm. On January 29, 1919, he formed and incorporated the General Construction Company and, four months later, the Boschke Miller Grier Company, both with offices in the Northwestern Bank Building in Portland, Oregon. His partners were George W. Boschke and Richard B. Miller, who had been chief engineer on the North Bank project with Twohy Brothers.

GRIER–HAVENS MARRIAGE, 1920

On the evening of June 20, 1920, Grier and his wife Laura attended the wedding of his cousin Thomas Johnston ("Tommy") Grier, Jr. and Sally Havens, daughter of Mr. and Mrs. Wickham Havens, at Sally's grandparents' home, "Wildwood Gardens," in Piedmont, California. Milt's cousin Victoria ("Muddie") Grier was a bridesmaid, while her brothers Lisgar Patterson Grier and Ormonde Palethorpe Grier served as ushers. A dinner dance was held in the home after the ceremony.

Built by Sally's grandfather Frank Colton Havens as a tribute to his wife Lila Rand Havens, "Wildwood Gardens" was designed by Bernard Maybeck and modeled after a maharajah's palace.[1]

Following Frank Havens's death at "Wildwood" on February 9,

---

1. Frank Colton Havens was a successful businessman in the Oakland and East Bay area.

1918, the city of Piedmont named its elementary school in his honor; both his great-grandson Thomas Johnston Grier 3d and William Milton Grier, Jr. were students at the Frank C. Havens School during the 1930s.

NEW PARTNERSHIPS, 1921–1923

On October 23, 1921, Milt's mother Georgie Orr Grier died of uremia following an operation for uterine cancer at Providence Hospital in Oakland, California. Milt, his sister May Grier Borman and her second husband Charlie, and his aunt Mrs. Mattie Orr Barber attended the funeral at Albert Brown Company, 584 13th Street and were present as her ashes were placed beside those of her husband William John at the Oakland Columbarium in Oakland, California.

Two months later, in December 1921, Grier purchased his partners' interests in the Boschke Miller Grier Company and moved its headquarters to San Francisco; the offices were located in the Monadnock Building at 681 Market Street, next to the Palace Hotel.

At this time, he also acquired a forty percent interest in the old San Francisco engineering and contracting firm of Erickson Petterson Company, which was already headquartered in the Monadnock Building. Changing its name to Erickson Petterson Grier Company, he ran the firm from December of 1921 until the fall of 1925.

BLUE CANYON–EMIGRANT GAP, 1923

In January of 1923, Erickson Petterson Grier was awarded the $614,000 contract for Southern Pacific Railroad Company's Blue Canyon–Emigrant Gap project, designed to improve railway passage through the famous Emigrant Gap in the Sierra Nevada, near Donner Pass—a rugged and precipitous location, nearly 7,000 feet in elevation, which offered a spectacular panorama of mountains and canyons.

Several hundred men were employed by Grier's company for this project, which began in March 1923. Using huge steam shovels and other equipment, they widened an existing tunnel and laid 5.2 miles of double-track over the original lines laid in the late 1860s by Central Pacific

---

In partnership with F.M. Smith of Borax fame, he bought and developed thousands of acres in and adjacent to Oakland. The project was facilitated by his construction of an interurban transportation system—the Key Route—which included the Claremont Hotel in Berkeley and the Key Route Inn in Oakland. He also developed the water system in Oakland. By the early 1900s, he owned land and utilities valued at $72 million.

Railroad.[2] (The original tracks had formed the western arm of the first transcontinental railroad, which was completed at Promontory, Utah in 1869. Central Pacific's pioneer locomotive, the Collis P. Huntington—named after one of railroading's Big Four who built the Central Pacific—passed through Emigrant Gap en route from San Francisco to Ogden, Utah that same year.) The majority of the construction materials used on this project were brought in by rail, as was the food provided to the crews in on-site kitchens and dining areas.

With the help of one construction manager, a lead foreman, and several assistants, Grier directed and supervised the work's progress from his office in a private railroad car. Complete with kitchen, living, and dining facilities, this Pullman car was Grier's "home," as well, until construction was completed in September 1923.

During a typical week, Grier would spend one or two days in his San Francisco offices. He would travel by Southern Pacific passenger train from the work site, often stopping in Sacramento before proceeding to the Oakland Mole depot and catching the ferryboat to San Francisco. From the Ferry Building, his office was then a short walk up Market Street. He also conferred regularly with Southern Pacific's representatives in both their Sacramento and San Francisco offices.[3]

---

2.   Today these tracks are still used as part of the Southern Pacific Railroad's route over the Sierra Nevada through Blue Canyon, Emigrant Gap, and the Donner Summit to Nevada and Utah. Emigrant Gap is 166 miles from San Francisco.

3.   More than fifty years after Grier completed this project, his eldest son, Bill, and wife Joan traveled by train over Donner Pass and Blue Canyon–Emigrant Gap, while en route from Denver to visit his mother and Lannon relatives in Sacramento.

Milt Grier (facing camera) and Erickson Petterson
Grier Company equipment on-site during the Blue
Canyon-Emigrant Gap project in 1923

Sally Havens Grier

Georgie Grier with her daughter May Grier Borman
and granddaughter George Ann, c. 1920

Monadnock Building in
San Francisco, with
Palace Hotel at left
*(Courtesy of the Society of
California Pioneers)*

Northwestern National Bank Building in Portland, Oregon,
c. 1911 *(Courtesy of the Oregon Historical Society)*

91

9

GRIER AND MEAD
1925–1931

In mid-1925, the three directors of Erickson Petterson Grier Company—Gust Petterson, H. White, and William Milton Grier—decided to dissolve the firm, effective November 2, 1925. (Erickson had recently died, and Petterson was ready to retire.) With its dissolution, Grier next organized a new company under his control.

That fall, he formed a partnership with Winfield Scott Mead, an experienced construction and railroad contractor who had completed projects in Oklahoma, Texas, California, and Mexico.[1] The offices of this new firm—Grier and Mead—were first located in San Francisco at 593 Market Street, Room 241, a block east of the Monadnock Building. In 1927, however, the offices were moved to the Ray Building in Oakland, at 1924 Broadway, Rooms 303 and 317, where the company remained until 1931. The building was acquired by Henry J. Kaiser for his construction company on November 20, 1944.

CLAREMONT TUNNEL, 1926–1929

In July of 1926, Grier and Mead secured a contract with the East Bay Municipal Utility District for the construction of the inter-county (Alameda and Contra Costa counties) Claremont water tunnel. Beginning in Orinda at a height of 340 feet above sea level, the transmountain tunnel gradually sloped to a 328-foot level at Rockridge district in Oakland, conveying 200 million gallons of water daily.

The Claremont project was one of three tunnels constructed between Oakland and the San Joaquin River to bring water from the

---

1. Grier's partner Winfield Scott Mead, a Kentucky native, was an active contractor in Kern County, California before opening a San Francisco office when they formed Grier and Mead. His work on grading the Kern River canyon–Walker's Pass road, for example, was hailed as an engineering feat and involved removing 40,000 tons of rock from a cliffside location.

Mead and his wife Annette B. had two sons—Winfield Scott, Jr., who died in the 1940s, and John Stanley, now an attorney with Mead, Bradley and Kennan in San Francisco. From the late 1920s through the 1940s, the Meads lived at 110 Mesa Avenue, one block east of the Griers' home at 107 Highland Avenue in Piedmont, California.

Mokelumne River, in northern California's Calaveras County, into the East Bay district. It was the longest underground link in the Mokelumne project, which diverted the river's water from San Pablo Creek in Orinda, Contra Costa County, up to the Rockridge district in Oakland, Alameda County, and thus directly into the distribution area for the city of Oakland.

The East Bay Municipal Utility District, which granted the contract to Grier and Mead, was organized in 1923, the year the O'Shaughnessy Dam on the Tuolomne River in Yosemite National Park was completed to impound water for San Francisco. In addition to the Claremont tunnel, the utility district constructed both the Walnut Creek tunnel, a half-mile bore, and the Lafayette tunnel, which ran just over three miles in length.

The Claremont project had originally been awarded to the firm of MacDonald & Kahn, which had submitted the lowest bid of $1,068,140. After beginning work, however, they discovered that they had miscalculated their bid and asked to be relieved, whereupon the contract was awarded to Grier and Mead, the next lowest bidder at $1,374,374. Grier's firm was chosen over twelve other companies, including W.A. Bechtel Company, Twohy Brothers, and Utah Construction Company.

Grier and Mead directed construction of the Claremont tunnel from two field offices, one at the north entrance in Orinda and the other at the south entrance on Chabot Road in the Oakland hills.

In the course of completing the project, Grier and his colleagues overcame a number of major engineering obstacles. The rugged terrain of the coastal hills prevented them from using vertical shafts for excavating, which was the conventional (and far simpler) technique. Instead, the 3.6-mile inter-county bore had to be constructed by working inward from its two ends, and all materials were hauled through its nine-foot, horseshoe-shaped entrances.

Because of the unusual construction techniques, special measures were needed to insure adequate ventilation while work progressed. Three huge blowers were installed at each end of the bore to deliver fresh air to the workers. Giant compressors were also set up at Orinda and Rockridge district in Oakland, furnishing 2,000 cubic feet of compressed air to operate the drills with which the men were forging their way through the earth.

The crews also had to contend with coal, gas, and oil deposits, various fossilized formations, and large quantities of water which accumulated within the tunnel.

Grier and Mead's crews worked round-the-clock in three eight-hour shifts, first removing 100,000 cubic feet of dirt to hollow out the bore, then constructing the tunnel itself— a 3.6-mile-long concrete pipe, nine feet in diameter. The entire project would require more than 22,000 cubic yards of concrete.

THANKSGIVING NIGHT TRAGEDY, 1926

Tragedy struck the Claremont project on Thanksgiving night, November 25, 1926, shortly after Grier and Mead Company had hosted a holiday meal. Flood waters, attributed to several days of heavy rains, broke the coffer dam on San Pablo Creek at Orinda, inundating a four-foot connecting conduit that ran into the Claremont tunnel. Eleven of Grier's men had just descended a seventy-five-foot shaft, some 800 feet from the mouth of the tunnel at Orinda, when a six-foot wall of water plunged down and filled the tunnel. The swirling waters caused a cave-in, trapping the eleven men. Only one survived.

The horrified town of Orinda kept vigil for two days while rescue workers tried to recover the bodies. Dr. George C. Pardee, president of the Board of Governors of the East Bay Municipal Utility District, paid tribute to the ten workmen who had lost their lives:

> The march of progress claims many lives. The men who thus died were the unsung heroes of this nation. We grieve for them; we honor them. May their souls find eternal peace in the great beyond.[2]

The broken coffer dam was located on the portion of the project under contract to Smith Brothers, Inc. An investigation of the tragedy assigned liability for the disaster to Smith Brothers, and the firm of Grier and Mead was absolved of any responsibility.

TUNNEL PROJECT PROCEEDS, 1927–1929

When the Claremont tunnel was completed, water flowed through pipes and conduits from the Lancha Plana reservoir on the Mokelumne River to the Claremont reservoir ninety miles away, coming to the surface at only one point for aeration purposes. At the Oakland end, a concrete building was erected above the buried standpipe to function as a control house and laboratory. Three fifty-four-inch steel pipes and giant gate valves controlled the flow of water at both Orinda and Rockridge; at the latter point, the water emptied into the "balancing" Claremont reservoir. The water flowed from the Mokelumne pipes into the Claremont tunnel at Orinda, near the site of the Orinda County Club, and through the chlorina-

---

2. *Oakland Post Enquirer*, 26 November 1926.

94

tion plant and cistern. It then ran into mains for general distribution from that point, passing directly from the western end of the Lafayette tunnel into the mains that conveyed it to the faucets of Oakland and East Bay residents.

The nine-foot-high Claremont tunnel, shaped like a horseshoe, was hailed as an engineering feat when it was completed in 1929. Extending 3.6 miles in a straight line, it cut through hills which, at their highest, were 1,650 feet above sea level. Under the Claremont hills from Orinda toward Oakland, it was constructed on a twenty-five-degree slope.

The project's actual cost was $1,712,535, exceeding the original bid by $338,161. The overrun was calculated at cost plus fifteen percent, a portion of which included extra work required to rectify the November 1926 flood damage.

During the course of construction, Grier and Mead made some interesting archeological discoveries, as well. Their crews unearthed the fossilized shinbone of an *Eohippus*, a miniature prehistoric horse, as well as a sabre-toothed tiger, which is normally found only in tropical climates.

Both Erickson Petterson Grier Company and Grier and Mead had completed large and technically demanding projects during the 1920s. These successes had, in turn, established Milt Grier's reputation for mastery in engineering and construction.

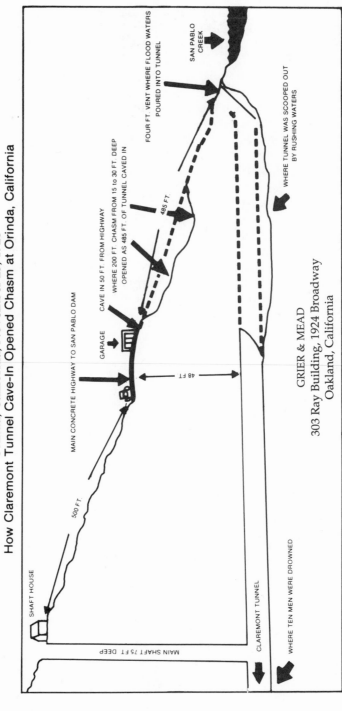

CLAREMONT TUNNEL CAVE-IN
Orinda, California, November 25, 1926
How Claremont Tunnel Cave-In Opened Chasm at Orinda, California

SHAFT HOUSE

500 FT.

MAIN SHAFT 75 FT DEEP

MAIN CONCRETE HIGHWAY TO SAN PABLO DAM

48 FT

GARAGE

CAVE IN 50 FT. FROM HIGHWAY

WHERE 200 FT. CHASM FROM 15 to 30 FT. DEEP
OPENED AS 485 FT. OF TUNNEL CAVED IN

485 FT.

FOUR FT. VENT WHERE FLOOD WATERS
POURED INTO TUNNEL

SAN PABLO
CREEK

WHERE TUNNEL WAS SCOOPED OUT
BY RUSHING WATERS

CLAREMONT TUNNEL

WHERE TEN MEN WERE DROWNED

GRIER & MEAD
303 Ray Building, 1924 Broadway
Oakland, California

Diagram shows location and effect of the cave-in which closed 485 feet of the Claremont tunnel's Orinda portal (dotted lines), after the tunnel was flooded by waters from San Pablo Creek on November 25, 1926. At the time of the cave-in, crews were searching for the bodies of the ten men drowned in the Thanksgiving flood. Above ground, the Mokelumne garage hangs precariously on the brink of a 200-foot chasm opened when the tunnel beneath collapsed.

Milt Grier and W.S. Mead at the site of the Claremont tunnel project, c. 1927

Winfield Scott Mead

Ray Building (left) in Oakland, California, c. 1925
(Courtesy of the California Historical Society Library)

10

MARRIAGE AND FAMILY

In 1921, Grier's marriage to Laura Watson ended in divorce; they had had no children.[1] Two years later, while in the offices of Southern Pacific Railroad to discuss the Blue Canyon-Emigrant Gap project, he met an attractive young secretary named Elo Theresa Lannon. After a four-year courtship, Milt and Elo were married on November 9, 1927 in a civil ceremony in Reno, Nevada. George Bartlett, a Nevada district judge, officiated, and Harlan L. Heward and Bessie Ellsworth witnessed the ceremony. The couple then honeymooned at the newly opened Ahwahnee Hotel in Yosemite National Park.[2]

ELO LANNON GRIER

Seventeen years younger than her husband, Elo was born on September 26, 1895 in Sacramento, California, the second of Patrick Joseph and Julia McDermott Lannon's children. She was baptized on October 27, 1895 in the Cathedral of the Blessed Sacrament at 11th and K Streets in Sacramento.

Her parents were of Irish descent, both born in Strokestown, Roscommon, Ireland. They emigrated to the United States in the 1880s and were married in Sacramento on October 3, 1892, in the church where Elo would be baptized three years later. (See Allied Families: Lannon)

Elo was educated in Sacramento's public and parochial schools, graduating from the John Marshall School, Mary Jane Watson Junior High School, and Saint Joseph Academy before entering the business world.

In mid-December 1926, Elo took a six-week winter vacation in the East. She went by train to New York City to visit her uncle John A. Lannon and his wife Sarah (nee Walsh) and to Providence, Rhode Island to visit her aunt Margaret McDermott O'Rourke (her mother's sister), Margaret's husband James, and Elo's cousin Elizabeth McGreevey. After celebrating

---

1. From 1922 to 1924, Milt Grier lived in San Francisco at 645 Leavenworth Street; from 1925 to 1927, at 2337 Chestnut Street. During this period, Laura A. Grier lived near Golden Gate Park, at 301 Carl Street.

2. Ahwahnee is an Indian name meaning "deep, grassy valley." The hotel's architect was Gilbert Stanley Underwood, a Harvard graduate who also designed two other high-country hotels: Timberline Lodge at Mount Hood, Oregon and Sun Valley Lodge in Idaho.

the holidays with her relatives, she boarded the Southern Pacific Steamship Lines' *Creole* in New York City for its January 15 cruise to New Orleans, where she enjoyed several days of sightseeing before returning to San Francisco by train.

During the spring of 1927, Grier took his bride-to-be and her younger sisters—Ferdinand ("Ferdy") and Julia—to the Del Coronado Hotel in Coronado, California for a week of swimming, sailing, and sight-seeing in San Diego and Tijuana.

PIEDMONT HOME, SONS

For his first home with Elo, Grier bought a ten-room, English-style house in fashionable Piedmont, California.[3] Located at 107 Highland Avenue, the two-story, grey-stuccoed and timbered home had leaded win-dows, two dining rooms, a wine cellar, and a roof garden over the garage. While Elo helped select furnishings at antique shops and W&J Sloane in San Francisco, Anna Jorgens, a designer and neighbor of May Grier Borman, created its interior plan. Elo eventually had a cook and maid, a nanny and gardener to help her there.[4]

Two sons were born to the Griers: William Milton, Jr., on Septem-ber 23, 1928 in the Fabiola Hospital in Oakland, and Eloyd John, on July 4, 1929 in the St. Francis Hospital in San Francisco. They were baptized on March 22, 1930 at Trinity Episcopal Cathedral in Phoenix, Arizona, where the family rented a winter home. Edwin S. Lane, Dean, was the officiant at the baptism; witnesses included Grier's sister May and brother-in-law Charles J. Borman.

THE YACHT *ELOGRIER*

In 1927, Grier retained Nunes Brothers Shipyard in Sausalito to design and construct a diesel-powered yacht to sleep ten passengers.

---

3. In 1820, the Piedmont, Oakland, Berkeley, Alameda, and San Leandro areas were part of a Spanish land grant called Rancho Antonio, which was given to Don Luis Peralta, a Spanish soldier. Peralta, never living on the Rancho, eventually divided it among his four sons. The first known settler in the Piedmont area, Walter Blair, came to San Francisco from Vermont. In 1852, he camped at what is now the corner of Blair and Highland Avenue, a block from William Milton Grier's home at 107 Highland Avenue.

4. After an attempted robbery at the Grier home in 1930, Milt installed a security alarm system between his home and his neighbors, the Joseph C. Merrick family, who lived on the corner of Park Way and Highland Avenue and often watched after young Bill and Eloyd.

Named for his wife, the *ELOGRIER* was completed in 1929. It was finished in Philippine mahogany and Chinese teak and was powered by a seventy-five-horsepower, six-cylinder diesel engine. Fifty feet long by eleven feet wide, the yacht featured a raised deck and trunk cabin and had a cruising range of 1,000 miles; its official number was 229179. Anna Jorgens also oversaw the yacht's furnishings, including glass- and dishware, draperies and fabric coverings.

Garland Rotch, a San Francisco ship's captain who had sailed widely in the South Pacific islands and the Orient, was employed by Grier to operate the yacht and oversee its maintenance. The *ELOGRIER* was moored in San Francisco's marina at St. Francis Yacht Club, where the adjoining berth slip was occupied by Templeton Crocker's yacht *Zaca*.[5] Grier was a member of the St. Francis Yacht Club from 1927 to 1935.

The family cruised in San Francisco and San Pablo Bays, on the Sacramento River, and along the Pacific Coast to Monterey, where they slept aboard the yacht or at the Del Monte Hotel.[6] They also cruised to San Diego and Coronado, where they were guests at the Del Coronado Hotel.

May and Charles Borman and their daughter George Ann were frequent passengers. Some ten years older than her cousins Bill and Eloyd, George Ann often watched after them during these family excursions.

LIFE IN PIEDMONT

In 1927, Grier bought new dining and living room furniture for Elo's parents' turn-of-the-century Victorian home at 5314 J Street in Sacramento. In the same year, he hired his young brother-in-law, Raymond James Lannon, to build a wine and beer cellar in the Griers' Piedmont home, where beer was brewed in large crocks and bottled, capped, and stored. He

---

5.   A philanthropist and heir to his father Charles Crocker's Central Pacific Railroad fortune, Templeton Crocker attended Yale and supported the California Academy of Sciences, the oldest scientific institution in the West. Crocker's yacht *Zaca* (the Samoan term for peace) was used on the Academy's expeditions in Alaska, Panama, Asia, Africa, Australia, New Zealand, South America, and many of the Pacific islands.

The yacht was also used by actor Errol Flynn during the 1940s to entertain young starlets. Following one such excursion, Flynn was accused of statutory rape, leading to a sensational court trial in 1942 and '43 which made front-page headlines across America. Defended by attorney Jerry Geisler, Flynn was finally acquitted on all charges.

6.   Pebble Beach, 125 miles south of San Francisco, was once a picnic ground for guests at Charles Crocker's Del Monte Hotel in Monterey. Crocker was one of the "Big Four" of the Central Pacific Railroad; his development firm, Pacific Improvement Company, later became Del Monte Properties.

also financed sister-in-law Ferd Lannon's education at San Jose State College and hired her to care for his infant sons.

The Griers often entertained in their Piedmont home and at the St. Francis Yacht Club in San Francisco. When Grier and Mead had offices in the Ray Building in Oakland, Milt often hosted lunches at the Leamington Hotel on 19th and Franklin Streets and at Hotel Oakland on 13th and Harrison, as well as at the Palace Hotel in San Francisco.

On July 20, 1929, Milt was saddened by the tragic death of his young cousin, Thomas Johnston ("Tommy") Grier, Jr. (1897–1929). He and a friend, Theron P. Stevick, were driving in the early evening in Tommy's Pierce Arrow near San Rafael, California, en route to the Bohemian Club summer encampment and its "Hi Jinks"—the annual play performed in the club's outdoor theatre at Bohemian Grove in northern California. The car overturned on a curve, instantly killing the thirty-two-year-old Grier. (His passenger was thrown from the car and escaped serious injury.)

Tommy and his wife Sally Havens had lived in Los Angeles following their Piedmont wedding in 1920. While there, he had been president of Citizens Guaranty Loan & Investment Company, a firm he founded in 1925. After the birth of his son Thomas Johnston Grier 3d in Los Angeles on August 20, 1926,[7] the Griers returned to San Francisco, where Tommy became an officer with Fireman's Fund Insurance Company at 401 California Street. At the time of his death, Tommy was assistant treasurer, and his family lived in San Francisco's Sea Cliff district at 2801 Lake Street. Milt, his wife Elo, and sister May attended the funeral in San Francisco.

During the holiday season, the Griers and May Borman enjoyed taking young Bill and Eloyd to see the Santa Clauses and toylands at San Francisco department stores: The White House; City of Paris, with its dazzling Christmas tree rising above balconies to a glass dome and its Louis XVI window frames of white enamel and carved, gilded wood; and The Emporium, with an immense glass-domed rotunda, ringed by a pillared gallery, rising through four stories to the roof garden. Amongst the glittering toys, the boys eagerly pointed out electric trains, bright red tricycles, fire trucks, and automobiles.

Between 1928 and 1933, the Griers celebrated Christmas and New

---

7. Thomas Johnston Grier 3d (1926–1982) was a compact man—5' 6 1/2" tall and 140 lbs.—with brown eyes and hair and a ruddy complexion. During the Second World War, he served in the U.S. Navy from August 18, 1944 to May 23, 1946. After completing Landing Craft School in San Diego, he worked in amphibious operations and saw duty in the Pacific for a year aboard the U.S.S. *Auburn* from 1945–1946. From May 31 to June 21, 1945, he participated in the occupation of Okinawa Gunto-Ryukyu Islands, and in July of 1945, he completed the radar operations course at Camp Catlin.

Year's in their Piedmont home, which was decorated with holly, evergreens, and a ceiling-tall tree. Presents were opened on Christmas Eve; afterward, before retiring, the children hung stockings on the mantle over the fireplace, then fetched and emptied them early Christmas morning. Later in the day, family and guests had a festive dinner, and the Griers hosted a reception on Christmas night. After the holidays, from 1930 to 1933, the Griers spent winters in rented homes in the Camelback Road area of Phoenix, Arizona.

TRAITS

Milt Grier, who possessed a keen intelligence and a captivating charm, inspired devotion and loyalty. He was 5' 8" tall and fair, with blue-gray eyes. In middle age, his brown hair receded and thinned, and he became stocky. He wore tailor-made, single-breasted suits, favored French and Italian food and wine, and smoked cigarettes, cigars, and pipes. (He had a handsome pipe collection, some of which he had bought while in the Philippines and Japan during 1898-1899, and an elegant mahogany humidor.)

When living at a construction site, he often took along books of Emerson, Keats, Sir Walter Scott, and Dickens, and when time permitted, he enjoyed walking in the country, savoring and observing nature's beauty and wildlife.

Politically, Grier was a Republican, a conservative who believed in private enterprise and individual initiative. He admired Herbert Hoover's mining engineering achievements, his public service, humanitarian work in Europe during World War I and turn-of-the-century relief work in China during the Boxer Rebellion, and his efforts to promote the Panama-Pacific International Exposition from 1912 to 1914.

Grier was a Mason for nearly thirty years. On March 4, 1907, he had joined Wasco Lodge Number 15, Columbia Commandery Number 13 in The Dalles, Oregon; on May 27, 1907, he became a Master Mason; on December 1, 1911, he received the Order of the Red Cross; and on February 9, 1912, he was made a Knight of the Malta and Knight Templar. While working in Montana from 1913 to 1915, he was an active member of the Algeria Temple in Helena. Grier retained his membership in the Masons until his death in December 1935.

In his leisure hours, Grier enjoyed woodworking at his bench in the garage of his Piedmont home—a skill passed down to him from his grandfather James, a carriage-maker—producing toy locomotives, railroad cars, and ships for his two sons with wood drills, saws, planes, files, chisels, and hammers. He also played cribbage, whist, poker, gin rummy, and dominoes. (While in Japan in 1899, he had purchased a set of ivory dominoes in a rectangular oak box with sliding lid which he took with him when living at construction sites.)

A sharp judge of character and ability, Grier selected able partners and associates in his companies, men of talent and integrity. He gave them broad responsibilities and compensated them well. Although bold and aggressive in directing his enterprises, Grier was unfailingly considerate and courteous in his personal relationships.

Elo Lannon Grier as a new bride in
Reno, Nevada, November 1927

Elo in the late 1920s

Elo Theresa Lannon Grier, c. 1927

Elo in front of the Griers' Piedmont home in the late 1920s

Three Lannon sisters—Julia, Ferd, and Elo—at the Hotel Del Coronado in the spring of 1927

Elo, Julia, and Ferd at Hotel Del Coronodo, spring 1927

Milt and Elo's first home, in Piedmont, California

St. Francis Hospital in San Francisco, c. 1922
(Courtesy of the California Historical Society Library)

Fabiola Hospital in Oakland, California, 1928
(Courtesy of the California Historical Society Library)

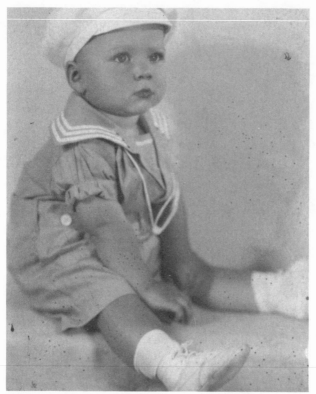

Bill Grier, 1929

Rear view of the *ELOGRIER* at St. Francis Yacht Club on the Marina, San Francisco, 1929

110

Side view of the *ELOGRIER* at St. Francis Yacht Club, on the Marina, San Francisco, 1929

The *ELOGRIER* under construction in 1928 at Nunes Brothers Shipyard in Sausalito, California, with Charlie, May, and George Ann Borman and Milt and Elo Grier

Milt with niece George Ann and her friend Wallace Hoover aboard the
ELOGRIER, 1929

Milt, c. 1929

Milt, Bill, and Elo in 1929

T.J., Jr. and wife Sally with son Thomas Johnston Grier 3d, 1926

Thomas Johnston Grier, Jr.

Eloyd, Gerry Lannon, and Bill
in rear garden of Lannon
grandparents' home in
Sacramento, summer 1934

Bill and Eloyd in the fall of 1933

Bill and Eloyd on lawn of their Piedmont home in the early 1930s

Milt at Sacramento's William Land Park, 1927

Bill (center) at his fifth birthday party, Piedmont, September 23, 1933

Milt and Elo on the steps of the Lannons' Sacramento home, 1927

11

FRIENDS, COMPETITORS, '29 CRASH

Milt Grier modestly attributed his success to luck and help from family and friends—his parents and his uncle T.J., Phoebe Hearst, and Judge John Twohy. Yet while he was doubtlessly helped by them, his ascendancy was, above all, the product of his own genius and industry.

A.P. GIANNINI

Grier was a lifelong friend of Amadeo Peter ("A.P.") Giannini, who, in 1904, founded the Bank of Italy (renamed Bank of America in 1930) at the corner of Washington Street and Columbus Avenue in San Francisco.[1] The two men had met during the bank's first year, while Grier was working as manager with Twohy Brothers, contractor on the Southern Pacific Railroad Company's Bayshore Cutoff project. They soon developed a close business relationship, and in future years, as a client of Giannini's bank, Grier would build tunnels, bridges, water systems, and dams and lay many miles of railroad track.

Giannini admired Grier's achievements and entrepreneurial abilities; Grier esteemed Giannini's original banking practices that helped the common man—practices that laid the foundation for his bank's future growth and success. Giannini, in fact, proudly dubbed his Bank of Italy "the Little Fellow's Bank." Laborers, small businessmen, anybody with a little vision and a lot of determination could walk into Giannini's bank and walk out with a loan.

Grier also applauded Giannini's daring immediately after San Francisco's disastrous earthquake in April 1906, even though many of Giannini's fellow bankers considered him a radical and would have nothing to do with him. While the majority of the city's bankers wrung their hands and declared they could not reopen until November, Giannini astounded everyone by announcing that the Bank of Italy would be ready for business the next day. Moreover, he set up a "bank" at a desk in a waterfront

---

1. A.P. Giannini, eight years Grier's senior, was born on May 6, 1870 in San Jose, California. A consummate businessman, A.P. had a philosophy concerning the accumulation of wealth: "I don't want to be rich....No man actually owns a fortune; it owns him." At his death in 1949, he left an estate of $489, 278, a relatively modest amount for a person in his position.

shack, where he loaned money liberally to area workers and quickly saw his faith rewarded. Soon after, he extended a loan to Grier, representing Twohy Brothers, to repair the damages on the Bayshore Cutoff project caused by the quake. Giannini's timely actions helped transform the city's pessimism into optimism.

Eschewing the trappings of corporate power and wanting to be in contact with his customers, Giannini did not have a private office at the bank's main branch at 1 Powell Street in San Francisco. Rather, he worked at his desk in the midst of the main floor, where he could readily greet and assist his customers. When Grier entered the Bank of Italy, Giannini would rise and walk over to welcome him with a warm embrace, affectionately calling him "Giamo." After Grier relocated his company to San Francisco at the end of 1921, he, Giannini, and others often lunched together at the Palace and downtown restaurants.

In 1922, '25, and '28, Giannini asked Grier to become a director of the Bank of Italy, but, already burdened with responsibilities, Grier respectfully declined each offer. Later, Grier also became a business friend of A.P.'s son Mario, a law graduate who was named president of the Bank of America in 1936.

HENRY KAISER AND WARREN BECHTEL

Grier was also a long-time friend of Henry J. Kaiser and Warren A. Bechtel.[2] Like Grier, these construction entrepreneurs had begun working at an early age, gradually making their way up through the ranks and founding their companies after gaining field experience with other firms.

Kaiser, the son of German immigrants, left school at thirteen to enter the business world. He began with a $1.50-a-week job in upstate New York; within ten years, he was the owner of a photographic firm with stores in New York, Florida, and the Bahamas.

In 1906, however, he decided to head to the fast-growing western states, where he secured a job with a hardware company in Spokane,

---

2. Henry J. Kaiser (1882–1967) was born in Sprout Brook, New York and left home in the eighth grade to help support his family. His first company, Henry J. Kaiser Company, Ltd., a construction firm, was formed in 1914 in Vancouver, British Columbia. His son Edgar (1908–1981) became president of Kaiser Industries Corporation in 1956.

Warren A. Bechtel (1872–1931) was born in Freeport, Illinois. His firm was originally headquartered in Oakland, California, but later relocated to San Francisco. In 1926, W.A. Bechtel Company lost the bid on the Claremont tunnel project to Grier and Mead.

Grier also knew the sons of these company founders—Stephen, Kenneth, and Warren, Jr. Bechtel and Henry, Jr. and Edgar Kaiser.

Washington. Six years later, he began work in the construction industry, joining a Pacific Northwest firm as a salesman and manager.

At the age of thirty-two— in the year 1914—he founded the Henry J. Kaiser Company, Ltd. By the time his firm relocated to its permanent headquarters in Oakland, California in 1921, Kaiser had completed millions of dollars worth of construction projects across California and the northwest—highways, dams, and sand and gravel plants.

In 1927, Kaiser was awarded a $20 million contract to build over 200 miles of roads and 500 bridges in Cuba. His company was also a member of the Six Companies, Inc., a consortium of builders who completed the Hoover Dam in the 1930s. Other projects in that period included the Shasta, Grand Coulee, and Bonneville dams and the San Francisco Bay Bridge piers.

Like Kaiser and Grier, Warren Bechtel—known to friends as "Dad" —was a self-starter from humble beginnings. An Illinois native, he was a muleskinner in his early years and had an unprofitable tenure in the cattle business before entering the heavy construction industry. By coincidence, he founded his own firm—W.A. Bechtel—in the same year that Kaiser had launched his business, 1914.

Over the next half-century, Bechtel's company, incorporated in 1925 in Oakland, would expand dramatically, building bridges, rail lines, dams, and natural gas lines, and was a member of the consortium that built the Hoover Dam.

Although Grier, Kaiser, and Bechtel were often competitors bidding on the same project, neither their friendship nor their mutual respect was affected by the outcome. During this period, they often talked by telephone and sometimes lunched together to discuss the exigencies of construction and future projects.

Since then, the companies formed by Kaiser and Bechtel in Oakland and San Francisco have grown into international firms—Kaiser Industries and Bechtel Group, Inc. The founding fathers' sons and grandsons have succeeded them and today continue to direct these enterprises.

Unlike Kaiser's and Bechtel's children who were grown and experienced in the business, Grier's sons Bill and Eloyd—only seven and six years old when he died—were, of course, too young to succeed their father, and thus his enterprise ended with his death in 1935.

AFTERMATH OF STOCK MARKET CRASH

Milt Grier's professional life and prosperity in the first third of the century reflected the nation's unprecedented growth. The United States was then producing twenty-five percent of the world's goods and services, and in this climate, all but the least efficient firms grew rich, especially those in manufacturing, construction, and real estate.

Accompanying this growth and prosperity was a strong spirit of optimism, leading many people to invest their money in the corporations that were making America great. Sound investment decisions, however, soon gave way to rash speculation. Between 1923 and 1929, speculative fever gripped the market, driving stock prices higher and higher. The vastly inflated prices of corporate equities soon bore little resemblance to actual corporate asset value and profitability.

Free of debt and enjoying a high income during the 1920s, Grier, too, invested in the stock market. Among the stocks soaring in price at this time were Giannini's Bank of Italy and Transamerica Corporation,[3] of which Grier accumulated 20,000 shares. Other holdings included U.S. Steel, Standard Oil of New Jersey, Petroleum Corporation of America, North American Oil Company, Inter Coast Trading Company, City Service Company, and various railroads.

When the bull market crashed on October 29, 1929—"Black Tuesday"—it brought ruin to many. For Grier, who was at the peak of his career as his Claremont tunnel project neared completion, the Crash seriously reduced his wealth and impaired his participation in future ventures, including the Hoover Dam (1931–1936), the San Francisco-Oakland Bay Bridge (1933–1936), and the Golden Gate Bridge which was started on January 14, 1933 and completed in May of 1937.

The Crash also took its toll on Grier's health, and in 1930, he suffered his first heart attack. Attended by nurses round-the-clock in his home, he recovered, but remained under the care of two San Francisco physicians, Drs. Daniel W. Sooy, a surgeon, and Laird M. Morris, an internist, until his death five years later.[4]

After surviving a second heart attack in 1933, Grier sought a change of pace and tried unsuccessfully to exchange his yacht *ELOGRIER* and the Piedmont home for an operating fruit ranch, with considerable acreage, in Walnut Creek, California.

Compounding the trauma of illness and the '29 Crash, Grier was kidnapped and robbed by three men and a woman in downtown Sacra-

---

3. From 1928 to 1929, Transamerica Corporation was formed as a holding company to absorb the assets of the Bank of Italy.

To acquire other banks through the exhange of stock, Transamerica held two California branch-banking systems, as well as a New York bank, two large insurance companies, and controlling interest in General Foods Corporation.

4. Both physicians had their offices in the medical-dental building at 490 Post Street. Dr. Sooy was in room 216; Dr. Morris, in room 644.

mento in 1934. They forced him into a car near Seventh and J Streets, knocked him unconscious, took a diamond stickpin, other jewelry, and cash, and threw him from the car in Yolo County, near Sacramento. Neither the jewelry and money nor the kidnappers were ever found.

12

MAY GRIER AND FAMILY

Grier's children Bill and Eloyd were devoted to his sister May Grier Borman, who adored them. From 1928 to 1934, she regularly visited them in Piedmont, commuting by ferry from San Francisco to Oakland Mole depot, then boarding the Key Route electric train to 41st Street and Piedmont Avenue. There she transferred to a streetcar that climbed up the wooded hills of Piedmont to the Griers' home at 107 Highland Avenue. The boys treasured her joyful visits and loving hugs, her amusing stories, games, and trinkets.

FAMILY VISITS

Bill and Eloyd were equally excited to visit their aunt May, uncle Charlie, cousin George Ann, and the Bormans' affectionate Irish terrier, Whiskers, in their San Francisco home near Golden Gate Park and the Pacific.

Their playful pet, a liver-colored mutt, was much loved by the boys. He accompanied May on her afternoon walks to market at nearby greengrocers on Balboa Street, went on fishing and camping trips, and slept in the basement in a wicker basket cushioned with old pillows and blankets.

George Ann played popular music on the family's upright piano and taught her cousins the scales and chords. She liked Irving Berlin's and Jerome Kern's compositions, George and Ira Gershwin's jazz harmonies, Harold Arlen's melodies, Cole Porter, Oscar Hammerstein II, and Lorenz Hart. Many of these songs were popularized by Bing Crosby, although the most important indicator of popularity then was the weekly radio show "The Lucky Strike Hit Parade," to which George Ann and her cousins faithfully listened.

FLEISHHACKER PLAYFIELD AND ZOO

During these visits, May planned all manner of excursions to delight the children: picnics, rides on street and cable cars, ferryboats, and interurban electric trains (both the orange-colored Key Route and red-colored Southern Pacific in Oakland and East Bay), tours to the Ghiradelli chocolate factory, and visits to Playland-at-the-Beach, Fleishhacker Playfield and Zoological Gardens (now San Francisco Zoo), and toy departments of downtown stores.

The zoo was named after Herbert Fleishhacker, a San Francisco banker and former president of the San Francisco Park Commission who donated the pool and Mother's House, a resting place for mothers and their offspring. Located on 128 acres a block from the Pacific Ocean, the 1,000-animal zoo, patterned after Germany's renowned Hagenbeck Zoo, featured man-made streams, waterfalls, islands, cliffs, and caves—natural habitats separated from spectators by moats.

For the boys, Fleishhacker was paradise—a bucolic site of greenery where the smell of eucalyptus and pine always seemed to wash the air. They enjoyed the animals (especially the expressive apes, monkeys, and penguins) and loved to watch the feeding of the lions and tigers. They played on the swings and spiraling slides and built fortresses in the sand. They gleefully rode the carousel's colorful, hand-carved wooden horses while it turned to the lively sound of its band organ.[1] They rode ponies and the thrilling miniature railroad. An engineer, dressed in blue-and-white striped bib overalls and visor cap, sat in the diesel-powered locomotive and ran the train. After shouting "All aboard!" he sounded his whistle, started the engine, and the train would soon disappear from the view of people at the depot; chugging about the gardens and groves of tall eucalyptus, pine, and cedar trees, it passed through a tunnel and over a bridge before the whistle sounded its return to the station.

There also were picnics on the lawn and wading and swimming in the warmed saltwater of the outdoor pool for fifteen cents. When built in 1925, the pool was considered the largest in the world. Measuring 1,000 feet long and 150 feet wide, its depth ranged from three to fourteen feet, and it accommodated several thousand swimmers in its 6.5 million gallons of water.[2]

William Milton Grier, by this time a successful businessman in his fifties, was especially proud to be a father and to experience the childhood pleasures of his sons at a time in life when his career was well established.

---

1. The merry-go-round was constructed in 1925 by William H. Dentzel of Philadelphia, whose family was famous for producing intricate wood carvings of animals.

2. Opening on April 23, 1925, the pool was first used for the American Amateur Union (AAU) men's championships, where Johnny Weismuller won the four-day competition for his team, the Illinois Athletic Club.

On annual visits to San Francisco as an adult, Bill has enjoyed returning to the zoo and gardens, an oasis of serenity and nostalgia: strolling its lush glades and viewing its animals; watching mothers and their frolicking children; picnicking and reading by a pond; savoring its beauty and recapturing his boyhood play there under the loving gaze of his aunt May Grier Borman. He was saddened, however, at the removal of the miniature railway and the unique outdoor swimming pool, which had added such excitement to his adventures there.

The Bormans' pet "Whiskers" on the deck of the *ELOGRIER*, c. 1929

Grandmother Borman, May, George Ann, and Charlie at the famed redwood tree tunnel in Yosemite National Park, 1927

129

Milt and his boys in Piedmont, c. 1931

13

GRIER AND FONTAINE
Gold Mining in the Sierra Nevada
1934–1935

In 1934, Milt formed Grier and Fontaine with William R. Fontaine, a brilliant Oakland civil engineer and consultant who assisted Grier and Mead in constructing the Claremont tunnel.[1] Their venture was prospecting for gold in Placer County, California, where the company had taken leasehold options on acreage tracts near the towns of Loomis and Lincoln.

With his work now centered in this area, Grier leased the home in Piedmont, stored its furnishings with a company in Oakland, and moved his family to Sacramento, fifty miles away from his work site. Initially, they shared the home of Elo's parents Patrick and Julia Lannon, at 5314 J Street. Later, however, Milt and Elo lived in a motel in Loomis, while the boys remained with their grandparents. In September of 1934, they enrolled in El Dorado Elementary School, Bill in high first grade and Eloyd in kindergarten. They remember that during this period their father gave them vials of gold, after the crushed rock samples from his dredgings were assayed for gold content at laboratories in Sacramento.

On July 4, 1934, in celebration of Eloyd's fifth birthday, his father bought a variety of fireworks which he set off in front of the Lannons' Victorian home on tree-lined J Street. Family and friends enjoyed the display from ladder-back rockers and a swing on the second-floor pillared front porch, which was reached from the sidewalk by wide steps. The family also watched the State Fair's nightly fireworks in August from the Lannons' rear porch .

While living in Sacramento in the mid-thirties, the boys often swam and picnicked during summer vacations at Southside Park, located on 6th and T Streets. They also visited the zoo and miniature railway in William Land Park.

---

1. William Fontaine lived in Oakland's Regillus Apartments at 244 Lakeside Drive, overlooking Lake Merritt. He also had an office in the nearby Ray Building, where Grier and Mead was headquartered.

SAN FRANCISCO VISITS

During 1934 and 1935, Grier traveled to San Francisco to see his doctors, conduct business, and visit with his sister May, brother-in-law Charlie, and niece George Ann. The Bormans adored his visits. A good conversationalist, "Billy" (as May called him, or "Uncle Milt" to George Ann) entertained them with stories of his activities and family. He also took them to dinner at favorite restaurants and for cruises on San Francisco Bay aboard his yacht *ELOGRIER*, which was berthed in the marina at St. Francis Yacht Club. (During this period, Charlie occasionally helped captain Garland Rotch aboard the yacht.)

From May's home on October 3, 1934, Milt wrote a letter — the only one that has survived—to his wife Elo: "My dearest sweetheart: I was just leaving for downtown when your dear letter was handed to me...I was glad to hear from you. Mighty glad to know Eloyd is OK, and hope he is back in school now. I was very much pleased when I opened my grip to find everything so nicely arranged, just like you. Won't write more now, just wanted to answer as soon as your dear letter was received and before going downtown. All my love to the dearest girl in the world. Love and kisses to the boys and folks. I am, yours lovingly—Billy."

GRIER'S DEATH, 1935

Grier and Fontaine Company continued gold prospecting until Milt succumbed to a third heart attack in Sacramento on December 8, 1935 at the age of fifty-seven. His ashes were placed near those of his father and mother, William John and Georgie, in the Oakland Columbarium near Piedmont.

William Milton Grier's untimely death left incomplete his promising gold exploration project in the Sierra Nevada. He left behind a young wife and two small boys of six and seven. But he left, too, a rich legacy of love and accomplishment that has inspired and brightened the lives of his family and friends to this day.

Bill (second row, extreme left) at Frank C. Havens School, Piedmont, California, June 1934

133

PART TWO

ELO GRIER AND HER SONS

CHRONOLOGY OF ELO LANNON GRIER

1895	Born in Sacramento, California on September 26
1901–1907	Attends and graduates from John Marshall School in Sacramento
1907–1910	Attends and graduates from Mary Jane Watson Junior High School in Sacramento
1910–1913	Attends and graduates from St. Joseph Academy in Sacramento
1923	Meets William Milton Grier while working in Southern Pacific Railroad Company's Sacramento office
1927	Marries William M. Grier in Reno, Nevada on November 9; moves into Piedmont, California home on November 19
1928	Son, William M. Grier, Jr., born in Oakland, California on September 23
1929	Son, Eloyd John Grier, born in San Francisco, California on July 4
1935	Husband dies in Sacramento on December 8; widowed at age forty
1936	Enrolls in Sacramento business school; works for California State Motor Vehicle Department, then joins John Deere Plow Company in San Francisco
1937	Sons join her in San Francisco; lives first on Jackson Street, later on Clay Street
1940	Joins Fireman's Fund Insurance Company in marine insurance underwriting; learns to drive
1941	Moves to 888 31st Avenue in San Francisco during summer
1947	Returns to live in Piedmont home, with sons; continues with Fireman's Fund

1948	Eloyd moves to Pennsylvania in August
1952	Bill leaves home to join Air Force unit in Minneapolis, Minnesota in January
1953	Visits Bill in Washington, D.C. in June; travels with him to New York City
1955	Bill visits her in Piedmont during June
1958	Granddaughter, Shelby W. Grier, born in Harrisburg, Pennsylvania on April 6
1959	Grandson, William M. Grier 3d, born in New York City on November 11
1950s	Sells Piedmont home; moves to San Francisco; continues with Fireman's Fund
1960	Retires from Fireman's Fund at age sixty-five; works part-time in San Francisco
1961	Bill and family visit her in San Francisco during May
1962	Buys and rents out home in Sacramento in October
1968	Retires; moves to Sacramento home on April 1
1987	Dies in Sacramento at age 91 on July 16

14

ELO CARRIES ON

Suddenly widowed at the age of forty, Elo became the source of support—both financial and moral—for her two young sons during the Great Depression years. Although buoyed by the love of her Lannon family and Borman in-laws, what truly carried the family through this trial was Elo's own resourcefulness, humor, energy, and resolve.

After their father's funeral, Bill and Eloyd lived in Santa Maria, California with Elo's youngest sister Ferdy and her attorney husband Fred Shaeffer. (Fred had two children from a previous marriage: Marie, a student at the University of California at Berkeley, and Freddie, a student in the local high school.) Among Bill's memories of this period are Freddie's many pets and the scent of eucalyptus logs burning in their living room fireplace. The boys celebrated Christmas 1935 there, but, after attending elementary school in Santa Maria from January to June 1936, they returned to live with their Lannon grandparents in Sacramento and re-entered El Dorado Elementary School in September of that year.

En route from Santa Maria, Bill and Eloyd visited their mother and her older sister Marie and husband Walter Hall in San Francisco, staying with the Halls in their apartment at 610 Leavenworth Street. Marie took them to Fisherman's Wharf, Crystal Palace market, and her husband's optometry office on the upper floor in Weinstein's department store, facing Market Street. On the last leg of their trip to Sacramento, she took her nephews on an exciting overnight trip aboard the *Delta Queen*—a riverboat with large stern paddle wheel, richly paneled lounges, dining and game rooms, and three decks. The boys shared a room with portholes looking out on the water. (Shortly thereafter, the *Delta Queen* and its sister ship *Delta King* ceased operations on the Sacramento River after fifty years of service. The *Delta Queen* now plies the Ohio River from Cincinnati to New Orleans, and the *Delta King*, converted to a hotel and restaurant, is berthed on the Sacramento River at K Street, in Old Sacramento.)

ENTERING THE BUSINESS WORLD

While settling her husband's estate, Elo lived with her parents, enrolled in a Sacramento business school, and worked for the California

State Motor Vehicle Department. After William Milton Grier's estate was settled in the Superior Court of California in Sacramento on May 7, 1936,[1] Elo accepted a secretarial and bookkeeping position with the John Deere Plow Company in San Francisco, at 424 Townsend Street. She resided for a few weeks with in-laws May and Charles Borman at 818 41st Avenue, then rented a furnished downtown apartment and returned by train on weekends to her family and sons in Sacramento.

Always prudent, Elo lived within her salary, saved a portion of it, and used credit sparingly.

Her dress was stylish and conservative, complemented by hats and gloves. On evenings out, she favored suits or dark-colored dresses, a pearl necklace, and fox or other furs. She patronized I. Magnin, City of Paris, White House, the Emporium, and Hale Brothers.

During the workweek, Elo rose and retired early, reserving Fridays and Saturdays for "evenings out." On the weekends, she liked dining at restaurants in the city with her sons, friends, and dates, among them Emil Wilmunder. Before dinner, she enjoyed a bourbon highball, an old fashioned, or a Manhattan and after the meal, a brandy Alexander with coffee. (Elo only imbibed socially— never alone, nor every day.) She also hosted cocktail and dinner parties and took in films and stage shows at San Francisco's theatres.

She also managed the family home in Piedmont, which was first leased out in the summer of 1934 when her husband formed a partnership with W.R. Fontaine (Grier and Fontaine) in Placer County. She negotiated leases, oversaw repairs, and kept the books. While there, Elo often visited and lunched with Piedmont friends—Annette Mead (widow of her husband's late partner), who lived a block east of the Griers; the Dreyers (founders of the ice cream company), who lived across Highland Avenue; the Cheathams (owners of the Sweet Shop in Piedmont); and the Merricks, next door neighbors on the corner.

From the time Elo settled in San Francisco in 1936, and in 1937 when her sons moved there to be with her, she and the boys visited her family in

---

1. Grier's will had been drawn and signed on February 26, 1930 in San Francisco. Less than a week later, on March 3, in Phoenix, Arizona (Maricopa County), a codicil was added in which a $20,000 trust fund was established for Laura A. Watson, Grier's first wife. The executor of the trust was to be A.P. Giannini's Bank of Italy National Trust and Savings Association. Given Grier's financial state at his death, neither this trust nor those established for his second wife and children were put into effect.

The ELOGRIER was sold to Arthur E. Nystrom on November 2, 1936. During World War II, it was requisitioned by the War Shipping Administration. In 1947, the yacht was redocumented and renamed JAN; in 1956, it was purchased by Joseph A. Giuffre of 32 Hillsdale Avenue, Daly City, California, who renamed the vessel EMA-RON and, in 1961, added a 671 GNC diesel engine and flying bridge for fishing.

Sacramento over weekends, taking the ferryboat to Oakland Mole where they transferred to Southern Pacific trains. Seeing her parents, brothers Joe and Raymond, her cousins Deirdrie Knapp and Helen Flanagan, and old friends was always a pleasant respite from her responsibilities in San Francisco.

Elo and her sons, c. 1940

Elo, Bill, Eloyd, and Emil Wilmunder dining out in San Francisco, c. 1938

15

THE BORMAN FAMILY

Over Thanksgiving week of 1936, Bill and Eloyd stayed in San Francisco with their aunt May, uncle Charlie, and cousin George Ann Borman. Arriving at the vast Oakland Mole depot by train from Sacramento, then going by ferryboat to the Ferry Building, the boys were met in the swirling crowd by George Ann and her Lux School classmate Carmen Aquado. In her family car, George Ann took them to lunch and a matinee performance at the Golden Gate Theatre, where they saw the Fred Astaire and Ginger Rogers film *Follow the Fleet* and a stage show.

Before returning to Sacramento, the boys enjoyed a host of activities in San Francisco. At Playland-at-the-Beach, they reveled in being by the ocean, in the carnival rides, arcade games, the small automobiles, the Big Dipper, and the Funhouse with its long undulating slides, round spinning platforms, mirrors, and mechanical laughing lady. They roller-skated at an indoor rink and played "kick the can" on George Ann's 41st Avenue block with her friends: Wallace Hoover, his cousins Robert and Edith, Gloria Binns, Janet Leavitt, and George Ann's Lux School classmate Virginia ("Ginger") Klute from 682 39th Avenue. The boys also watched George Ann ride horseback and take equestrian instruction in Golden Gate Park, and, with friends Duane Harder and Billy Binns, rode handmade coasters (whose wheels were automobile ball bearings) down 41st Avenue between Cabrillo and Fulton Streets.

CHEZ BORMAN

In May Grier Borman's two-story, white-stuccoed home, the family lived on the second floor, while the ground level housed the garage and basement; the front door was reached by an exterior brick staircase. The living room, with fireplace, bookshelves, and three bay windows, faced west; the rear sunroom overlooked a luxuriant flower garden to the east, enclosed by a weathered cedar fence, which had two goldfish ponds, a birdhouse, pink concrete walks, and a rough-hewn cedar gazebo in the rear. The interior was furnished in contemporary and period pieces, Oriental and Indian rugs; a large French tapestry hung on a living room wall. Milt Grier's wedding gifts also graced their home—a dining room set and Chinese rug from an antique shop and W & J Sloane and china, crystal glasses, and silver flatware from Shreve & Company. Later, when the Griers moved from Piedmont to Sacramento and stored their furniture, Milt gave the Bormans his family's English slant-top desk which May had always admired.

MAY GRIER BORMAN

In the midst of morning chores (preparing breakfast and tidying the kitchen, writing letters, paying bills, gardening, telephoning friends, and making appointments), May listened to two popular radio serials, "Helen Trent" and "The Goldbergs."

An ardent gardener, she was an officer of the San Francisco Garden Club, participated in their shows and programs, and brightened her home with flowers from her own yard. While gardening, May wore a dark-green visor to shield her eyes from the sun and often stopped to chat over the fence with her next-door neighbor, Mrs. Leavitt, another devoted gardener.

May went downtown on business or to shop, to meet friends or her daughter for lunch several times a week. She kept both her family's and her husband's business books and deposited checks or withdrew funds at the downtown Bank of America, at 1 Powell Street, or at the Balboa Street branch near her home. She also was her family's correspondent, writing her letters in clear and elegant penmanship.

After starting dinner and awaiting husband Charlie's return from work, May sometimes played solitaire, a game that held her rapt attention, at the dining room table, rearranging the cards and analyzing her moves. Before dinner, Charlie always worked the crossword puzzle in the *Call Bulletin*.[1]

After dinner, the Bormans listened to radio programs—the Jack Benny, Bob Hope, Walter Winchell, and Fred Allen shows; "Amos and Andy"; "Abbott and Costello"; "Kay Kyser's Kollege of Musical Knowledge"; "Gangbusters"; "Lucky Strike Hit Parade"; "I Love a Mystery"; and Joe Louis's championship fights. With Bill, Eloyd, and friends, they also played cards and games—canasta, hearts, gin rummy, poker, Chinese checkers, dominoes, and bingo.

---

1. Charles John ("C.J.") Borman was born on January 28, 1888 in Seymour, Indiana. He had two brothers, Earl and Elmer.

CHARLES BORMAN

When not entertaining, the Bormans read books and magazines, articles on gardening and art. Both May and Charlie were skilled painters of oil and watercolor still lifes and landscapes; they painted in their garden and sunroom, as well as during fishing and camping trips.

Charlie, an avid trout fly-fisherman, had honed his skills in nearby Golden Gate Park's fly-casting ponds and in the streams of northern California. At home, wearing bifocals, he tied flies, using Chinese dusters and other materials. He also cared for the goldfish and the two ponds which he had designed, built, and landscaped in the garden.

Automobile design was another lifelong interest for Charlie. He closely followed the annual model and engineering changes in trade journals and through his friends in the auto dealerships on Van Ness Avenue, near his shop. His avocation became his vocation, as well, for his firm, Borman and Company, specialized in designing and building "autobeds," reupholstering automobiles, and recovering convertibles.[2] The autobed concept—Charlie's own—provided a double-bed extension from the rear seat into the trunk of a four-door sedan. Another Borman innovation was a convenient dressing area addition—a folding, hinged wooden frame with canvas which formed a tent between the opened front and rear passenger doors, thereby creating a stand-up dressing space opened by a zipper on the front.

As a side line, Charlie also designed and built Art Deco club chairs, lounge chairs, and sofas. For his daughter George Ann and nephews Bill and Eloyd he built child-sized upholstered armchairs which they used through their early years.

May, Charlie, and George Ann drove to Detroit every other year from 1935 to 1941 to trade in their car for a new model. En route, they also camped in national parks and visited Charlie's brother Elmer, his wife Minnie, and sons Harold and Bobby in Cincinnati. (See Part Three: George Ann Borman Palmer)

May Grier Borman died at her home on the evening of March 21, 1947, the victim of a heart attack; she was seventy-one years old. Her husband, twelve years her junior, died at seventy-five on October 14, 1963.

---

2. Charles Borman's business partnerships in San Francisco included: Borman & Dahneke (Harry L.), 1656 Pine Street (1920s-1930s); Borman & Decker (Elmer), 1355 Bush Street (1931-1933); and Borman & Company, 1355 Bush Street (1934-1950s).

May Grier Borman

16

CITY LIFE
1937–1941

Elo and her sons celebrated Christmas in 1936 with the Lannons and their large family in Sacramento.[1] However, when the winter school term ended in Sacramento in January 1937, Elo decided to move to a first-floor walk-up apartment on Jackson Street in San Francisco, where Bill and Eloyd were enrolled in Spring Valley School, directly across from their apartment. Elo hired helpers to supervise her sons' after-school play and homework and to start dinner.

During the late afternoon, the boys listened to radio serials—"Dick Tracy," "Captain Midnight," "Jack Armstrong," and "Little Orphan Annie." On Saturday mornings in 1937 and 1938, they took tap-dancing and singing lessons at a studio on Market Street, near the Fox Theatre, performing to popular songs like "A-Tisket A-Tasket" and "Stop Beatin' Round the Mulberry Bush." Saturday afternoons were devoted to film matinees at one of the Polk Street theatres—the Royal or the Alhambra—which ran two features, a newsreel, a cartoon, and long-running serials, including "The Adventures of Wild Bill Hickok," all for a dime.

On Sunday mornings, Bill and Eloyd read the *San Francisco Examiner*'s sports and comics sections, then walked six blocks on Nob Hill to Episcopal services and Sunday school at Grace Cathedral. The Griers sometimes dined out on weekend evenings, with Elo's boyfriend Emil Wilmunder. The boys also accompanied Elo and Emil to the Saturday afternoon horse races at Bay Meadows and Tanforan, a short train ride south of the city. For Christmas in 1937, Elo gave her sons bicycles which they rode when they visited their aunt May. Billy Binns, a 41st Avenue friend, often rode with them around Golden Gate Park and the beach.

The Griers' family dentist at this time was Dr. Lew E. Wallace, a tall and genial man whose greeting was always a broad grin and a firm

---

1. All from California, the guests were Ferdinand Henrietta ("Ferdy") and her husband Fred Shaeffer from Santa Maria; Norma Winifred and Herb Pope Langton, from Berkeley; Mary Elizabeth ("Marie") and Walter George Hall, from San Francisco; Joseph Martin, Gerald ("Gerry") Joseph and Wilhelmina ("Mina") Lannon, from Sacramento; and Raymond James Lannon, bachelor and youngest Lannon child, from Sacramento.

handshake. His office, across from the St. Francis Hotel in the Elkan Gunst building at 323 Geary Street, Room 708, overlooked Union Square. Dr. Wallace had admired the boys' father, whom he treated from 1922 until Grier's death in 1935, and took a special interest in the boys' welfare. Bill's orthodontic work was done by Dr. Wallace from 1941 to '43.

HOLIDAYS, VACATIONS

Between 1937 and 1946, the Griers celebrated Christmas Eve at the Bormans' home. Presents were opened after dinner and Uncle Charlie later drove them about the city—to St. Francis Wood, Pacific Heights, and Marina districts— to see the colorfully lighted gardens and homes. Elo also hosted Thanksgiving and Christmas dinners and New Year's parties, as well.

During their summer vacations in 1937 and 1938, Bill and Eloyd were at Tilly's Roost, a camp in the Santa Cruz mountains near Boulder Creek and Ben Lomond, California. The following three summers, the boys alternated six-week visits with their Lannon grandparents in Sacramento.

The summers with the Lannons were idyllic times for the boys. Bill remembers waking early to a chorus of their crowing roosters. After a breakfast of rolled oats or cream of wheat, fruit, toast, and milk, the boys sometimes helped their grandfather Lannon feed the chickens and fetch eggs. Located inside a vine-covered, wire-fenced yard several hundred feet to the rear of the Lannon home, the chicken shed was reached from the back lawn by a path through a grape arbor and a cluster of quince, apple, cherry, and apricot trees.

To the side and rear of the shed were vegetable gardens, planted with tomatoes, turnips, cantaloupe, corn, strawberries, honeydew melons, squash, carrots, and cucumbers. Some of these crops were stewed, then bottled, capped, and stored in the basement. The boys helped to cultivate and pick crops, mow lawns, and trim shrubs around their grandparents' Victorian home, and with the Lannons' equipment, Bill also developed a profitable lawn-cutting service with a number of the neighbors.

After lunch, the boys and their grandparents took naps. In the evenings, using their wall blackboard, their grandmother sometimes tested the boys with spelling and arithmetic exercises; even though Bill and Eloyd disliked these sessions, they doubtlessly helped them in school.

All was not work, however, during these summers with their grandparents. Bill and Eloyd took hikes with their grandfather to parks and along the levees of the Sacramento and American Rivers. They played on the El Dorado softball team, competing against other Sacramento playground teams, and enjoyed croquet, ping pong, and crafts. They went on group outings—to the State Capitol, Sutter's Fort, Coca-Cola bottling plant, and elsewhere. Frequently, they picnicked and swam at McKinley Park and the American River and attended professional baseball games of the Sacramento Solons.

The boys also accompanied their grandmother on her "first of the month" bill-paying trips to downtown Sacramento, where they stopped at the telephone company, Pacific Gas & Electric, and City Hall.

At the Public Market at 13th and J Streets, where many stores were gathered under one roof, Bill and Eloyd weighed themselves on the huge produce scales in the rear of the building. Then, for a nickel, they usually had a glass of buttermilk—all they could drink—at Henderson's.

While waiting for the home-bound streetcar in front of Country Maid Ice Cream on 12th and J Streets, their grandmother treated them to a milkshake or a cornucopia, as she called ice cream cones.

Bill and Eloyd went to movies at the Alhambra theatre, an exotic Egyptian-styled structure, where they walked up its long entryway and went through the gardens and over the little bridges spanning the ponds and fountains. (Today, alas, "progress" has replaced this unique building with a Safeway supermarket.) Next door to the Alhambra, the boys could get delicious cones at the Shasta ice cream shop.

Late in the summer, they went to the State Fair on Stockton Boulevard, a short streetcar ride south of the Lannons' home on J Street. They explored the Counties Building, with its animated exhibits depicting each county's choicest products, and the Flower Building, humid, fragrant, and breath-taking in its natural splendor. They were intrigued by the Machinery Building, where huge pumps forced water down a canal in the middle of the building; the mind readers; the organ grinders with their penny-grabbing monkeys; the souvenir hawkers; the nighttime horse show in all its grandeur; the midway, brightly lighted by its many rides; and the grandstand show, complete with dazzling fireworks which could also be seen from the Lannons' rear porch.

TREASURE ISLAND

During 1939 and '40, the boys also visited Treasure Island (the Golden Gate International Exposition) in San Francisco Bay—the world's fair of towers and pavilions. They reached Treasure Island by taking the Jackson Street cable car near their apartment to the Ferry Building, then a ferryboat to the exposition. It was there that they heard Republican presidential candidate Wendell Willkie make a campaign speech in 1940.

The boys were especially captivated by the marionette shows, with their magical stage sets and amusing plays, and the exciting model railway

149

layouts, featuring large, multi-tiered displays. They inspired Bill to build a portable puppet theatre in their Clay Street apartment and create his own marionettes, directing and producing *Hansel and Gretel* for the family and his Spring Valley School classmates. He also constructed an HO gauge train layout on large plywood panels in his aunt May's basement in San Francisco.

WILMA HENN AND GERRY LANNON

During these summers, Bill and Eloyd also saw their older Sacramento cousins, who would later become public school teachers there: Wilma Henn, the only child of Elo's oldest sister Marie Lannon Henn (1893–1965), and Gerry Lannon, the only child of Elo's brother Joseph Lannon (1899–1955). Wilma, some thirteen years older than Bill, occasionally took care of her Grier cousins during these summer visits.

Gerry Lannon lived with his parents Joe and Mina at 820 41st Street. His father, a graduate of McGeorge School of Law (now part of the University of the Pacific), was a detective for the Sacramento County district attorney's office and a local real estate investor. In summer 1941, he took his nephew Bill to a special Sacramento Solon baseball game —an evening honoring Pepper Martin, the team's popular manager and former star with the St. Louis Cardinals.

SACRAMENTO SUMMER NIGHTS

After dinner, the Lannons usually retired to their ladder-back rockers or a canvas-covered swing on their home's columned front porch, facing the cool north side. Patrick Lannon often smoked his pipe as they read, enjoyed the evening's breezes, and entertained friends. At mid-evening, Julia Lannon served tea and dessert.

The Lannons' unmarried daughter, Julia Margaret (1897–1970), a registered nurse and supervisor of nurses at Sacramento County Hospital, lived with her parents and sometimes joined them in the evening, and their youngest child, Raymond James (1911–1945), a mechanical contractor, was also occasionally present. On other evenings, Julia Lannon took her grandsons on walks about the neighborhood, where she called on friends in their homes.

For the boys, summer in Sacramento was a treasured time. The city's cool and shady streets were sun-dappled by day, soft and beguiling at dusk, and beckoning and mysterious tunnels by night. Summer flowed as lazily as the Sacramento and American Rivers between their cottonwood-shaded banks at the west and north ends of town. Night came slowly, as the sounds of frogs and crickets dominated the air, and the fireflies winked along the darkening streets and trimmed lawns like a sky full of stars brought down to earth for the season. (See Allied Families: Lannon)

Eloyd and Bill, c. 1937

Bill and Eloyd, c. 1938

May Grier Borman at Treasure Island in 1939, with Eloyd and Bill

May with her aunt Mattie Orr Barber, 1939

Eloyd, Gerry Lannon, Wilma Henn, and Bill, with Grandfather Lannon in background, in Sacramento, 1933

17

SAN FRANCISCO YEARS
1940–1943

In 1939, the Griers moved two blocks away from Jackson Street to a larger, third-floor walk-up apartment on Clay Street. Part of the Griers' Piedmont home furniture was taken out of storage and used in both the Jackson and Clay Street apartments.

REDDING SCHOOL

After school in 1940, Bill and Eloyd sold popular magazines door-to-door in their neighborhood, and *Evening News* and *Call Bulletin* newspapers on street corners—Bill at Sacramento and Polk Streets, Eloyd at Hyde and Sutter.

After graduating from Spring Valley School in January 1940, Bill entered the seventh grade at Redding School, on Larkin and Pine Streets. Like Spring Valley, this school had a rich ethnic mix of Oriental, Italian, Portuguese, Hispanic, and Anglo students. Bill joined Boy Scout Troop 146, which met in the school auditorium on Friday evenings. Dallas Brock, later a San Francisco attorney, was a classmate and fellow scout. He and Bill also belonged to the school's camera club and attended Sunday school at Grace Cathedral, where Dallas sang in the choir.[1]

Eloyd entered Redding in February 1941. The boys, members of the school's traffic patrol, played on volleyball and soccer teams which competed against other city schools.

ELO'S FIRST CAR, 1941

Elo's workweek during the pre-World War II years was five and one-half days—forty-four hours. When she joined Fireman's Fund Insurance Company in 1940, in marine underwriting, she no longer worked on Saturday mornings, cutting her schedule to thirty-seven and one-half

---

1. After reading Dallas's name in the Menlo School and College Directory, Bill contacted him and they lunched in April 1987 with friends at Fiore d'Italia in San Francisco.

hours.

That same year, tutored by her brother-in-law Charles Borman, Elo learned to drive a car, at age forty-four. When licensed, she bought a 1941 maroon-colored Chrysler New Yorker sedan, with "fluid drive" (the first automatic shift). Now driving to work in downtown San Francisco and visiting family and friends (including Alicia Schroeder, a former co-worker at John Deere Plow Company, her husband Oscar, and their two children on San Francisco Peninsula), Elo and her family also drove to Sacramento, Russian River, Santa Cruz, and northern California. A cautious driver, Elo's slow pace on the highways sometimes caused anxieties for her sons, who, with gentle urging and humor, could usually induce her to increase her speed during these trips.

Elo and the boys also drove to Hillsborough to visit her sister Norma and brother-in-law Herb Langton. Norma was a successful homebuilder in the Berkeley hills during the 1930s and early forties; Herb was a financial executive with a San Francisco steamship firm.[2]

Because Elo's job in marine underwriting—insuring military ships—was essential to the war effort, she had a "B" gas rationing card, providing a greater monthly gasoline allowance than the three-gallons-a-week "A" card, but less than the coveted "C" card. Nonetheless, it proved more than enough for her family needs.

In summer 1941, the Griers rented the second-floor flat at 888 31st Avenue, off Fulton Street and a few steps from Golden Gate Park. The following summer, Bill worked as an office boy in the financial district for Hinchman Rolph & Landis, insurance agents, at 345 Sansome Street, earning seventy-five dollars a month. And in 1941 and '42, Eloyd delivered the *Evening News* in Sutro Heights.

CAMPING WITH THE BORMANS

For a week over Labor Day 1941, Bill and Eloyd went fishing and camping near Mount Shasta and Mount Lassen with their aunt May, uncle Charlie, and cousin George Ann. The youngsters slept in portable canvas tents, while May and Charlie enjoyed the comfort of their autobed.Their

---

2. During World War II, when Norma operated a women's clothing shop at 1417 Burlingame Avenue in Burlingame, the Langtons moved to Hillsborough from their Berkeley hills home at 1020 Miller Avenue. In the 1950s, Norma subdivided land and built homes in Los Altos, where she and Herb occupied two houses, first at 301 and later at 261 Langton Avenue.

meals were cooked over open fires and a portable gas stove. There, they packed their provisions on a burro and rode horseback, with a guide, to a remote log cabin complete with a fireplace and a front porch overlooking a lake, green meadows, and forests. In this tranquil setting, they hiked and fished from a rowboat, catching trout which were sauteed for breakfast and dinner. Charlie also shot a deer, which provided many venison meals that fall. This was one of several such outings in northern California, the redwoods, and Yosemite National Park that the Bormans and Grier boys made together in the thirties and forties.

PRESIDIO JUNIOR HIGH SCHOOL

In September 1941, Bill and Eloyd transferred to Presidio Junior High School, entering the high eighth and high seventh grade, respectively. Both boys played intramural basketball and baseball. Eloyd was on the track team, running the 50- and 100-yard dashes and the 220-yard relays. During lunch period, Bill worked in the school cafeteria.

It was during this first year at Presidio that the boys and their classmates gathered in the school auditorium to hear President Roosevelt's radio address on December 8, 1941, declaring war on Japan.

After school, Bill, Eloyd, and neighborhood friends—Bill Degenhardt and his older brother John, the Cohn brothers, Monroe Johnson, Jack Anderson and his younger sister Jane—played touch football outside the Griers' flat on 31st Avenue.

Madeline and Grace Gilmore, who lived around the corner at Cabrillo Street and 32nd Avenue, were also frequent cohorts for Bill and Eloyd. The girls attended Sacred Heart School, a Catholic girls' school on Broadway in Pacific Heights. Grace liked giving the Grier boys and others rides around Golden Gate Park in her dark blue, three-wheel motor scooter with sidecar passenger seat.[3]

During weekends between 1941 and 1943, Bill worked at Sutro Baths and Ice Rink, assigning lockers and dispensing towels for the pools or collecting tickets at the rink.

Built in 1896 by Adolph Sutro, the baths had six indoor swimming pools of both fresh and salt water, varying in size, depth, and temperature. It was reported that on one day 25,000 people had visited the baths, which also accommodated 7,000 spectators. A Victorian glass-roofed structure

---

3. Their father William Gilmore, president of Gilmore Steel Corporation in San Francisco, was an avid polo player and owned land near Menlo School and College, which was sold to Menlo after his death in the 1960s.

built on a cliff overlooking the Pacific Ocean, the facility also had an enclosed ice rink and featured wide-tiered galleries and promenades, bordered with palm trees, tables, and chairs. Tragically, this unique building was destroyed by a fire in 1966.

From 1943 to '45, Bill and Eloyd delivered the *San Francisco Shopping News* to residences near their home on Wednesday afternoons and Saturday mornings; later, Eloyd became captain and administrator of several routes, supervising other carriers.

Dallas Brock and Bill at Fleishhacker Zoo,
San Francisco, May 1941

The interior of Sutro Baths, c. 1912 (*Courtesy of the California Historical Society Library*)

159

18

HIGH SCHOOL YEARS
1943–1947

In 1943, Bill entered George Washington High School (GWHS), where he studied a college preparatory curriculum that included Spanish, history, physics, algebra, and geometry. He also lettered in basketball and played football.[1] As a junior, he joined the popular Omega fraternity, and he and other members attended sorority receptions and dances after their weekly evening meetings.

Bill was a substitute quarterback on the varsity football team in 1945, in coach Milt Axt's T formation.[2] Duane Harder, Bill and Eloyd's boyhood friend from 41st Avenue, played halfback. The games were held in GWHS stadium, where one could see the Golden Gate Bridge, or in Kezar Stadium in Golden Gate Park, where college ball and the Shriners' East-West games were played.

JOBS, WHEELS

From June of 1943 to July of 1945, Bill worked two days a week after school and on Saturday mornings in the shipping department of Ingram Laboratories, Inc., a small pharmaceutical firm located off Union Square at 278 Post Street. He and two other San Francisco high school students wrapped products for shipment; before closing, the packages were put in canvas mail bags and carried on a dolly a block away to the basement post office in the White House department store at Grant Avenue and Sutter Street. Bill also delivered orders to nearby medical offices.

During the summers between 1944 and 1948, Eloyd worked in San Francisco's Winterland Auditorium as head concessionaire, selling programs, novelties, and food items. The Ice Follies were staged at Winterland, and in time, he met and became friendly with some of the show's artists,

---

1. George Washington High School was the subject of a television report in San Francisco in the early 1980s—"The Kids at Washington High," produced by local station KOE—which outlined changes that had occurred there since 1955.

2. Bill's T formation quarterback heroes were Stanford's Frankie Albert, Notre Dame's Johnny Lujack, and Chicago Bear's Sid Luckman.

including Russ Tuckey, a performer and transportation manager for the Follies.[3] Eloyd also worked evening events at Winterland throughout the school year.

In the fall of 1944, Bill withdrew $500 from his savings to buy a 1935 gray De Soto coupe, with rumble seat, from a dealer. His uncle Charlie Borman, after checking its condition, recommended its purchase; he also taught Bill how to drive and parallel park near the beach. Bill obtained his temporary operator's permit at age fourteen, his license two years later.

In his sporty car, Bill drove to school and athletic events and parties, to dances at Larkspur in Marin County, and to the Hillsborough home of his aunt Norma and uncle Herb Langton. By the end of 1945, Bill had sold the car to his brother Eloyd.

EXTRACURRICULAR

In mid-summer 1945, Bill resigned from Ingram Laboratories to begin work as an assistant groundskeeper at Kraft Foods in south San Francisco (where he cut and edged lawns, pruned trees, and watered the grounds) and as an office boy during his Christmas vacation in 1945.

Between 1944 and 1945, Bill also worked three evenings a week at Presidio Junior High School as a gym assistant to Josh S. Faulkner, director of physical education. Earning seventy-five cents an hour, he succeeded Jack Anderson, an older neighborhood friend and basketball player at George Washington High School who later received both bachelor's and master's degrees in education from Stanford University. When Bill resigned a few weeks prior to graduating from GWHS in 1946, his brother succeeded him in the position, a job which Eloyd held until his own graduation in 1947.

On Saturday evenings, Bill, Jack Anderson, Glen Barry, and other GWHS friends occasionally attended professional basketball games at San Francisco's Civic Auditorium or films, big band performances, and stage shows at the Golden Gate Theatre. Afterward, they stopped at cafes for sodas and desserts.

On balmy spring days, Bill, Eloyd, and their classmates often went to China Beach in the stately Sea Cliff district, eight downhill blocks from school. The view from the cove-shaped beach encompassed the Golden Gate Bridge to the east, the headlands of Marin County to the north, and the

---

3.   Russ Tuckey, a native of Harrisburg, Pennsylvania, had been a basketball star at Gettysburg College.

George T. Campbell, manager of Winterland, lived on 41st Avenue, a few doors south of Bill and Eloyd's aunt May Grier Borman. In earlier years, the boys had played with Campbell's two sons, who had a large electric train layout in their basement.

Pacific Ocean to the west. There, the boys swam, played volleyball and touch football, and eyed and talked to the girls. On summer weekends, they sometimes went to Russian River, staying with friends in Guerneville or Monte Rio.

Graduating from George Washington High School in 1946, Bill then studied for a year at Menlo Junior College in nearby Menlo Park, while Eloyd enrolled at San Francisco State following his high school graduation in 1947.

Bill, 1944

Bill (second row from top, third from left) and his graduating class at Presidio Junior High School, 1943

Eloyd (third row from top, second from right) and Presidio Junior High's graduating class of 1944

19

BACK HOME IN PIEDMONT
1947

Elo and her sons returned to live in their Piedmont home in the summer of 1947. Still with Fireman's Fund, Elo now commuted by train across the San Francisco-Oakland Bay Bridge to her office in the financial district.

ELO'S LIFE

The previous year, Elo had traded in her Chrysler for a De Soto sedan, and in 1949, she bought a two-door De Soto coupe—her last automobile—which she drove until selling it in 1969. (In her later years in San Francisco, she drove less often, preferring taxis and buses.)

Although Elo had savings accounts at other San Francisco banks, her checking account and safe deposit box were always with Wells Fargo Bank, in its imposing building at Grant Avenue and Market Street.

After moving back to Piedmont, Bill enrolled at the University of California at Berkeley, where he would earn a Bachelor of Arts in chemistry and zoology.

When Bill and Eloyd's Sacramento cousin Gerry Lannon attended St. Mary's College in nearby Moraga, California, he was a frequent guest at their Piedmont home. In the late 1940s, Bill and Gerry both dated students at Mills College, and Bill hosted parties in his mother's home. Later, Gerry took his Master of Arts in English and literature at the University of San Francisco.

ELOYD AND BILL LEAVE HOME

In August of 1948, Eloyd, unhappy and in conflict with his mother, decided to continue his education in the East. Urged by Russ Tuckey, an acquaintance from the Ice Follies and an alum from Gettysburg College, he moved to Harrisburg, Pennsylvania and attended York Collegiate Institute and, later, Gettysburg College.

Elo, her brother Joseph Lannon, and family friends attended Bill's graduation from Berkeley in June 1951, followed by a reception hosted by Elo in her Piedmont home.

After Bill left home in January 1952 to join his Air Force unit at Fort Snelling in Minneapolis, Elo continued to live in Piedmont and commute to her job in San Francisco. She took occasional vacations with friends to Carmel and Lake Tahoe and visited her sisters. During the workweek, she often dined out and attended shows with business friends.

In early June of 1953, Elo flew to Washington, D.C. to visit Bill, who was working as a passenger agent with United Airlines at National Airport. After a week of sightseeing there, she accompanied him to Manhattan for a brief holiday and saw him off on the S.S. *Stavangerfjord* as he sailed for Norway.

After study and travel abroad, Bill received a Master of Science degree from Columbia University Business School in 1955. He then returned home to Piedmont for a six-week vacation before starting work in the finance training program of General Motors Overseas Corporation in New York City.

During this period, his brother Eloyd was also establishing roots in the East. After attending college in Pennsylvania, he joined the Federal Bureau of Investigation in Washington, D.C. and subsequently entered the insurance business in Pennsylvania.

Elo's sons both married during the second half of the fifties, and by the end of the decade, she had two grandchildren, as well: Eloyd's daughter Shelby, born in 1958, and Bill's son William Milton Grier 3d, born one year later.

Bill outside the family's Piedmont home, 1947

20

ELO ALONE

With her sons grown, married, and living in the East, Elo sold the large Piedmont home in the late 1950s and leased flats in San Francisco, first on 19th Avenue and later on Stanyan Street, both near Fireman's Fund Insurance Company's new complex at 3333 California Street in Richmond district.

After retiring in the fall of 1960 at age sixty-five, and too energetic to remain idle, Elo worked part-time in the offices of several downtown San Francisco firms, including the Fairmont Hotel. She now had time for friends and for visits with her three sisters and a brother-in-law: Marie Hall Henn, a widow, who lived in a San Francisco apartment at Leavenworth and Geary Streets; Norma and Herb Langton, who had moved in the 1950s from their Spanish colonial home in Hillsborough further south on the San Francisco Peninsula to Los Altos, where Norma, a contractor, had built a tract of homes; and her younger, divorced sister Ferd Shaeffer, an elementary school teacher in Sacramento.

BILL AND FAMILY VISIT

In May of 1961, Elo's son Bill, daughter-in-law Joan Sears, and one-and-a-half-year-old grandson Billy visited her for three weeks from Boston. Accompanied by Bill's cousin George Ann, Elo met them at the airport and that evening hosted a dinner party for friends and family, including George Ann and her husband Sam Palmer and Elo's older sister Marie.

Bill's UC-Berkeley classmate Jay Martin, a San Francisco bachelor and lawyer, gave a party for the Griers in his two-level apartment, with striking views of the Bay. The young Griers were also entertained in the Berkeley hills home of the Palmers—George Ann, Sam, and their children Catherine, Charles, and Kenneth. Bill's uncle Charlie Borman— George Ann's father—came over from San Francisco to see his nephew and family. En route to Carmel and Big Sur, Bill and his wife had lunch with Norma and Herb Langton in Menlo Park, near their Palo Alto financial consulting office.

After the Griers visited Lannon relatives in Sacramento (Bill's aunts Ferd Shaeffer and Julia Lannon; his schoolteacher cousins Gerry Lannon and Wilma Henn Tamblyn; and Elo's cousin Deirdrie Knapp Berrigan, a music teacher and violinist with the Sacramento Symphony Orchestra), Bill and Joan toured Lake Tahoe and Reno, while grandmother Elo cared for young Billy. During Bill's years of residence in the East and in Denver, he annually visited his mother, family, and friends in California, sojourns of nostalgia and adventure that always exhilarated and refreshed him.

RETURN TO SACRAMENTO

Anticipating retirement in Sacramento, near her sister Ferd Shaeffer, Elo bought a one-story, two-bedroom stucco home at 5400 H Street in October of 1962, which she rented out over five years. Then, after forty-one years in San Francisco and Piedmont, Elo, nearing seventy-three, decided to resettle in her native city. After completing her move into her Sacramento home in April 1968, she gave a party for friends, neighbors, and family to celebrate her return.

In her later years, Elo lived in a nursing home in Sacramento. She died there on July 16, 1987—two months and ten days short of her ninety-second birthday. She was buried in East Lawn Cemetery—where her parents and several of her brothers and sisters had been buried, as well—five days later. Father Michael O'Hara of Sacred Heart Church officiated at the grave-side service. Among family members attending were her son Bill and his wife Joan, her niece Wilma Henn Tamblyn, and her cousin Michael Berrigan.

MEMORIES

Elo was kind, generous, tolerant, and scrupulously honest in thought and deed. As a young girl and mother, she was slight, pretty, bright-eyed, elfin, and gay. A brunette with a shapely figure—impulsive and flirtatious —she liked to dance and play the piano.

Yet behind the gaiety, a discernment and purposefulness directed her life—qualities that became evident after her husband's death. And while her vanity never deserted her, neither did her wit and courage. Indeed, these qualities never shone more luminously than when, emerging from her personal loss in the Depression, she forged a successful career and raised her two sons alone.

After eight years of a privileged life as the wife of a well-to-do entrepreneur, the plucky Elo—through her subsequent struggle and hard-won triumph—taught her sons a timeless lesson: in adversity, you neither forsake humor nor complain nor give up—rather, you persevere, you endure, and by endurance the garland is won.

In a conversation with her cousin Bill in April of 1983, Elo's niece George Ann spoke of the phone call that came to her mother early in the morning of December 8, 1935—Elo's call, informing the Borman family of Uncle Milt's death. She recalled Elo's first year as a widow, when she had lived for a few weeks with George Ann and her parents while establishing her career in San Francisco. She remembered that Elo would rise in the pre-dawn darkness, well before the household, and catch the nearby Fulton streetcar heading downtown, where she breakfasted before going to work at John Deere Plow Company on Townsend Street.

During this dolorous time, Elo bore her burdens lightly. As she grappled valiantly with a new life and job and enlarged family responsibilities, her humor lifted the spirit of family and friends. George Ann had poignant memories of her aunt Elo's endearing ways—her cheerfulness and dignity in the face of ineffable sadness—which deeply touched George Ann and her family and drew them very close to her. "From such anguish and pathos," Bill has said, "I believe my soul was born."

Many years later, Bill recalled a day in 1937 when he was sitting on his aunt May's lap and giggling at her stories as she asked him if he could keep a promise. When he agreed, she whispered in his ear, "Promise me you'll never forget your mother." Quickly, he reassured her, and, indeed, over the next fifty years of his mother's long life, Bill would remain lovingly devoted to her.

Elo Lannon Grier in Reno, Nevada,
1927

PART THREE

THE NEXT GENERATION

BILL AND ELOYD GRIER

GEORGE ANN BORMAN

DAVID GRIER

CHRONOLOGY OF WILLIAM M. GRIER, JR.

1928   Born in Oakland, California on September 23

1930   Baptized in Trinity Cathedral in Phoenix, Arizona on
            March 22

1934   Moves to Sacramento, California; enrolls in El Dorado
            Elementary School

1935   Father, William M. Grier, Sr., dies in Sacramento on
            December 8

1935–1936   Lives in Santa Maria, California with aunt and uncle

1936   Returns to Sacramento and El Dorado Elementary
            School in June

1937   Moves to San Francisco, California; enrolls in Spring
            Valley School

1937–1938   Summers at Tilly's Roost Camp, Santa Cruz Mountains,
            California

1939–1940   Summers with Lannon grandparents in Sacramento;
            visits Golden Gate International Exposition (Treasure
            Island)

1940   Enters Redding School in San Francisco (junior high
            years) in January

1941   Works during summer for Hinchman Rolph & Landis in
            San Francisco; camps with Borman family near
            Mt. Shasta, California over Labor Day; transfers to
            Presidio Junior High School in San Francisco in Septem-
            ber

1941–1943   Works part-time at Sutro Baths and Ice Rink

1943   Enters George Washington High School in San Francisco

1943–1945	Works part-time at Ingram Laboratories and as gym assistant at Presidio Junior High School
1945	Works at Kraft Foods during summer
1946	Graduates from George Washington High School; enters Menlo Junior College in Menlo Park, California; works at Yosemite National Park in August
1947	Returns to live in Piedmont home; enrolls in University of California at Berkeley
1948–1950	Works during summers at Lake Tahoe, at Hunt Foods, and at summer camp in Huntington Lake, California
1949	Joins Air National Guard, Alameda, California
1949–1951	Works as playground director for City of Oakland
1951	Graduates from University of California at Berkeley in June with B.A. in chemistry and zoology
1952	Joins California Air National Guard in January, on active duty in U.S. Air Force, Fort Snelling, Minneapolis, Minnesota
1953	Discharged from Air Force in February; moves to Washington, D.C. and works for United Airlines; studies on scholarship at the University of Oslo Summer School; travels in Scandinavia, Britain, and Europe; studies at the Institute of Touraine in October; travels in Europe over Christmas holidays
1953–1954	Studies at the Sorbonne
1954	Travels in Europe in spring and summer; enters Columbia University Graduate School of Business in New York City
1955	Receives M.S. from Columbia Business School; visits family and friends in Piedmont and California; joins General Motors Overseas Corporation in New York City

1959	Joins Previews, Inc. in New York City in spring; marries Joan Cecilia Sears in New York City on April 11; son, William M. Grier 3d, born in New York City on November 11; moves to Cambridge, Massachusetts; continues with Previews, Inc. in Boston in fall
1960	Forms Feature Arts, marketing museum art reproductions, books, and records
1962	Divorces Joan Sears Grier in November; forms real estate investment and management firm in Cambridge in December
1963–1969	Vacations in Europe and Mediterranean
1969	Joins Apache Corporation; relocates to New York City
1970	Joins Union League Club in New York City
1971	Vacations in England in May
1972	Vacations in Europe in February; marries Joan Grafmueller in Ketchum, Idaho on June 15
1972–1973	Lives in France; travels in Europe
1973	Visits East Africa in July; relocates to Denver, Colorado and founds Grier & Company in November
1976	Begins publication of *Real Estate West* in June
1980	Grier & Company edits, designs, and produces *Walter Judd: Chronicles of a Statesman*
1974–1988	Vacations in the United States, Canada, and Mexico
1987	Mother, Elo Lannon Grier, dies at age 91 in Sacramento on July 16

1989   Publishes *Grier of San Francisco: Builder in the West and His Family 1878–1988* and *The Griers: Pioneers in the American West and Canada 1818–1988;* compiles *The Lannons: Sacramento Pioneers 1888–1988*

21

WILLIAM MILTON GRIER, JR.
1928–

After graduating from George Washington High School in 1946, Bill enrolled in Menlo School and Junior College, a small, private men's institution in Menlo Park, California. Entering Menlo with older, returning World War II veterans, Bill, a callow seventeen—more interested in sport than study—was now challenged by eager classmates and a demanding curriculum. Menlo awakened his curiosity and stirred his imagination; spurring scholarship, it marked the beginning of his becoming a student.

MENLO

At the time Bill enrolled, Menlo Junior College had 192 students, and its secondary boys' school, 151. On campus, he lived in Upper House and in College Hall.[1] He studied French with Holbrook Bonney; western civilization with Donovan D. Fischer; physics with Dr. William Pomeroy; and biology and psychology with Dr. Paul Hurd.

It was at Menlo that Bill began a lifelong friendship with John D. Russell, the distinguished director emeritus of the College and its School of Business Administration. A Stanford University alumnus and lawyer, Russell began teaching business law at Menlo in 1938. Several years later, while serving in the Navy during World War II, he received frequent letters from servicemen whom he had taught at Menlo—letters which helped to persuade him that his true metier lay not in law, but in education. He became convinced that he could affect more change, do more good, and, in turn, enjoy a more rewarding life through teaching. During his fifty-year tenure at Menlo, his able leadership and inspired teaching helped advance

---

1. Several of Bill's classmates were from Hawaii, alumni of Punahau School: Allan and Bob Clarke; Bob Gibson, now a Honolulu dentist; and Larry Doolittle, Bill's first roommate in Upper House. Other Upper House classmates were Chuck and Fritz von Geldern from Sacramento; Truman ("Tony") De Lap from Stockton, now an artist in Corona del Mar, California; Russell Hael; Chauncey G. Behrens, now an anesthesiologist; and late Vern Purcell from Seattle. Classmates from physics were John Whipple; John Zeile, an environmental engineer with Ralph M. Parsons Company in Pasadena; Bill Sheridan; and Bob Lurie, real estate investor and owner of the San Francisco Giants.

the school's academic excellence and enhance the lives of legions of its students. Since his official retirement in 1977, Russell (fondly known as "Judge") has kept an office at the school and continues to guide and encourage a second and third generation of Menlo students.

Over the years, he and Bill have exchanged a good many letters and postcards, and since 1947, Bill has received his self-designed Christmas and birthday cards with personal greetings. Throughout this period, Bill has benefited from Russell's counsel, admired his humane spirit and liberal temper, and cherished his friendship.[2] In a letter to Bill in 1984, Russell revealed his philosophy:

> Don't worry about such things as memorials. Mine are living. My memories (memorial) and wealth consist of those special Bill Grier's, 'my boys,' close friends through the years, whose progress and productivity give me continuing pride and satisfaction. I consider myself a very wealthy person in essentials for the good life, my assets being my former students ('my sons'), and my income consisting of pleasure from continuing communication and contact and pride from their achievements. I therefore do not need to be further honored while I live or memorialized after I die. One Bill Grier already honors me sufficiently by taking time and trouble to send me cards, letters, examples of his works, and a complimentary subscription to *Real Estate West*.
>
> I have enjoyed a full life, forty-seven years of which were at Menlo where I have been able to participate in building a fine educational institution. I like to think that I have laid a constructive brick or two into the foundation of each of my boys, to help make their careers more significant and successful. Thus I have gained more than I have given in my Menlo relationship through the years.

Edgar Wise Weaver—"The Weav," as he was affectionately known—was a popular English professor at Menlo. Urbane, humorous, and tweedy, a pipe smoker and collector of jazz vocal recordings, he was dedicated to clear thinking and good writing. In 1946, he was Upper House dorm counselor, whose suite was near Bill's room; prior to dinner, "The Weav's" sitting room was the place where Bill and his classmates gathered to enjoy conversation and music.

Among Bill's other faculty acquaintances were E. Hutson Hart (chemistry), Leon T. Loofbourow (history and literature), and president William E. Kratt.

---

2.   Bill and his wife Joan attended a reunion picnic at Menlo School and College on Sunday, October 13, 1985; while seeing Judge Russell and other friends, they were entertained by the Kingston Trio, Menlo alumni of the mid-fifties.

ACTIVITIES

Bill played basketball at Menlo for coach Roy Hughes. Like the student body, the team was dominated by World War II veterans, several of whom were also graduates of George Washington High School: Bill Rose, Cliff Gerstner, Ken Berridge, Bob Durnal, and Harry Myers. Other teammates included Hank Needham, Byron VanAlstyne, Joe Greenbach, Harry Cusack (alumnus of Punahau School in Honolulu), Harry Morris (who became a three-star Air Force general), and Hobert Burns (former president of San Jose State University). After scoring well in early games, Bill was nicknamed "Points" Grier. "Points" also earned expense money by working as a bus boy at Menlo.

In August 1946, Bill worked as a bus boy with other college students in Camp Curry Company's dining room in Yosemite National Park. While there, he renewed his friendship with the vacationing Lloyd Leith, former GWHS basketball coach whom Bill had known briefly in 1943 before Lloyd entered the Navy. At Yosemite, Lloyd offered Bill the extra bed in his tent-cabin, which Bill used a few nights before moving to quarters provided by Camp Curry Company.

Working breakfast, lunch, and dinner six days a week, Bill's day began early, but he and the staff were free after lunch to rest or explore the park, hike, ride horseback, swim, fish, and raft on the Merced River. In the evenings, there were ranger talks and films, entertainment around the amphitheatre's campfire, and outdoor dancing to Bud Stone's band.[3]

BERKELEY

Bill transferred to the University of California at Berkeley in the fall of 1947 and earned a Bachelor of Arts degree in chemistry and zoology with the class of 1951. His chemistry professor was the renowned Dr. Joel H. Hildebrand, a brilliant scholar-teacher whose *Principles of Chemistry* was the textbook. A skier and environmentalist, he was the manager of the U.S. Olympic ski team in 1936 and president of the Sierra Club in 1937. Hildebrand died at the age of 101 in 1983.

From Berkeley's tradition of academic excellence, of vigorous dissent and free speech—a university tolerant of a diversity of views and expressions—Bill developed a creativity and a love of the arts, a questioning mind, an independence of thought and action which have shaped his life.

While at Berkeley, Bill pledged Pi Kappa Alpha fraternity, but

---

3. Bud Stone lived in Piedmont and attended the University of California at Berkeley.

179

chose not to become a member and lived at home in nearby Piedmont. Bill Hahn, Neville Rich, and Bill Bigelow, Bill's basketball teammates from GWHS, also attended UC-Berkeley, and both Hahn and Bigelow became members of Pi Kappa Alpha fraternity.[4]

On Thursday evenings during the school year, Bill attended San Francisco Symphony concerts, conducted by Pierre Monteux, in the War Memorial Opera House with Pi Kappa Alpha friends who had a box there.[5] The group often dined together in San Francisco restaurants prior to these performances.

Bill and his friends also attended Saturday "Cal" football games at Memorial Stadium and the Cal vs. Northwestern Rose Bowl game in Pasadena, California on January 1, 1949. Under coach Lyn ("Pappy") Waldorf, the Golden Bears won the Pacific Coast Conference Championship in 1948, '49, and '50 and went to the Rose Bowl, though losing each time.

While working his way through UC-Berkeley, Bill held a variety of jobs. He worked as a bellboy at Homewood Lodge and Cottages on Lake Tahoe in the summer of 1948. The following year, he worked at Hunt Foods' cannery in Hayward, California, where he lived with his cousin George Ann and her husband Sam Palmer. (The young couple owned and operated Palmer's, a combined pharmacy and variety store on Main Street in Hayward.) Later that summer, Bill worked in the San Francisco warehouse of Schwabacher-Frey, stationers, rearranging inventory.

Bill was a playground director for the City of Oakland Recreation Department during the 1949–1951 school years, working from 3 to 6 p.m. on weekdays and all day on Saturdays.

On June 17, 1950, Bill was an usher in the wedding of Philip Amos Crane, Jr. and Rosemary ("Rary") Pratt in Fresno, California. Phil's brother Bruce served as best man, and his sister Barbara was an attendant. The other ushers were Dick Miller, Ray Smith, Jay Martin, Stanley Pratt, and Bill Nordlund. The reception was held at the Sunnyside Country Club.[6]

During the summer of 1950, Bill and Ray Berg, a UC classmate,

---

4.   Bill and Diane Hahn have lived in Hawaii since the late 1950s; they visited Bill in Cambridge, Massachusetts in the sixties. Bill Bigelow, a golfer at UC-Berkeley, became a CPA.

5.   In 1978, Davies Hall was built in San Francisco for its symphony orchestra. Pierre Monteux was the conductor when Bill attended Thursday evening concerts from 1947–1950.

6.   Rosemary's mother and stepfather were Maude and Roy Paehlig.

Phil and Bruce Crane were raised near Chicago in Hinsdale, Illinois. Bill's classmates at UC-Berkeley, they were members of Pi Kappa Alpha and have been his lifelong friends. In the summer of 1966, Bruce and his second wife Barbara ("Basia"), a Polish emigre, were Bill's guests in his home at 220 Harvard Steet in Cambridge, Massachusetts; together, they toured Nantucket and Cape Cod.

worked as waiters at a girls' camp in Huntington Lake, some 100 miles northeast of Fresno.[7] (Ray had worked there the previous summer and persuaded Bill to apply in 1950.) With one day off a week and every afternoon free, Bill, Ray, and other student workers swam, sailed, canoed, or rode horseback. In the evenings, they read, wrote letters, or played games—ping pong, darts, and shuffleboard—or danced in the nearby lodge.

MILITARY SERVICE, 1949–1953

In 1949, Bill joined the California Air National Guard in Alameda, California. The unit trained on Monday evenings and for two summer weeks at Hamilton Air Force Base in Marin County. Bill's unit was ordered to active duty in the summer of 1951 and later assigned to Fort Snelling in Minneapolis, Minnesota, where he joined them in February 1952.

After his discharge as a corporal one year later, Bill traveled east to tour Boston, New York City, Philadelphia, and Washington, D.C., where his brother Eloyd lived and worked for the FBI Identification Section. In Washington, Bill rented a third-floor room in a nineteenth-century brick home, across from George Washington University Law School, and worked as a passenger agent for United Airlines at National Airport.

STUDY AND TRAVEL ABROAD, 1953–1954

While on duty at Fort Snelling, Bill had applied and was interviewed for admission to the University of Oslo Summer School in Oslo, Norway, and in May 1953, he received notification in Washington that he had been accepted and granted a scholarship, funded by a Norwegian hydro-electric company.

Prior to his June departure for Norway, his mother Elo, visiting him for a week in Washington, accompanied him by train to New York City for a short holiday.

On June 16, from Pier 42 in the Hudson River, Bill said goodbye to his mother and boarded the Norwegian American Lines' S.S. *Stavangerfjord* for the ten-day voyage to Norway. He and his fellow students traveled tourist class, though they moved freely between cabin and first-class lounges to enjoy teas, dances, films, and concerts.

---

7. Ray, an orthopedic surgeon, interned at St. Vincent's Hospital in Manhattan's Greenwich Village from 1956–1957.

After breakfasts of smorgasbord and American dishes, the students attended Norwegian language and orientation classes. Afternoons were devoted to games, reading, swimming, relaxing in deck chairs, and getting to know the classmates who came from thirty-seven states.

On the eighth and ninth days of the trip (June 24 and 25), the ship stopped for a part of each day in the Norwegian cities of Bergen, Stavanger, and Kristiansand. (At each port, including New York, both the Norwegian national anthem, "*Ja, Vi Elsker*," and "The Star-Spangled Banner" were played.)

They arrived in Bergen just a few days past midsummer night, the longest day of the year—a magical time when the northern sun casts its glow upon the night sky. Bill and his classmates were charmed by the beauty of the old Hanseatic city, with its pointed, tile rooftops stretching to the sky over a busy fishing harbor and its magnificent fjord views. The portside market was filled with flower vendors, fishmongers, and fruit and vegetable merchants.

Bill visited Bergenhus Fortress and Hakon Hall, the Hanseatic Museum and Wharves, Fantoft Stave church, and "Troldhaugen," Edvard Grieg's home. In late afternoon, he rode the funicular railway to the top of Mount Floien, where a terraced restaurant offered dramatic views of the town, its fjord, and the surrounding mountains. With Bill were fellow students Jake Jacobson of Providence, Rhode Island; Dick Cameron of Durham, New Hampshire; Karl Trygve Gundersen of Boston; Clayton Willis of Greenwich, Connecticut; and others. Exhilarated by the setting and their arrival in Norway, they toasted their good fortune with several rounds of Norwegian beer, chatting away and singing songs.

UNIVERSITY OF OSLO

On June 26, the ship docked in Oslo harbor. The University of Oslo campus, located on a wooded hill near Holmenkollen ski area (site of the 1948 Winter Olympics), was a fifteen-minute ride by "trikk" (electric tram) from downtown Oslo. The six-week session offered courses in Norwegian and Scandinavian history, politics, literature (Henrik Ibsen, Sigrid Undset, August Strindberg), music (Grieg), and art (Vigeland, Munch). There were also lectures and debates by leaders of Norway's political parties and government.

The program included two, three-day weekend excursions in Norway. By train, bus, and the nineteenth-century sidewheeler paddle steamer *Skibladner* (skib means ship in Norwegian, pronounced "ship"), the group visited Lillehammer, Hamar, Aulestad, and Eidsvoll and crossed Lake Mjosa, Norway's largest lake. They went on bus to Rjukan via Drammen,

Kongsberg, Rauland, Morgedal, Seljord, and Notodden.

On two other weekends, Bill, Jake, and Peter Steese were guests of Ragnhild ("Pusa") Strand at her parents' attractive country home in Aamot, Modum, a short train ride west of Oslo. Pusa's friend Margaret Thoraldson and her sister Tove were also there.[8]

Bill shared a three-room suite in Blindern Hall with Jake, Peter, and Stuart Chase. Peter, a student at Houghton College, was a minister's son from Rochester, New York; Stuart later succeeded his father as headmaster at Eaglebrook School in Deerfield, Massachusetts. Karl Gundersen and Dick Cameron shared the adjoining room at the end of the second floor.

Stuart, Karl, and Dick had met their future wives aboard the S.S. *Stavangerfjord*,[9] while Bill met Nancy Stevens of San Francisco, an alumna of the University of California at Berkeley and an acquaintance of several of Bill's friends from both UC and Piedmont.[10]

At a Blindern reception the weekend before classes started, Bill also met Lila Linkey, a talented, blue-eyed brunette, who had grown up in San Mateo on the San Francisco Peninsula and studied at the University of California-Santa Barbara. She was spending the year with a Norwegian shipowning family. Their elegant home above Blindern, where Lila hosted several dinners, overlooked the city and its beautiful fjord. An accomplished guitarist and singer, she played and sang a moving rendition of Rodgers and Hart's "Blue Moon" to Bill and others at a student show and accompanied him to dances and other events.

Bill and his classmates also attended concerts and art exhibits, swam and played tennis, explored Oslo, and savored local cafes, including Blom, known as "The Artist's Restaurant." On July 4th, the U.S. Embassy hosted a reception for Americans in Oslo, and a month later, Bill and other scholarship recipients were feted by the Norwegian Shipowner Association at a sumptuous evening buffet, with string ensemble, in the penthouse of "Redernes Hus," the shipowners' building overlooking Oslo's harbor.

---

8.   Pusa, a Norwegian scholarship student at the University of Maine (Orono), would later marry Karl Gundersen, a Boston native and Williams College alumnus; they met aboard the S.S. *Stavangerfjord* en route to Norway.

9.   Stuart met Edmonia Johnson, from Bedford, Virginia and Randolph-Macon Woman's College, while at the University of Oslo. Dick Cameron, a geologist from the University of New Hampshire, also met his wife Dorothy ("Dottie") Loew at the school; she was a student at the University of Indiana.

10.   Nancy A. Stevens had resigned a job in San Francisco to attend the University of Oslo and travel that summer. In June 1955, following his graduation from Columbia University Business School, Bill dined with Nancy in San Francisco.

183

THE CONTINENT AND ENGLAND

After successfully completing their examinations, receiving certificates, and attending a farewell dinner at Blindern on August 8, Bill and Karl Gundersen took a train to mid-Norway, near the Jotunheimen Mountains, the mythical home of the Nordic gods. (According to legend, Peer Gynt flew over the ridge here on his reindeer.) They spent several days at the old seacoast city of Trondheim, visiting the medieval Nidaros Cathedral, which is considered one of Scandinavia's most notable architectural masterpieces. They also stayed a few nights at "Sellanraa" in the Rondane Mountains, the summer home of Karl's American cousin Elizabeth Gundersen, who had married Norwegian doctor Harold Somerfeldt and settled in Norway. They also spent a night with Karl's uncle Borge Gundersen, who owned and operated a profitable farm, harvesting timber in Flisa, near the Swedish border.

Bill and Karl flew to Stockholm, where they remained for four days. They then went by train to southern Sweden, stopping for a night and a day at Sweden's colorful amusement park, Lisberg, and at various beaches before boarding a ferry to Denmark. While in Copenhagen, Bill and Karl lived in a youth hostel, savored smorgasbord in the elegant garden of the Royal Library, rode the trams, and walked about the city. They enjoyed Tivoli Gardens' cafes, concerts, entertainment, and nightly fireworks. They also visited Hans Christian Andersen's home in Odense and toured the Royal Palace, museum, waterfront (Nyhavn), and Carlsberg brewery. Before leaving, they went by train to Elsinore Castle, where they walked its ramparts and communed with Hamlet's ghost on a gloomy, rainy day.

From Copenhagen, they took the train to Hamburg, Germany for a two-day visit, then proceeded to Amsterdam. There they stayed in a small hotel near the station, rode canal boats, went to museums, and saw many of Rembrandt's paintings, including the "Night Watch." After a visit to The Hague and Rotterdam, Bill and Karl went on to Brussels, Ghent, Bruges, and Ostend in Belgium, then sailed across the channel to England.

In the summer of 1953, there was still evidence of World War II bombings around London, particularly near St. Paul's Cathedral, which was miraculously spared. Traveling in England and Europe at this time was a bargain for Americans—and especially for Bill, an impecunious student-adventurer!

While in London, Bill and Karl attended the theatre, and at a performance of Ibsen's *A Doll's House*, they met Clayton Willis, a fellow Oslo summer alum who was visiting friends and inquiring about admission to Oxford University.

Karl returned to the University of Oslo after a few days in London, to fly to Boston and his final year at Williams College. Renting a third-floor bedroom in a townhouse near Paddington train station, Bill and Clayton spent three weeks touring London and the English countryside. They visited museums and Fleet Street bookstores. They rode double-decker buses, trains, the underground, and boats on the Thames. They strolled through Kew Gardens and Regent's Park (known as Queen Mary's Garden) and the romantic St. James Park, with its sinuous lake, dreamy willows, and fountains. They also toured Eton School and its playing fields, Windsor Castle, and Oxford University.

Bill and Clayton flew to Paris for a few days in early September, then took a train to Montpellier, France, where they lived in a hotel near downtown and the University of Montpellier. From there, they toured Nimes, Arles, and Avignon and attended Sunday afternoon bullfights.

INSTITUTE OF TOURAINE

At the end of September, Bill boarded a train for Tours, where he enrolled in a French language course at the Institute of Touraine, housed in an elegant eighteenth-century home with marble stairways, marquetry floors, and a walled garden.

He rented a third-floor room in the home of the Jacob family at 13 rue de Vinci, a few blocks from school.[11] Here, Col. and Mrs. Jacob, Bill, and two other students—a young Italian foreign service officer and a Swedish postal executive—were served exceptional lunches and dinners, and their lively conversations improved Bill's French. At mid-evening, their maid brought trays of tea, toast, butter, and jelly to the guests' rooms; Bill usually shared this time with the genial Swede.

The Institute of Touraine's morning course was conducted entirely in French, covering grammar, reading, writing, and oral responses to their instructors' questions. In the afternoons, Bill and his friends sometimes bicycled about Tours or along the Loire River and the countryside,

---

11. Colonel Jacob, a St. Cyr graduate (the West Point of France), was retired, having served in World War II, Algeria, and French Indochina. In April 1973, when Bill and his second wife Joan were living in Tours, they visited the Jacobs' home and its new owner (the Jacobs had died) and lived in Tours with Mrs. Jacob's sister Madame Maupa.

visiting chateaux and the Vouvray wine cellars; they also went to museums and cafes. On Saturday evenings, they attended the opera at the baroque opera house in Tours, after which they met other students for drinks in nearby cafes.

The Institute had students of all ages and nationalities. Bill became a close friend of Cecilia Larson, a native of Oslo, whose father was the publisher of *Dagbladet*, a Norwegian newspaper. Cecilia's French host family repared to their attractive country home on the weekends. Bill, a guest there with others on two Sunday afternoons, enjoyed fine wines amidst much bonhommie, gaiety, and grand luncheons.

SORBONNE

At the end of October, Bill departed for Paris, where he enrolled at the Sorbonne in a French language and civilization course for foreign students. He found a fourth-floor walk-up room in a Left Bank hotel on rue Monsieur Le Prince, near Boulevard San Michel, the Sorbonne, and Luxembourg Gardens. Bill's classmates included Richard Wright, the black American author whose books, *Black Boy* and *Native Son*, Bill had read and admired in high school. They saw each other at popular Left Bank cafes, where Bill also met the American writer James Baldwin.

During this period in Paris, the dollar was so strong that Americans could live comfortably on $15 to $20 a week. Receiving $110 a month from the G.I. Bill of Rights, Bill availed himself fully of Paris's cultural life, attending the theatre, opera, ballet, concerts, films, and museums at low student rates.

Bill, Dermott Doyle, Clayton Willis, and others often attended receptions at the American Cathedral on Sunday evenings. On one occasion, they met U.S. Senator William Benton's family, including his three stepchildren—Louise, Helen, and John—who were attending a preparatory school in Paris.[12] On Sunday afternoons, Bill sometimes took in plays at the Odeon or went to Montmartre to hear singers and comedians.

Over the Christmas holiday, Bill traveled with John Emmerich (from McComb, Mississippi) and his wife Celia in their Renault sedan, touring Luxembourg, Germany, Austria, and Switzerland. On Christmas Day, they walked and dined in Heidelberg, and after driving through Bavaria, Garmisch, and Berchtesgaden, they celebrated New Year's Eve in

---

12. After his unsuccessful campaign for election to the U.S. Senate from Connecticut, William Benton had taken his family to Paris for a year, 1953–1954.

Benton and Chester Bowles, Yale classmates, founded Benton & Bowles, the advertising agency, in 1929. Later, he acquired and published the *Encyclopedia Britannica*.

186

an Austrian inn, singing and dancing until dawn. Bill and the Emmerichs returned to Paris by way of Liechtenstein, Zurich, and Basle.

Over Easter vacation in 1954, Bill and Dermott Doyle hitched a ride on a vegetable truck from Les Halles market in Paris to the Riviera, then proceeded by bus and train along the French and Italian Rivieras to Pisa, Florence, and Rome, where they saw Louise, Helen, and John Benton and their parents.

Desiring to return to Paris by plane, Senator Benton engaged Bill and Dermott to drive his family's large black Citroen sedan back to Paris, expenses paid. Accepting with alacrity, they returned to Paris in style, touring Venice, the Italian lakes, Locarno, Lugano, Geneva, Zurich, and Basle while en route. Back in Paris, spring greeted them with greening trees, blossoming flowers and chestnuts.

SPAIN, PORTUGAL, AND GIBRALTAR

At the end of June 1954, having completed classes at the Sorbonne, Bill and another American toured Bordeaux, Biarritz, and the lovely beaches of the Cote d'Argent before taking the train through the Pyrenees to San Sebastian, Spain, on the Atlantic Ocean.

In July, they were in Pamplona for the annual fete—the running of the bulls—and the bullfights and life in the cafes which Ernest Hemingway recorded in *The Sun Also Rises*. They then traveled to Barcelona and the islands of Majorca and Ibiza before returning to mainland Spain at Valencia and journeying by bus to Madrid. After several days in the capital, they boarded an overnight express train to Lisbon, where they toured the city, Estoril, and nearby towns. Returning to Spain, they stopped in Seville, Cordova, Granada (the Alhambra), and finally the Andalusian city of Malaga on the Mediterranean. After his American friend returned to Portland, Oregon, Bill lived in Malaga for three weeks with a Swedish family whose villa was a short trolley ride east of town.

After lunch and a siesta, Bill, the Swedish family, and their guests swam in the Mediterranean, relaxed, and read on the beach. He enjoyed Spanish food (particularly paella) and watching performances of Spanish folk dances. After visiting Gibraltar and Morocco, Bill returned to the United States by ship from Algeciras, Spain, with a port call at Halifax, Nova Scotia en route to New York City.

COLUMBIA

In September 1954, Bill entered Columbia University Business School, where he completed a Master of Science degree in 1955. While there, he lived in John Jay Hall, sharing a two-room suite overlooking Hamilton Hall and Low Library with Jim Syrett, Gene Dimet, and Tosiharu Terashiki, a Japanese scholarship student who was an officer with Sumitomo Corporation in Tokyo. There, Bill also met John Watts, who was studying for his Ph.D. in economics. Both men earned A's in international economics and remained friends until Watts's death in March of 1988.[13]

During his year at Columbia, Bill worked part-time in the university's Career Placement Office. In the spring semester, he was elected president of the Business School's Foreign Trade Association and subsequently planned activities, arranged for speakers, and conducted dinner programs in John Jay Hall.

EARLY CAREER, 1955

Following his 1955 graduation, Bill accepted a finance trainee position with General Motors Overseas Corporation (GMOC) in their New York City headquarters, starting in accounting.[14] At the end of three to five years, Bill and his fellow trainees were to be promoted to treasurer or finance manager at one of GM's foreign manufacturing and assembly plants.

During the GM period, Bill shared a one-bedroom apartment on Riverside Drive and 107th Street with Jim Syrett, his roommate at Columbia, and Arthur Kimball, an advertising space salesman for *Vogue*. Furnishing the apartment, they occupied it through the summer of 1957. When

---

13. In Tokyo, Terashiki lived at 24 Kagegaoka-cho, Shibuya-Ku. He received his B.A. in 1944 from Keio University in Tokyo. Syrett, from Rock Island, Illinois, received his B.A. from Augustana College. Gene Dimet, a Miami University (Ohio) graduate, grew up in Niagara Falls, New York.

John Watts, from Norman, Oklahoma, held a B.A. from the University of Minnesota, an M.A. from the University of Pennsylvania, and a Ph.D. in economics from Columbia University. John taught economics at the University of Rhode Island, Michigan State University, Brooklyn College, St. John's University, and Iona College. A bachelor, Dr. Watts lived in a Greenwich Village apartment at 135 Waverly Place in Manhattan from the late 1950s until his death there of a heart attack on March 16, 1988.

14. Bill was one of four men selected for GMOC's program. The other three included: James P. Thompson, Bill's classmate at Columbia who came from Georgia; a graduate of the Amos Tuck School of Business at Dartmouth College; and a Harvard Business School alumnus.

Jim married Ruth, an apartment neighbor, Bill and Arthur leased a one-bedroom, fifth-floor apartment in a stately townhouse off Fifth Avenue at 9 East 84th Street.

In early 1956, another Columbia Business School colleague, Norman Allan, then with Compton Advertising Agency, had the foresight to buy eight tickets to the opening night's performance of *My Fair Lady*. Thus, Norman, Bill, and other friends were present at the dazzling musical's Broadway debut on March 16, 1956. Afterward, they celebrated over drinks at Sardi's and listened to the reading of the New York newspaper critics' rave reviews. The *World-Telegram and Sun* called it "the biggest thing of the century in musical theatre."[15]

Unsatisfied with the financial work at GM, Bill resigned in the spring of 1959 and accepted a real estate sales position with Previews, Inc., an international real estate marketing firm with headquarters in Manhattan, at 49 East 53rd Street, and other offices across the United States and Europe.[16] In this post, Bill inspected and evaluated large residential, commercial, and farm properties in New York, New England, and eastern Canada; sold the firm's marketing services to owners; prepared property reports covering saleability, highest and best use, and value; and assisted brokers in property promotions and negotiating sales. The service required a retainer fee, payable at the time of the property's listing, to cover advertising, brochure and newsletter preparations, mailings, owner and broker consultations, and sale negotiations.

FIRST MARRIAGE, 1959

On April 11, 1959, Bill married Joan Cecilia Sears of Devon, Connecticut. The Manhattan ceremony was held in the "Little Church Around the Corner"—the Episcopal Church of Transfiguration. George S. Banks, Jr., a GM associate and an alumnus of University of Pennsylvania's Wharton School, was best man; Mrs. Ronald F. Dobson was matron of honor. A reception was held in the Library Suite of Manhattan's St. Regis Hotel. In addition to family members, Dr. John Watts, James P. Thompson, Wayne W. Hartley (a GM associate from Seattle and the University of Washington), and Louise H. Benton attended.

Joan was born on July 3, 1935 in Bridgeport, Connecticut, the only

---

15. *World-Telegram and Sun*, 17 March 1956.

16. Ten of Bill's GMOC associates gave him a farewell luncheon at the New York Athletic Club on Central Park South in April 1959.

child of David and Edna Sears (Sesarsky). She graduated from Mary Burnham School in Northhampton, Massachusetts and received her Bachelor of Arts degree in 1957 from Skidmore College in Saratoga, New York. At the time of her marriage, she was working in the investment department of the Bank of New York. (See Allied Families: Sears)

A son, William Milton Grier 3d, was born to the couple in Manhattan on November 11, 1959 in the Harkness Pavilion of Columbia University Presbyterian Hospital.

CAMBRIDGE, MASSACHUSETTS, 1959

Later that year, the Griers moved to Cambridge, Massachusetts, where Bill worked for the Boston office of Previews, Inc. and had responsibility for operations in New England, eastern Canada, the Canadian Maritime Provinces, and Bermuda. In time, he became a manager and an officer of the firm.

In 1960, while in Cambridge, Bill also formed Feature Arts, a mail-order business which marketed museum reproductions of well-known paintings, sculpture, and antique jewelry, as well as art books and records. The business was closed in 1962.

DIVORCE, 1962

In November 1962, the Griers were divorced, and a prolonged dispute over custody of their son Billy ensued.[17] Angered by the divorce, which Bill had sought, Joan refused to allow him weekend or vacation custody, despite repeated court orders over the next six years. Consequently, Bill was able to see his son only once or twice a month on Saturdays or after school, driving four hours from Boston to the boy's home in Weston, Connecticut.

Irving Rappoport, the Sears family's attorney for many years, advised Joan not to obstruct the father-son relationship by denying Bill vacation custody. When she was unwilling to follow his counsel, he refused to represent her. She then retained a new attorney, Stephen E. Ronai (of

---

17. Joan, who had custody of young Billy, then lived with her family in Devon, Connecticut while teaching school in nearby Bridgeport from 1961–1962.

The following year, she married Dr. Edward Keelan, a Dublin-educated psychiatrist who had emigrated to Westport, Connecticut, where he later established a practice. They had a son, David, in 1966 and lived in Weston, Connecticut. In the late 1970s, Dr. Keelan, a manic-depressive, had a mental breakdown, which was exacerbated by financial reverses and the loss of their home.

Gitlitz, Ronai and Berchem in Milford, Connecticut), who led her protracted legal effort to bar vacation custody from 1962 to 1972.

After each court order issued between 1962 and 1968 reaffirming Bill's custody rights, Joan immediately filed motions to modify those orders, thereby thwarting any solution.

For Bill, it was anguishing to have his son periodically taken out of school to appear in court, where, sometimes in tears, he submitted to questioning by attorneys and judges. To spare his son further agony, and distraught over Joan's intransigence and the futility of litigation, Bill suggested that Joan and her second husband, Dr. Edward Keelan, adopt young Billy, a proposal which she promptly rejected. To end the debilitating impasse, Bill reluctantly agreed, when his son was nine in 1968, to forego weekend and vacation custody until the boy was older. He continued day visitations, and Joan agreed to support Billy and provide for his education through college.

After Bill's move to Manhattan in 1970, his son spent one weekend with him there, but Joan refused to permit such visits in the future, claiming the boy suffered "separation anxiety"—an argument that was repeatedly rejected by the court. When Billy entered his teenage years, his father again attempted to arrange for overnight visitations, as well as longer stays during his son's school vacations. Joan, however, remained opposed, despite the fact that her attorney acknowledged, in a letter to Bill's lawyer, that Billy was "amenable to occasional weekend visitation."[18] Unfortunately, Joan's unwillingness to cooperate prevailed throughout Billy's high school years.

In the fall of 1973, when Billy was fourteen, his father and stepmother moved to Denver, and thereafter they saw each other in the East over Christmas holidays. Now, Bill's letters to his son were censored or discarded by Joan (a practice that would continue even in 1988, when twenty-eight-year-old Billy used his mother's address for mail while he was working in New York City).

It was not until Billy's senior year in college that Joan began to relent a bit. Regrettably, by then both father and son were effectively deprived of any normal relationship—a loss they carry with them today.

REAL ESTATE INVESTMENT

Shortly after his divorce in 1962, Bill formed a real estate investment

---

18. This letter, dated April 5, 1972, was sent from Joan's attorney Stephen Ronai to Bill's attorney James R. Healey (of Sturges and Mathes in Southbury, Connecticut).

and management firm, while continuing in his position with Previews, Inc. From 1962 to 1970, his firm acquired, renovated, and managed six Cambridge apartment buildings; all were three-story, frame walk-ups in Central Square, between Harvard University and Massachusetts Institute of Technology. The first acquisition was a six-unit structure on Western Avenue, a half block from the Charles River, where Bill occupied a unit until purchasing a three-story Victorian with mansard roof at 220 Harvard Street; he lived in this house from 1964 to 1969. At that time, Boston area real estate was greatly undervalued. With urban renewal and Harvard's real estate development in Cambridge during this period, the value of Bill's holdings appreciated substantially. Their gain was realized when Bill sold his properties in the late sixties and early 1970.

Over the Christmas holidays during this period, Bill usually visited his family in San Francisco and friends in Los Angeles. Annually, from 1963 to 1969, he also enjoyed three-week spring vacations in Europe, primarily in northern Italy, southern France, Switzerland, Austria, and Germany. In the spring of 1967, he went to Italy, Yugoslavia, Greece, and Turkey; from Venice, he sailed aboard a Yugoslav ship for five days along the Dalmatian Coast, stopping for visits in Trieste, Dubrovnik, and other cities before arriving in Greece. After a week on the mainland of Greece, Bill took a cruise to the Aegean Islands, Istanbul, the Bosphorus, the Dardanelles, and the western coast of Turkey, including Ephesus.

RETURN TO NEW YORK CITY, 1969

At the end of 1969, Grier returned to New York City and worked in investment sales with Apache Corporation, a New York Stock Exchange firm with headquarters in Minneapolis. In this post, Bill sold tax-sheltered, limited partnerships in oil and gas and real estate to high-income individuals. During this period, he also became a member of the Union League Club at 38 East 37th Street, where he entertained clients and friends, played squash, and used the library.

Unfortunately, the proliferation of oil and gas tax-shelter programs being marketed in the late sixties caused increased competition which, along with a bear market in 1971, forced Apache to begin to phase out its offices, including the one in New York. Bill, therefore, left the firm with the intention of acquiring or founding his own business.

TRAVEL ABROAD, 1971–1972

In May 1971, Bill vacationed in England, crossing the Atlantic on the S.S. *France*, on the next to last voyage of the venerable French ship. Aboard, he met British actress Hermione Gingold and accompanied her to a rerun of her winning role in "Gigi" in the ship's theatre. From Southhampton, he drove through Thomas Hardy's West Country and the Cotswolds. In Bideford, he bought a George III mahogany flap table and four nineteenth-century mahogany dining chairs from J. Collins and Son; the furniture was shipped to New York City, with three oil paintings purchased in London galleries. Branching out from London, he visited Cambridge, Canterbury, and Winston Churchill's home, "Chartwell," in Kent. During the last week of his holiday, Bill was joined in London by Joan Grafmueller, who was visiting a classmate from Ethel Walker School— Elaine Domingues Rawlinson (Lady Peter Rawlinson), whose husband was then serving as attorney general in Prime Minister Edward Heath's cabinet.

The following February, Bill went to Europe for three weeks, visiting Turkish friends in Munich, Germany; skiing in San Anton, Austria and San Moritz, Switzerland; then sightseeing in Madrid, where he visited the Prado and, in a gallery in the capital, bought two paintings; and finally, touring Lisbon and nearby Estoril and Cascais.

SECOND MARRIAGE

On June 15, 1972, Bill married Joan Grafmueller in Ketchum, Idaho, next to Sun Valley. The ceremony took place in the home of Presbyterian minister Curtis M. Page, where the windows and terrace overlooked Mt. Baldy and Sun Valley's downhill ski runs, a deep green at the time.

Prior to their wedding, Bill and Joan had traveled through the Black Hills of South Dakota, visiting the Homestake Mining Company and seeing the statue of Bill's great-uncle Thomas Johnston ("T.J.") Grier, Homestake's superintendent for thirty years, in Lead, South Dakota. The couple had also traveled to Yellowstone and Grand Teton National Parks and to Helena, Montana.

The newlyweds flew from Boise, Idaho to Portland, Oregon after the ceremony. Following a few days of sightseeing there, they rented a car and drove along the Oregon and California coasts, past the redwoods to San Francisco and Sacramento, where they visited Bill's family. Later, they drove to Monterey, Carmel, and Big Sur, then proceeded south along Coastal Highway One to William Randolph Hearst's estate, "San Simeon," and to Brentwood, where they were the guests of Bruce and Barbara Crane. A two-week holiday in Mexico City followed, with visits to Oaxaca and Acapulco.

Bill and Joan had met in Manhattan in November of 1968 through Nadia Von Hurt, a mutual friend in Cambridge, Massachusetts. A native of New York City, Joan was born on September 21, 1935 in Columbia Univer-

193

sity Presbyterian Hospital, the only child of Charles Edward and Barbara Rose Grafmueller (nee Brownlee). When she was three-and-a-half, her mother died of a brain tumor. (See Allied Families: Grafmueller/Brownlee)

Until the age of ten, Joan lived in Scarsdale, New York; Danbury, Connecticut; and Grosse Pointe, Michigan with her father, her stepmother Edith Colby de Rham, and her stepsister and stepbrother, Edie and Charlie. (See Allied Families: de Rham) In 1945, the Grafmuellers moved to Greenwich, Connecticut, where Joan graduated from Greenwich Country Day School four years later. In 1953, she graduated from the Ethel Walker School in Simsbury, Connecticut.

Following three years at Sweet Briar College in Lynchburg, Virginia (1953–1956), Joan settled in New York City, where she worked at *Look* magazine for eight and a half years as an assistant to the director of personnel and ran a training program for thirty-seven editorial trainees. Later, Joan worked for Rock Resorts and the JDR III Fund (John D. Rockefeller III's personal investments); Young & Rubicam advertising agency; and, until 1972, as an executive secretary for Doubleday & Company.

FRANCE AND EAST AFRICA

When Bill's financing to purchase a business fell through in September of 1972, the Griers decided to take a year off. They spent that year in France, studying the language, traveling extensively, and considering a relocation from Manhattan to the West upon their return. After buying an Audi in Germany, they lived in Aix-en-Provence from November 1972 to March 1973 and in Tours, deep in the chateaux country of the Loire Valley, from May to August 1973. They studied French at the University of Aix-En-Provence and at the Institute of Touraine and traveled in France, Italy, Switzerland, Germany, and Austria. From Tours, they often visited Joan's cousin Barbara Bolton and her French husband Jerome Gratry in Paris and toured Brittany and Normandy, as well.

In July, inoculated and properly outfitted, Bill left Joan behind in Tours and took a trip to East Africa, visiting Kenya, Tanzania, and the islands of Zanzibar and Pemba. He flew to Nairobi, Kenya with eighteen French professionals; armed with sleeping bags and a restless spirit of adventure, the group and an Indian guide toured Kenya and Tanzania game reserves in two Volkswagen vans. They saw Nairobi National Park, the Masai Mara, Serengeti National Park, the Olduvai Gorge, and Seronera.

Roughing it, the group slept in huts, in a museum, in the workers' quarters at parks, and in modest hotels. They swam and bathed in streams and lakes, often with a vista of Mount Kilimanjaro as a backdrop. They retired early each evening and rose with the sun, as a crease of orange transformed the night into shrimp-colored hues of dawn.

From the Serengeti, Bill and his companions spent a day at the Ngorongoro Crater, a spectacular caldera. Perched on the crater's edge, the Ngorongoro Wildlife Lodge had a view of the crater's floor some 2,000 feet below. At the center was a large alkali lake of a dazzling jade color, accented by thousands of pink-winged flamingos, crowned cranes, and storks with neck pouches.

En route from Serengeti to Ngorongoro, the group surmounted the Great Rift Valley wall and saw Masai herdsmen guiding their cattle along. After ten days in the vans, they then traveled by Tanzania's trains and buses to visit an agricultural research center and a model Tanzanian community, as well as Dar-es-Salaam, the capital, where Bill bought a dozen primitive (naive) oil paintings.

After a two-day visit in Zanzibar and a brief stop on the island of Pemba, they flew to Mombasa, Kenya. There, Bill visited his great-uncle Thomas Johnston Grier's stepdaughter—Margaret Eliza ("Madge") Christie (nee Ferrie). The widow of James Carron Christie, a Scot who had been the Queen's counsel in Kenya for almost fifty years, Madge was born in Scotland and had settled in Africa after her marriage on October 7, 1924 in her mother's Los Angeles home at 1675 Buckingham Road, Lafayette Square.

Over lunches, dinners, and teas in her comfortable house near the Indian Ocean, Madge recalled many events, people, and places from the past: her early years in Edinburgh and the Black Hills of South Dakota; her stepfather T.J. Grier and her mother Mary Jane Grier (nee Palethorpe); her student days at Lead High School and Columbia University; her life in Los Angeles after T.J.'s death in 1914; and her friendship with Phoebe Hearst. She spoke of her brother James William Ferrie, her half sister Evangeline Victoria ("Muddie") Grier, and her three Grier half brothers—Tommy, Lisgar, and Ormonde. She reminisced about Homestake Mining Company and the times when she had been a guest in Phoebe Hearst's California residences, "Hacienda" and "Wyntoon." Madge also gave Bill several family papers and photos.

In her English Ford, Madge drove Bill around Mombasa's large port, its downtown and residential areas, and nearby shorefront resorts. She entertained him at the elegant Mombasa Club, with its view of lush gardens and the Indian Ocean. Bill also met Madge's daughter and son-in-law, Jean and Ian Mills, who were vacationing at a resort to the north of Mombasa.

Bill had been corresponding with Madge for more than a year before his 1973 visit. Mildred Fielder, the author of *Homestake Gold*, had referred him first to Madge's half sister Muddie Grier (Mrs. Edwin Nelsen) in Sausalito, California; Muddie, in turn, urged Bill to contact Madge. For

Bill, meeting her in July of 1973 was like meeting an old friend.

DENVER

When the Griers returned to New York in August of 1973, they decided to relocate in Colorado. After arranging their affairs in early October, they began a leisurely drive west, stopping to visit Gettysburg, Charlottesville, Great Smoky Mountains National Park, Knoxville, Memphis, Oklahoma City, Santa Fe, Taos, Colorado Springs, and Boulder on the way.

Arriving in Denver in November, the Griers rented an apartment, and soon after, Bill leased an office suite in the Empire Building in downtown Denver. Here, he founded Grier & Company, a management consulting, marketing, and publishing firm.

The following July, the Griers purchased one side of a duplex at 443 Marion Street—an attached, 1904 two-story brick house near the Denver Country Club, where they reside today.

GRIER & COMPANY

During the early months in Denver, Grier & Company prepared executive resumes, corporate brochures, and advertising, while Bill explored the possibility of starting a commercial real estate newspaper. In June of 1976, that concept became a reality with the publication of the first monthly issue of *Real Estate West.*

Now in its fourteenth year, the paper covers news and trends of income-producing real estate development, financing, leasing, sales, and investment from the Midwest to the Pacific Coast and includes a *California Real Estate* section. In addition to city reviews and special features, the tabloid paper reports on the office, multi-family, shopping center, and industrial markets. Its subscribers include developers, investors, brokers, building owners, officers of financial institutions, and corporate real estate executives.

In 1980, Grier & Company edited, designed, and produced a 432-page book, *Walter Judd: Chronicles of a Statesman,* for the Center for Science, Technology, and Political Thought in Boulder, Colorado. Bill and his staff worked on the project with Professor Edward J. Rozek, the Center's founder and director, a Polish emigre, Harvard University Ph.D., and political science professor at the University of Colorado.

In the summer of 1984, Grier & Company relocated to a larger downtown Denver office at 909 17th Street, Suite 607, and in November

196

1988, the firm moved again to a corner suite at 444 17th Street, Suite 918, a few steps from the Brown Palace hotel.

INVESTOR

When Bill sold, at a profit, his apartment properties in Cambridge, Massachussetts in the late sixties and 1970, he invested the proceeds in corporate stocks, thereby launching a secondary career as an investor that has continued for two decades.

Initially a short-term trader and speculator, he sometimes bought stock on margin (using borrowed funds) and on broker recommendations with little, if any, independent assessment of the companies involved. This strategy, steadily eroding his portfolio's value, soon lead Bill to reappraise his approach. He began to view a share of stock as a part-interest in a business, rather than a speculative medium, to stress business values instead of stock market values.

In analyzing the methods of money management, Bill was soon drawn to the basic value approach of Benjamin Graham, the esteemed professor of investments at Columbia Business School, father of modern security analysis, and founder of the Wall Street firm of Graham-Newman. In 1934, he and colleague David L. Dodd published their pioneering text, *Security Analysis*. In 1949, Graham also published *The Intelligent Investor*. (As a student at Columbia Business School, Bill's emphasis was on foreign trade; therefore, he did not take their courses. However, his roommate Jim Syrett, a finance major, had talked enthusiastically about them.)

Successful investing, Graham said, requires patience and discipline; stocks should be bought with the curt calculation we apply to prices at the grocery store, not with the hopes and dreams we bring to the gambling casino. He also believed that emotion, whims, and changes of fancy in the market sometimes caused specific stocks to sell for less than their true value.

In developing a portfolio, he wanted companies with more equity than debt, and he liked to buy stocks at or below net current asset value (current assets minus current liabilities and debt). He would buy such bargains among various companies and industries for diversification and safety. Thus, the key was to buy stocks selling at low prices relative to current earnings and to apply Graham's test of assets divided by liabilities to determine how much real value existed.

Since Bill began to practice Graham's principles in 1974, he has had rewarding results—buying undervalued companies for the long term.

OTHER INTERESTS

Since the late seventies, Joan Grier has designed and produced sachets and lingerie for Bergdorf Goodman, Lord & Taylor, I. Magnin, and D. Porthault, Inc., the French linen firm.

In the summers, the Griers have vacationed in Nantucket, Maine, and Vermont, and in August 1979, they sailed for several days with Bill's Montreal cousin, David Grier, on his sloop on Lake Champlain. At other times, they have been guests of Joan's Cleveland cousins, the Boltons, in Prouts Neck, Maine. From 1980 to 1984, for a month each year, the Griers rented homes in Nantucket, Massachusetts, and in the spring of 1984, they explored the old houses, plantations, and gardens of Charleston and Savannah.

The Griers visited Bill's mother each year until her death in 1987 and saw his family in San Francisco and Sacramento. Since settling in Denver in 1973, they have traveled extensively in the West, including trips to Taos, Santa Fe, Portland, Seattle, and Victoria and Vancouver, British Columbia. They have also alternated Christmas-New Year's vacations with both of their families—Bill's in California and Joan's in Connecticut. While visiting the Grafmuellers, the Griers have sometimes rented apartments in Manhattan.

WILLIAM MILTON GRIER 3d
(b. November 11, 1959)

The only child of William Milton, Jr. and Joan Sears Grier, young Billy spent his first two years in Cambridge, Massachusetts. In May of 1961, he and his parents visited his grandmother Elo Grier in San Francisco, his great-aunt Ferdy Lannon Shaeffer in Sacramento, and his Palmer cousins— Cathy, Charles, and Kenneth—in Berkeley.

Following his parents' divorce in November 1962, Billy and his mother shared the home of her parents, David and Edna Sears, in Devon, Connecticut.

Billy's mother remarried in 1963, and in 1966, she and her second husband, Dr. Edward Keelan, had a son, David, some seven years Billy's junior. The family first lived in Westport, Connecticut, where Dr. Keelan had a psychiatric practice. In the mid-sixties, they bought a home in Weston, Connecticut, where they lived until the late 1970s.

Billy attended public schools in Milford, Westport, and Weston until the fourth grade. From the fall of 1968 until his graduation in June 1977, he attended Greens Farms Academy, a private school in Greens Farms, Connecticut.

The following September, Billy enrolled in the freshman class of Rollins College in Winter Park, Florida. In his sophomore year, however, he transferred to Colgate University in Hamilton, New York, where he majored in fine arts and was on the university's tennis team. During his college summers, he worked as an assistant tennis pro at clubs in Connecticut, including Wee Burn Country Club in Darien.

Billy was awarded a B.A. in fine arts from Colgate in May of 1981, and his father and stepmother attended the commencement ceremonies. In a letter sent to Billy shortly before graduation, Bill shared with his son three particularly relevant quotes. He wrote of Adlai Stevenson's caveat to the 1954 graduating class at Princeton University—"Don't forget when you leave why you came"—and his wise assessment that "what a man knows at fifty that he didn't know at twenty is, for the most part, uncommunicable. The knowledge he has acquired with age is not the knowledge of formulas, or forms or words, but of people, places, actions—a knowledge not gained of words but of touch, sight, sound, victories, failures, sleeplessness, devotion, love—the human experiences and emotions of this earth and of oneself and other men; and perhaps, too, a little reverence for things you cannot see." Bill also passed on the advice that Henry James gave to his graduating niece: "Be kind to people, be kind, be kind...."

After receiving his degree, Billy continued to work as a tennis pro at clubs in Connecticut's Fairfield County. Two years later, he accepted a sales position with a Manhattan firm that organized tennis tournaments in New York and Florida, assisting in marketing and selling sponsorships to corporations. Today, he works in Manhattan as a broker in commodity futures, primarily trading the United States dollar in world currency markets.

"Judge" John D. Russell

Menlo faculty members: Leon T. Loofbourow, E. Hutson Hart, Christopher Conner, President William E. Kratt, and Holbrook Bonney

Bill (seated, second from left) and the Menlo basketball team, 1946

Bill (right) and friends Ray Smith, Margie Mason, and Carol Keeler at the Hotel Claremont in Berkeley, California, September 1949

At the 1950 Crane-Pratt wedding: Jay Martin, Richard Miller, Bill, Bruce Randall Pratt, Jr., Ray Smith, and Bill Nordlund

Bill (in background) at Huntington Lake Camp, 1950

Bill and Marie Bertillion at San Francisco's Fairmont Hotel, 1951

Bill and Cecilia Larson in Tours, France, 1953

Bill in Pisa, Italy, Easter 1954

Bill in Venice, Italy, April 1954

Bill in Cannes, France, April 1954

Bill and roommate Tosiharu Terashiki on the steps of Columbia University's Low Library, 1954

Bill (right) with Clayton Willis and a Norwegian friend on the Eiffel Tower, June 1954

Bill and colleague
Alvin Cohen from the
Foreign Trade
Association at
Columbia Business
School, 1955

Bill, Tosiharu, and Melvin Brown in John Jay Hall at Columbia, 1954

The Grier-Sears wedding reception on April 11, 1959: Wayne Hartley, Bill, Joan, Mr. and Mrs. Ronald Dobson, and James Thompson

Bill (center) with Wayne Hartley and James Thompson on Narragansett Bay, aboard Jamestown Ferry en route to Newport, Rhode Island, August 1956

Bill and six-week-old Billy in Devon, Connecticut, Christmas 1959

Billy in Cambridge, Massachusetts, 1961

Billy, 1963

210

Bill and Billy (age 7), November 1966

Bill in Cambridge, 1966

Bill on New Year's Day 1966 in Sun Valley,
Idaho

 Bill in Trieste, Italy in April 1967

Bill meeting the ship's captain on Aegean cruise, April 1967

Bill (second from left in front row) at the June 1968 New England Real Estate Convention at the Mt. Washington Hotel in Bretton Woods, New Hampshire. Also attending were A. Pelham Stevens (extreme left, second row) and Roland Hopkins (third from left, second row), publisher of *New England Real Estate Journal*.

George Banks and Bill in Bermuda over the 1969 Christmas holidays

On Rearing Children From Crib To College

October 1970

PARENTS'

MAGAZINE & BETTER FAMILY LIVING

More than 2,100,000 Circulation

Must We Legislate Family Size?

The Middle Years of Childhood

First Baby in the House

Hidden Handicaps to Learning

Billy on the cover of *Parents'* magazine in October 1970

Billy and Bill, 1969

Billy in 1972

Billy and Joan Grafmueller Grier at Round Hill
Club, Greenwich, Connecticut, September 1973
(Photo by Bill Grier)

Joan Grafmueller Grier

Newlyweds Bill and Joan Grafmueller Grier after marriage
ceremony in Sun Valley, Idaho, June 1972

Billy at 16

Billy, Joan, and Bill in August 1972

220

Bill and Ferd Shaeffer in Denver, September 1976

Joan and Bill in Denver, November 1973

California Real Estate News (Section B)

Los Angeles Report P.A7	Fort Worth Report P.A12	Office Market P.A17

RealEstate West

THE JOURNAL OF COMMERCIAL & INVESTMENT PROPERTY

PUBLISHED BY GRIER & COMPANY

VOL. 12 NO. 5   OCTOBER 1987

Denver, Dallas, Houston

S.F. Fund Takes $100 Million Write-Down

A major real estate investment pension fund manager has taken a substantial write-down on two Denver office buildings a move experts said may follow in the Mile High City's depressed real estate market.

San Francisco-based RREEF Fund has taken a $100 million write-down on nine properties located in Denver, Houston and Dallas a write-down of 40% of the properties' value at Dec. 31, 1986.

The two Denver properties are 400,000 sq. ft. of office space at 410 17th St. and 100,000 sq. ft. of office space at Orchard Place in Englewood. RREEF didn't specify the value of the Denver properties, but the write-downs averaged 25%.

Realistic

"We just felt we should be more realistic in realizing what was the bottom of the market," said John Dayton, a principal with RREEF, which has $3.1 billion in real estate under management. "We felt that our external appraisals were lagging the leasing markets."

Denver's downtown office vacancy rate was 29.5% in June, one of the highest in the nation, according to a survey by Coldwell Banker. At the Denver Tech Center, vacancy rates were running 21.9%.

50% Value Drop

Appraisers and real estate brokers said they wouldn't be surprised if other write-downs follow RREEF's move. Accountants said most property owners, however, are not required to adjust property values to current market until the property is sold. In some cases, today's market value is 50% below what was paid four years ago.

"I agree with you one 100% that

some of the properties that are out there are overvalued," said Cliff Cryer with Cryer and Company Appraisers Inc. "$100 million is a drop in the bucket from what should be written down out there, but financially if we did that we'd be shaking the pillars of the financial temple."

Paid Inflated Prices

Part of the problem is investors paid inflated prices for office buildings several years ago. Sales prices were not discounted for free rent or cash concessions. At the time, office space was leasing at $20 to $25 a sq. ft. But today, brokers are having trouble selling space at $8 to $10 a sq. ft.

In hope that the market rebounds institutional fund managers and property owners have resisted write-downs. "It's kind of like having a cavity and waiting until it gets so bad that the tooth has to be pulled," said John Bixer, vice prsident with Fuller and Co., a Denver real estate brokerage.   □

County, City & State of L.A. Become Civic Center Partners

The Los Angeles County Supervisors have approved RCI as developer of a $125 million, 21-story, 600,000 sq. ft. commercial office building on the 4.6-acre Civic Center site at First and Broadway. The County of Los Angeles is the lead agency along with the State of California and City of Los Angeles who will be 66-year partners in what is heralded by the County as one of the most significant projects nationally in a downtown civic area. Ground breaking is planned for mid-1988 with completion in 1990. Murphy-Jahn of Chicago is architect.

MCI Building Opens In Downtown St. Louis

The newest addition to St. Louis' growing downtown skyline is the MCI Building, which will serve as MCI's Southwestern Division headquarters. Developed by The Forsythe Group, the 12-story building overlooks the Mississippi River and the city's Gateway Arch grounds. The St. Louis area has undergone an economic renaissance over the past several years and is now one of the most active business development markets in the country. St. Louis is ranked seventh by Forbes magazine as a headquarters location for "Forbes 500" companies. Approximately 360 of the "Fortune 500" companies operate major offices or facilities in the St. Louis area.

Securitized Mortgage Assets Skyrocket

NEW YORK—The securitization of financial assets accelerated dramatically in 1986 and the first pan of 1987, according to a new Salomon Brothers report, "Securitization and the Mortgage Market." The maturity of this market is perhaps best illustrated by the fact that the issuance of new residential mortgage pass-through securities more than doubled in only one year—reaching $263 billion during 1986.

This is part of a long-term trend that has seen the aggregate amount of mortgage pool certificates mushroom from $92 billion of mortgage debt in 1979 to more than $580 billion in March 1987, according to the report. This burgeoning market includes commercial mortgage securities, which the survey projects will grow to a volume of $8 billion by year's end.

Among other findings contained in the report, the issuance of collateralized mortgage obligations (CMOs) has climbed to a peak of $82 billion in the past 18 months. □

INSIDE

Regular Departments

Special Section

October 1987 issue of *Real Estate West*, (Vol. 12, No. 5)

William Milton Grier 3d, 1981

Billy receiving his Bachelor of Arts degree from Colgate
University on May 31, 1981

Colgate University's
Memorial Chapel

Madge Ferrie at the Hearsts' "Hacienda" in Pleasanton,
California, c. 1916

CHRONOLOGY OF ELOYD JOHN GRIER

1929	Born in San Francisco, California on July 4
1930	Baptized in Trinity Cathedral in Phoenix, Arizona on March 22
1934	Moves to Sacramento, California; enrolls in El Dorado Elementary School
1935	Father, William M. Grier, Sr., dies in Sacramento on December 8
1935–1936	Lives in Santa Maria, California with aunt and uncle
1936	Returns to Sacramento and El Dorado Elementary School in June
1937	Moves to San Francisco; enrolls in Spring Valley School
1937–1938	Summers at Tilly's Roost Camp, Santa Cruz Mountains, California
1939–1940	Summers with Lannon grandparents in Sacramento; visits Golden Gate International Exposition (Treasure Island)
1941	Enters Redding School in San Francisco in February; camps with Borman family near Mt. Shasta, California over Labor Day; transfers to Presidio Junior High School in San Francisco in September
1944–1948	Works summers at Winterland Auditorium in San Francisco
1944	Enters George Washington High School in San Francisco
1947	Returns to live in Piedmont home; graduates from George Washington High School; enters San Francisco State College

1948	Completes freshman and half of sophomore year; moves to Harrisburg, Pennsylvania in August; attends York Collegiate Institute
1949	Attends Gettysburg College in Harrisburg
1950	Joins FBI in Washington, D.C. as fingerprint trainee in January
1950–1952	Serves in U.S. Army Military Police, in West Germany; graduates from intelligence school with superior commendation
1952	Discharged from Army, returns to FBI while studying Spanish and law at George Washington University in Washington, D.C.
1956	Marries Patricia Warrington Bender in Valley Forge, Pennsylvania on September 1
1957	Joins John Hancock Life Insurance Company in Harrisburg in January
1958	Daughter, Shelby Warrington Grier, born in Harrisburg on April 6
1959	Promoted to assistant district manager; relocates to Jacksonville, Florida
1962	Becomes assistant district manager for Hancock's Tampa, Florida office
1966	Made district manager for Hancock's Atlanta, Georgia office
1968	Resigns from Hancock; relocates to West Chester, Pennsylvania where he buys and operates a delicatessen near West Chester University
1983	Retires in March
1984	Divorces Patricia Bender Grier

1987	Mother, Elo Lannon Grier, dies at age 91 in Sacramento on July 16
1989	Continues to live in West Chester; enjoys weekends and summers of boating at waterfront home in Chestertown, Maryland

22

ELOYD JOHN GRIER
1929–

William Milton Grier's second son, Eloyd John, would remain in his native California until the age of nineteen. After graduating from George Washington High School in 1947, he studied for one-and-a-half years at San Francisco State College (later named San Francisco State University), while living in the family's Piedmont house. During this period, Eloyd, unhappy at home, began to consider continuing his education in the East.

Since 1947, Russ Tuckey, a Gettysburg College alumnus and member of the Ice Follies, had been encouraging Eloyd to attend his alma mater in Pennsylvania. Anxious for a change in his life, Eloyd moved to Harrisburg, Pennsylvania in late summer of 1948, where he attended York Collegiate Institute for one semester and became president of the YMCA and the Linguistics Society. The following year, he completed three semesters at Gettysburg College and joined Sigma Chi fraternity.

FBI, 1950

In January 1950, Eloyd accepted an appointment as a fingerprint trainee in the Technical Section of the Identification Division of the Federal Bureau of Investigation (FBI) in Washington, D.C. That fall, however, he was drafted into the Army, and after basic training at Fort Knox, Kentucky and eight weeks of military police (MP) school at Camp Gordon, Georgia, he was promoted to corporal and transferred to West Germany, where he served as a military policeman aboard passenger trains. He later graduated from intelligence school with a superior commendation. Following his honorable discharge in late 1952 at Indiantown Gap, Pennsylvania, Eloyd returned to the FBI as a fingerprint classifier, while studying Spanish and law in the evenings at George Washington University.

MARRIAGE AND CAREER

While with the FBI, he met his future wife, Patricia ("Pat") Warrington Bender; they were married on September 1, 1956 in the Valley Forge Memorial Chapel, Valley Forge, Pennsylvania. The daughter of J. Herbert and Laura Warrington Bender, Pat was born on November 27, 1934 in West Chester, Pennsylvania.

With his marriage, Eloyd also made a career change, becoming a sales agent with John Hancock Life Insurance Company in Harrisburg, Pennsylvania in January 1957. The following year, a daughter, Shelby Warrington, was born to the Griers on April 6, 1958 at Polyclinic Hospital in Harrisburg. A second child, a son, died in infancy. Eloyd was promoted to assistant district manager and relocated to Jacksonville, Florida in 1959. Three years later, he became assistant district manager in Hancock's Tampa office, where his district ranked thirty-seventh nationally. By 1966, he had risen to district manager and supervised forty-eight sales agents in the Atlanta, Georgia office until 1968. During his tenure with Hancock, Eloyd rose to the top in management and sales in each of his districts, becoming a member of the company's prestigious Regional and President's Clubs. At the time of his resignation in 1968, his southeastern district ranked twelfth in national sales.

ENTREPRENEUR, 1969–1983

Despite his success with Hancock, Eloyd, like his father before him, yearned to be an independent businessman—an entrepreneur. Hence, after a family trip to California that included a visit to his native San Francisco, Eloyd and his family settled in West Chester, Pennsylvania, where he purchased a delicatessen one block from West Chester University. He successfully operated this business for fourteen years—from April 1969 to March 1983, when he retired.

Eloyd and Pat were divorced in 1984. Today, they both continue to live in West Chester, where Pat works for John Harland Company. On weekends and in summers, Eloyd enjoys his waterfront vacation home in Chestertown on Maryland's eastern shore.

SHELBY GRIER MACKRIDES
(b. April 6, 1958)

Shelby Warrington Grier, Eloyd and Patricia's surviving child, received her early schooling at St. John's Episcopal School in Tampa, Florida and in Atlanta, Georgia and West Chester, Pennsylvania. She graduated from Henderson High School in West Chester, where she was an honor roll student, a cheerleader, and a member of the school's ski club, varsity track, and gymnastics teams.

230

Shelby received a Bachelor of Arts in Spanish and English, with honors, in June of 1980 from Allegheny College in Meadville, Pennsylvania. During college, she was an Alden Scholar and a member of Alpha Chi Omega sorority. She also received an award for excellence in Spanish from the National Conference of Foreign Language Teachers and was named best Spanish student for 1980. In her junior year, she studied at the University of Madrid; as a senior, she tutored Spanish, was an assistant in the language laboratory, and, with a third-class operator's license, worked for the college radio station, WARC.

After graduation, Shelby was a bilingual executive secretary for Pennsylvania State Export Corporation, then became an administrative assistant in Plymouth Meeting, Pennsylvania with Woodward-Clyde Consultants, engineers with extensive Latin American business. In 1985, she became personnel manager for a health care firm in Bryn Mawr, Pennsylvania, while studying in the evenings for an M.B.A. at Villanova College. Shelby also served as a financial advisor to her sorority, Alpha Chi Omega (Zeta Tau Chapter), while attending Villanova and has been the secretary of the Pi Pi Alumnae Chapter for two years.

Shelby Warrington Grier Mackrides
(*Courtesy of Eloyd J. Grier*)

In September 1988, Shelby married Brian Marc Mackrides. Her husband, the son of former Eagles football player Dr. William Mackrides and his wife, holds a degree in geology from Bucknell University and a civil engineering degree from Drexel University. He is a project manager with R.M. Shoemaker Company in Princeton, New Jersey. Curently living in Newton, Pennsylvania, the couple expects their first child in December 1989.

Eloyd John Grier in 1947

23

DAVID DENHAM EYRE GRIER
1932–

The first Grier born outside North America since his great-grand-father James, David Denham Eyre Grier was born on April 12, 1932 in Johannesburg, South Africa, the only child of Charles Denham and Ruby Stephenie Grier (nee Coote). (See Part One: 7)

David's father, a mining and metallurgical engineer, had traveled extensively across the United States before relocating to South Africa in 1925, where he became the managing director of a subsidiary of American Cyanamid Company in Johannesburg. He met his wife, a native of Armagh, Northern Ireland, in South Africa. They were married on February 26, 1927.

FAMILY

Ruby's mother was Mary Emilie Wolfe, the eldest daughter of the venerable John Charles Wolfe, archdeacon of Cloger, Ireland. One of the Wolfes of Fornaght (an estate on what is now the border between Ireland and Ulster), he is reputed to have been a descendant of the General Wolfe who died—and gained fame—on the plains of Abraham at Quebec. Mary Emilie married Albert Augustus Eyre Coote, the youngest son of the late Major Coote, on August 9, 1882. The couple produced eleven children (remarkable, since Mary Emilie also acted as manager of the Armagh Savings Bank). Ruby Stephenie's sisters included Violet, Sylvia, Emmy (twin of brother Tom), Olive (Ruby's twin, known as "Polly"), Beatrice, Claire, and Grace. Her brothers were Albert, Tom, and Eyre.

David never knew his mother, for she died in childbirth. He was raised first by his grandmother Frances Margaret Mills Grier and then, from the age of five, by his father's second wife, Kathleen Augusta McKiel Zwicker.[1] The family home was located at 11 Pallinghurst Road in Parktown, South Africa.

---

1. Kathleen was born April 20, 1898 in Lunenburg, Nova Scotia. After graduating from high school there, she received a teacher's certificate in violin and voice from Ladies' College in Halifax. She taught music in Lunenburg, then earned a certificate in nursing from Royal Victoria Hospital in Montreal, Quebec, where she began her career as an operating room

VOYAGES

Young David accompanied his parents on two trips to North America, the first in 1938 and the second in 1944–1945. The wartime voyage was a considerable adventure in itself for twelve-year-old David and his parents. On the first leg of this trip, the family boarded a neutral Argentinian ship in Capetown, South Africa in early June 1944. For twenty-one days, the small, 3,500-ton ship plowed through the notoriously rough seas of the South Atlantic's "Roaring Forties" before docking in Buenos Aires. The Griers then took a Pan American DC-3 across the Andes Mountains to Chile, up the western coast of South America, and across the Caribbean to Miami.

They returned to South Africa via a Portuguese ship, setting sail for Lisbon from Philadelphia on March 10, 1945. They were forced to wait for some weeks in Lisbon—then a hotbed of spies, both Allied and Axis— before proceeding south to Capetown.

The journey to the United States and Canada in mid-1944 was an arduous one, and Kathleen's nursing skills were called upon not only because Denham's health was already damaged (one of the trip's purposes was medical testing in the States), but because both Denham and David contracted pneumonia and were admitted, one after the other, to a hospital in Buenos Aires. To make matters worse, the Argentinian authorities, sympathetic to the German cause in World War II and hostile to British subjects, initially refused to permit Kathleen to disembark from the ship, for she was traveling on a Canadian passport. Denham, by dint of bribery and string-pulling, managed to extract her from this predicament some days after the ship docked, sneaking her off the ship—sans luggage—in a rowboat. (Her suitcases were later retrieved.)

The return to South Africa via Lisbon came to a conclusion on V-E Day, May 8, 1945, when the ship arrived in Capetown harbor. No porters or taxis were available, as the whole town was celebrating the Allied victory, but the Griers nonetheless boarded the train for Johannesburg and home.

David was educated in Johannesburg through high school. From 1940 to '45, he attended the Ridge Preparatory School and from 1945 to '48, the King Edward VII School. Upon graduation, he entered an electrical

---

nurse. In 1928, she was chosen by neurosurgeon Dr. Wilder Penfield to become his personal surgical nurse. When Dr. Penfield founded the Montreal Neurological Institute in 1934, Kathleen became chief neurosurgical nurse there, in charge of the operating room nursing staff. She continued in this post until she left Canada in February 1937 to marry Grier in South Africa.

Kathleen and Charles Denham Grier were married on April 3, 1937 in St. George's Church (Anglican) in the Johannesburg suburb of Parktown.

engineering program at the University of Witwatersrand in Johannesburg. However, six months after his father's death on December 2, 1948, David left at mid-year to return to Canada with his stepmother and grandmother.

MCGILL, STUDY IN INDIA

Settling in Montreal, David continued his studies at McGill University. He changed his major from pre-science/engineering to English and philosophy and received his Bachelor of Arts degree in the spring of 1953. While at McGill, David was editor-in-chief of the *McGill Daily*, the school newspaper, where his writing won the Bracken award for the best editorials in a Canadian student paper. He also held vacation and part-time jobs in summer theatre and as a technician at a local radio station.

Following his graduation, David received a Ford Foundation scholarship to attend a six-week seminar at the University of Mysore, India. The seminar was organized by the World University Service and concerned "The Human Implications of Development Planning." Three weeks of planned travel in India and West Pakistan followed the seminar, and the participants then had two additional weeks of independent "tourist" travel. After a stopover in Paris and London, David returned to Montreal and a master's program in comparative religion at McGill.

CAREER AND MARRIAGE

Following a year of graduate work, David left school in 1954 to become a reporter for Montreal's morning daily paper, the *Gazette*. That October, he became assistant editor of McGill's Graduate Society alumni magazine and designed direct mail fund-raising materials for the university, as well.

On May 24, 1955—Victoria Day—David married Deena Marion Stern, a McGill classmate, in Montreal. They had three children, all born in Montreal: Jon Denham, on January 20, 1958; Wendy Ruth, on June 24, 1961; and Robin Anne, on December 5, 1962.

In November of 1955, David became the editor of two monthly trade magazines, one for women's-wear and one for children's-wear. The following year, tiring of the newspaper business, he joined DuPont of Canada, Ltd., where he edited the employee paper and prepared product publicity on plastics, textile fibers, and explosives. David left DuPont in February of 1959 to become a copy editor for *Weekend Magazine*, a national supplement in Canada similar to America's *Parade*. In time, he advanced to the number two position on the desk.

David returned to DuPont in September of 1961, when he was hired to explore the use of radio, television, and film in DuPont's public relations efforts. As manager of employee communications and community relations, he subsequently wrote, directed, produced, and edited a number of successful industrial films and appeared on many radio and television programs on behalf of DuPont.

David left DuPont in April of 1967 to establish a public relations department for the Royal Bank of Canada, the country's largest bank and the fourth largest bank in North America. After supervising the department for ten years, he became an advisor to the bank's top management and in 1980 was named vice president and chief advisor on government and corporate affairs. The Royal Bank transferred him to Toronto in 1983, where he continued in a similar position.

Separated from Deena in 1976 and later divorced, David married Annette Barbara Hebb, a Montreal social worker and expert in children's learning disabilities, on March 3, 1984. By coincidence, Annette had been born and raised in Lunenburg, Nova Scotia, the same fishing town from which his stepmother Kathleen had come.

OTHER INTERESTS

David has been a member of the Canadian Public Relations Society (CPRS) since October of 1969 and received his accreditation in 1973. From 1972 to 1974, he served as the organization's vice president and from 1974 to 1975, as president of the Quebec chapter. On several occasions, he received an Award of Excellence from the CPRS for public relations projects executed on behalf of his employer.

An avid sailor, David owned a twenty-five-foot sloop, which he moored on Lake Champlain near Essex, New York. Many summer weekends were spent sailing there, and today he and his wife Annette enjoy winter holidays sailing in the Caribbean, as well as keeping a twenty-seven-foot sloop on Ontario's Georgian Bay, some 100 miles north of Toronto, where the couple now resides.

CHILDREN

Jon Denham Grier (1958–)

Jon was born in Montreal on January 20, 1958. He graduated from Montreal's Westhill High School in 1975. A music major, he attended Vanier College in Montreal from 1976 to 1978 and Dawson College New School from 1978 to 1979. He also studied at the Guitar Institute of Technology in Hollywood, California from 1979 to 1980. After playing guitar and singing in his own rock band, with engagements across Canada, and working at a world-class recording studio in Morin Heights, Quebec, near Montreal, he is now working as a musician and computer music programmer in San Francisco, California. On December 29, 1987, in Montreal, he married Allison Louise Smith, a native of California. The couple then moved to Lafayette, near San Francisco, with Allison's six-year old son, Justin.

Wendy Ruth Grier (1961–)

Wendy was born in Montreal on June 24, 1961. After graduating from Montreal's Westmount High School in 1978, Wendy continued her studies at Dawson College New School. Today she is studying early childhood education at Montreal's Concordia University, and is the mother of two: Mathieu, born April 10, 1986, and Stephanie, born July 7, 1988. Their father, Wendy's "boy next door" Bruno Beauregard, is a professional photographer operating his own studio in Montreal.

Robin Anne Grier (1962–)

Robin was born in Montreal on December 5, 1962. A Westmount High School alumna (1979) and 1981 fine arts graduate from Montreal's Dawson College, she is now studying architecture at the University of Waterloo, in Kitchener-Waterloo, Ontario.

Denham and David outside their home
in Parktown, South Africa
(Courtesy of David Grier)

Denham and David Grier, c. 1942
(Courtesy of David Grier)

238

Denham, Kathleen, and David arrive in Capetown harbor on V-E Day,
May 8, 1945
(*Courtesy of David Grier*)

David and Annette Hebb Grier (center) at their March 3, 1984 wedding in Toronto, Canada
(*Courtesy of David Grier*)

Wendy Grier and Bill
on dock at Essex, New York,
August 1979
(Photo by Bill Grier)

David, sailing with Ellen Coolidge on Lake Champlain,
August 1979
(Photo by Bill Grier)

241

24

GEORGE ANN BORMAN PALMER
1919–1983

George Ann Borman, the only child of Milt Grier's sister May and her husband Charles J. Borman, was born on January 24, 1919 in the Good Samaritan Hospital in Detroit, Michigan. Like her mother, she was raised and educated in San Francisco.

After a brief stay in Oakland following the death of her maternal grandmother, Georgie Orr Grier, on October 23, 1921, George Ann and her family moved to a house at 818 41st Avenue in San Francisco, near Golden Gate Park and the Pacific Ocean. (This house would be the family home for over thirty years. After May suffered a fatal heart attack at home in 1947, Charles continued to live there until the 1950s.)

George Ann's bedroom in this home could be entered from either the inner hall or rear sunroom. On fair days, the room was brightened by morning sun pouring through the east window, which overlooked her mother's garden. Accented by two Oriental throw rugs, the white furniture was contemporary, and her walls were covered with photos, student memorabilia, and a red-lettered sign reading "Hi Toots!" Here she read, studied, wrote school papers and letters. In the adjacent sunroom, she played the piano and sang.

George Ann was shapely, fair, and pretty, of medium height with blue-gray eyes. She was vivacious, extroverted, and humorous, as well as a gifted musician and athlete.

SCHOOL YEARS, 1925–1937

Always a good student, she graduated from two public schools (Lafayette Elementary in 1931 and Presidio Junior High in 1934) and the private Lux School for girls in 1937, before completing a year at San Francisco State College (then located at 124 Buchanan Street) from 1937–1938.[1]

---

1. Lux School, founded in 1913, was privately endowed by Miranda Lux. Phoebe Hearst was an early Lux trustee. Located at 2450 17th Street in San Francisco, Lux was later consolidated with another institution, renamed Lick-Wilmerding High School, and privately endowed by James Lick and Jillis Wilmerding. It was located at 2250 17th Street. The school's three benefactors wished to integrate book knowledge with what Lick called "the practical arts of

George Ann pursued her interest in music and the piano throughout her school years. She was a member of the Presidio Junior High School Glee Club and played the piano in the school orchestra for the spring 1934 one-act operetta, "The Treasure Chest," and the school play, "Mr. Dooley Junior." She also performed at assemblies, parent-teacher association meetings, and in "Jinx," the school musical.

At home, George Ann enjoyed playing popular music on the piano and singing in the family's sunroom. Her cousins Bill and Eloyd recall the joyous occasions when they lent their voices to accompany George Ann: standing on each side of her, they peered over her shoulders to follow the lyrics of the sheet music, often improvising and ending in laughter. Some melodies of that time were trite and trivial, yet many have proved durable and still retain their beauty, wit, and charm, evoking not only nostalgia, but also wonder. Among these are: "Beyond the Blue Horizon," "I'm Confessin' (That I Love You)," "Let's Fall in Love," "Lullaby of Broadway," "Pennies from Heaven," "Blue Hawaii," "Sweet Leilani," "My Heart Is Taking Lessons," and, of course, "White Christmas."

An athlete, she played on intramural basketball, volleyball, and baseball teams. Later, while at Lux School, she swam each Wednesday afternoon at the YWCA and participated in the 1937 mid-term carnival, with its relay, balloon, and pigeon races. She also helped organize and took part in the Lux Athletic Association's hiking party on June 20, 1936. For that occasion, the group boarded a bus at the Western Women's Club in San Francisco, then rode a ferryboat to Sausalito and proceeded to Muir Woods in Marin County for a day of walking the wilderness trails and picnicking among the giant redwoods.

During these early years, George Ann's nickname was "Jo-Jo," and, according to the Presidio Junior High yearbook, *The Panther*, her ambition was to become a librarian.

Under her mother's tutelage, she became a skilled seamstress and cook. Her father taught her to drive, and in the year after she graduated from Lux, he let her drive his second car, which he acquired from a collector in distress—a sleek, dark green Pierce Arrow convertible sedan, with elegant wood dashboard and butter-colored leather seats.

Two of her closest school friends were Betty ("Bets") Calhoun and Virginia ("Ginger") Klute. George Ann and Ginger, who lived three-and-a-half blocks away at 682 39th Avenue, remained best friends through their years together at Lafayette, Presidio, and Lux Schools.

---

life," to train young women in marketable skills, and to help them become "modern homemakers." George Ann took college preparatory courses at Lick-Wilmerding on Tuesday and Thursday afternoons from 1934–1937.

Another of George Ann's classmates was Judy Turner, better known by the stage name she would adopt years later—Lana Turner. Judy attended Presidio Junior High after being expelled from a nearby Catholic school, Visitacion.

George Ann attended Lux School from 1934 to 1937. In the fall of 1936, she was elected student body president. She presided over the party honoring George A. Merrill's seventieth birthday on September 9, 1936 in Lux's Merrill Hall. (Merrill had been the director of Lux, Lick, and Wilmerding Schools since their inception.) Ginger succeeded George Ann as student body president in the spring of 1937, while George Ann was elected secretary for the same term. Another close friend, Carmen Aquado, was an artist on the staff of the student yearbook, *L.W.L. Life*.

George Ann and Ginger also starred on the championship kickball and volleyball teams, and both served on the Lux School Athletic Association Board of Control in 1935.

COLLEGE AND CAREER, 1937–1942

After completing two semesters at San Francisco State College in 1937 and 1938, George Ann entered the business world. In her first position, she helped manage a one-man import office near the San Francisco Civic Center. In 1940, she accepted a secretarial and bookkeeping position with the San Francisco office of D.C. Heath & Company, educational publishers, at 182 Second Street (second floor). During the workweek, George Ann would occasionally lunch with her mother and friends at downtown restaurants.

In 1941, George Ann took a short leave of absence from her job to join her parents on an automobile trip east. They stopped in Salt Lake City, where her mother May had been born in 1876; toured Yellowstone National Park in Wyoming and Rocky Mountain National Park in Colorado; and visited Seymour, Indiana, where Charlie was born on January 28, 1888. After buying a 1942 four-door Dodge in Detroit, the Bormans then visited Charlie's brother Elmer, his wife Minny, and his family in Cincinnati, Ohio.

FIRST MARRIAGE, 1942

George Ann became engaged to Bruce Quartly, a young Army Air Corps recruit from Rodeo, California, early in 1942. While in the service, Bruce left his Model A Ford, "Leapin' Lena," with George Ann, and one evening a week, she drove it across the San Francisco-Oakland Bay Bridge to visit Bruce's widowed mother in Rodeo, a few miles north of Berkeley.

244

Her young cousin, Bill Grier, sometimes joined her on these trips.

But fate intervened, and George Ann fell in love with a sailor, Stuart Alvin Burnham, whom she married on April 11, 1942. The ceremony, held in Reno, Nevada, was witnessed by M. Dowd and Drasnap J. Lowe.

Born on February 25, 1919 in Blanding, Utah, Stuart was a Machinist's Mate, First Class in the Coast Guard and was stationed in San Francisco. There, he and George Ann lived in an apartment at 1080 Bush Street. Their young marriage ended tragically on January 5, 1944, when Stuart died of spinal meningitis in San Francisco's Marine Hospital. He was buried in the Presidio National Cemetery. After settling Stuart's estate, George Ann continued her work at D.C. Heath & Company and moved back with her parents.

SECOND MARRIAGE, 1946

On December 27, 1946, George Ann married Samuel Lewis Dickens Palmer in the Episcopal church in Reno, Nevada. Sam, born on March 26, 1911, was raised in Knoxville, Tennessee. He received his Bachelor of Science degree in accounting from the University of Tennessee at Knoxville in 1934 and the following year was awarded a Master of Arts in linguistics from Gallaudet Teacher's College in Washington, D.C., a federally chartered institution and one of the world's foremost schools for the hearing impaired. Palmer taught deaf students in Honolulu from 1938 to 1945; at age twenty-seven, he became the principal and superintendent of the school—the youngest principal in Hawaii at that time.

FAMILY LIFE

From 1946 to 1947, George Ann and Sam lived in a San Francisco apartment at 801 Baker Street. They subsequently moved to Hayward, California, where Sam had opened "Palmer's," a large one-story-with-basement drug and variety store on the main street. George Ann resigned from D.C. Heath & Company to help her husband manage the store. In the 1950s, the Palmers opened a store in Berkeley, at Shattuck and University Avenues, just a block west of the University of California campus.

Three children were born to the Palmers: Catherine Ann, on October 15, 1949, in Hayward; Charles Arthur, on May 28, 1952, also in Hayward; and Kenneth Grier, on January 26, 1957, in Berkeley, where the family had moved in the 1950s. In the mid-sixties, the Palmers moved to 6 Garden Estates Court in Alamo, California. The children graduated from San Ramon High School in Danville, in 1967, '70, and '75, respectively.

During their vacations and weekends, they worked in the family's Berkeley store.

In September 1972, Sam died of a heart attack while asleep in bed at his home in Alamo, having returned from a family vacation the previous day.

Following Sam's death, George Ann bought a townhouse at 180 Lawnview Circle in Danville, California. Several years later, in 1977, she purchased a home in the Napa Valley (at 12 San Lucas Court, St. Helena, California), which she shared with Paul Wilcox, a retired musician who had played with bands in San Francisco and the West in the forties, fifties, and sixties.

George Ann's St. Helena home, by the Napa River, looked out upon the coastal mountains and was surrounded by vineyards. The subdivision had a clubhouse with game rooms and restaurant, putting green, swimming pool, woodworking shop, and art and craft studios. She and Paul were members of a nearby golf and tennis club and regularly played the nine-hole course.

After moving to St. Helena, George Ann continued to manage "Palmer's," commuting two days a week in her yellow Honda Civic. After selling the business in 1979, she and Paul traveled to Scandinavia, England, and Scotland, where they played a week of golf at St. Andrew's. Thereafter in winter, they rented condominiums and played golf in Kona, Hawaii.

After a five-year battle with cancer, during which she remained active, George Ann died in the Napa Hospital,on the day she was admitted, July 25, 1983. A member of the Neptune Society, she was cremated, and her ashes were scattered by plane over San Francisco Bay.

CHILDREN

Catherine Ann Palmer (1949–)

George Ann's daughter Cathy graduated in 1971 with a Bachelor of Arts in sociology from the College of Holy Names in Oakland. She taught in Oakland parochial schools for several years before moving to Willits, California, where she married Walter Camp. Now divorced, Cathy is a graduate student in education at Oregon State College in Corvallis.

Charles Arthur Palmer (1952–)

Charles Palmer received his Bachelor of Arts in business administration from Chico State College in 1975. Today, he lives in Willits with his wife Joanne Lee (nee Witte) and daughters Sarah Ruth (born August 24, 1983, in Oakland, California) and Casey Noelle (born December 20, 1985, in Willits). Prior to settling in Willits, Charles had managed a camera store in East Bay for seven years. (As a schoolboy, he had worked in the camera department of his family's drug and variety store in Berkeley.) In 1983, Charles acquired twenty-one acres of land in Willits, where he helped design and construct his family's home at 4809 Bear Canyon Road.

Kenneth Grier Palmer (1957–)

Kenneth, his wife Colleen Sue ("Teddy"), daughter Melissa Ann (born May 9, 1983, in Oakland), and son Andrew Cody (born January 22, 1989) live at 951 Stow Lane, Lafayette, California. Ken is a contractor and owner of Ken Palmer General Contractor, Inc., in the Oakland and East Bay area.

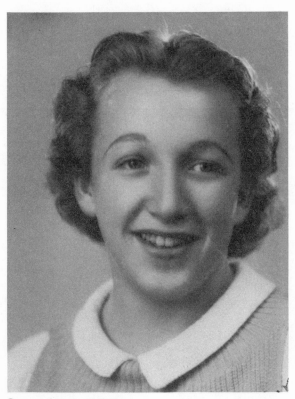

George Ann in 1937
(Courtesy of George Ann Palmer)

George Ann Borman
(Courtesy of George Ann Palmer)

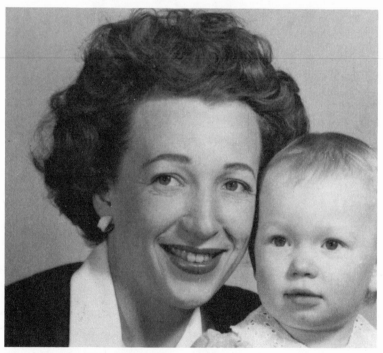

George Ann and daughter Cathy, c. 1950
(Courtesy of George Ann Palmer)

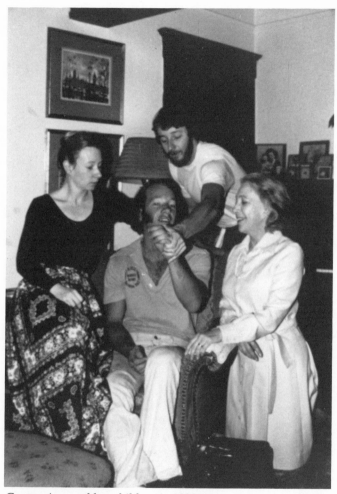

George Ann and her children in 1981:
Cathy, Kenneth, Charles, and George Ann
(Courtesy of George Ann Palmer)

PART FOUR

ALLIED FAMILIES

25

PATTERSON

Among the first of William Milton Grier's ancestors to live in North America were George and Anne Merrigold Patterson, who emigrated to Upper Canada in the early nineteenth century.

GEORGE (1782–1862) AND ANNE (1791–1867)

Born in Perth, Scotland in 1782, George Patterson was a sea captain who served seven years in the military before emigrating to Upper Canada in 1816.

He began his military career at the age of twenty-seven, volunteering for service in the British 37th Regiment of Foot Soldiers. He subsequently fought at Gibraltar during the Peninsular War (1808–1814) and in Upper Canada in the War of 1812. Three years later, at the Battle of Waterloo, he was wounded in the foot, but remained with his comrades while serving as a cobbler.

George's wife Anne Merrigold (later changed to Marigold) was born in 1791 in Worcestershire, England. She accompanied her husband on his military campaigns, giving birth to two children during this period. The first, a daughter, died in infancy and was buried on Gibraltar. Their second child, Walter, was sent to live with Anne's family in London.

On June 23, 1816, George Patterson was mustered out of the 37th Regiment. Having survived three major battles on two continents, he was rewarded by the British government with a land grant in Upper Canada, where he and Anne would make their home.

When the Pattersons moved to Upper Canada, the area was sparsely settled and truly a frontier to be conquered. Canada had been divided into its Upper and Lower provinces by the British government in 1791; Upper Canada (renamed Ontario in 1846) bordered the Great Lakes and had largely been settled by United Empire Loyalists fleeing the Thirteen Colonies during the American Revolutionary War. Further inland, most of the settlers were immigrants from Scotland and Ireland.

Amidst the constant challenges of frontier life, Anne and George Patterson raised two daughters and six sons: Walter (b. ?) who joined his parents in Upper Canada at age fourteen, Janet (1817–1901), James (1819–1902), Eliza Anne (1825–1884), Ephraim (1826–1892), Charles, Richard, and George (dates of birth unknown).

George Patterson, Sr. died on July 20, 1862 and was buried in the Episcopal cemetery in Perth, Ontario. His wife died some five years later on May 3, 1867 at the home of her eldest daughter and son-in-law in Balderson Corners. She was also buried in Perth's Episcopal cemetery, with the Reverend R. L. Stephenson officiating.

EPHRAIM (1826–1892)

George Patterson's son Ephraim had a long and prominent career with the Episcopal church. On August 19, 1849, he was made deacon at St. George's Church in Kingston, Ontario by the Right Reverend John Strachan, the bishop of Toronto, and on November 17, 1850, he was ordained a priest by the same bishop at Holy Trinity Church in Toronto.

Ephraim also served as curate to Dr. Bethune at the Church of England Theological College in Cobourge, Upper Canada from 1849 to 1850. He then served as a missionary in Portsmouth and on Wolfe Island from 1850 to 1851. Over the next forty years, he was rector of St. James Parish in Stratford, Ontario.

While serving as rector, Ephraim completed two university degrees. He received his B.A. degree from Trinity College in Toronto in 1859 and two years later was awarded an M.A. degree from the same institution.

During this period, Ephraim met and married Jane Wanchope Mackenzie. The wedding ceremony took place on October 22, 1852 at St. James's Anglican Church in Perth and was officiated by the Reverend M. Harris. Ephraim and Jane had fourteen children, only seven of whom survived infancy: Frederick William, Anna Maria, Wilhelmina Ashley, Edith Beatrice, Maud Mary, Henry Strachan, and George Mackenzie.

Ephraim witnessed many changes in the community of Stratford during his tenure as rector. When he arrived there in 1851, it was a rough frontier town of a mere 400 inhabitants. At the time of his death in 1892, however, the population had increased to 10,000. The quality of life improved dramatically in these years, and Ephraim himself contributed significantly to the development of early education in the Stratford area.

JANET (1817–1901)

Janet Patterson, born August 29, 1817, was the second surviving child of George and Anne Patterson, and married Andrew Allan in 1848. Nine years her junior, Andrew was born on Wolfe Island on July 31, 1826, the son of William and Eleanor Davis Allan. He had six sisters: Eleanor, Jane,

Hannah, Margaret, Anne, and Susannah.[1]

Andrew's father William Allan was, like George Patterson, a veteran of the Napoleonic Wars and fought under the Duke of Wellington at the Battle of Waterloo in 1815. Soon after, he settled on Wolfe Island, by Kingston, Lake Ontario. A stone mason by trade, William helped build Fort Henry at Kingston, near the United States border.

Andrew Allan settled around Perth with other British soldiers and later moved to Balderson Corners, where he became a charter member of the Presbyterian church. Over the years, he taught there and joined the Freemasons, as well.

Janet and Andrew owned a farm and lived in a large, red-brick house that he had built. The Allans had three daughters and four sons: Annie Marigold (January 30, 1849–August 9, 1930), William Hiram (September 29, 1850–August 9, 1936), Eleanor Davis (March 18, 1853–1910), George Constantine (January 19, 1855–May 5, 1931), Marshall Henry (May 12, 1857–September 29, 1923), Norman Grier (March 21, 1859–April 23, 1936), and Adaline Eliza (July 21, 1862–July 30, 1862).

Janet Patterson died on January 23, 1901 in Balderson Corners. Six-and-a-half years later, Andrew died and was buried in the Elmwood Cemetery in Perth, Ontario.

ELIZA ANNE (1825–1884)

Eliza Patterson married James Grier, a native of Northern Ireland who had emigrated to Upper Canada in the late 1830s. The wedding took place at Perth's Episcopal Church of St. James on July 4, 1844. (See Part One: 1)

After two years in Perth, the young couple moved to Pakenham, some thirty miles northeast. By 1851, they had relocated to Matilda Township, a small town on the St. Lawrence River which was later renamed Iroquois. James was elected to the community's first town council and became the Iroquois postmaster in 1860, a position he would hold for more than twenty-three years.

Eliza and James had ten children: James Richard Henry (1845–1911), George Edwin (1846–1925), Anne Marigold (1848–1935), Thomas Johnston (1850–1914), William John (1853–1909), Eliza Victoria (1855–1941), Margaret Armstrong (1857–1884), Albert Ephraim (1859–1907),

---

1. James Grier (1818–1892), a widower, married Andrew's widowed sister Susannah Allan (Mrs. Thaddeus Weatherhead, 1826–1909) in 1886 in Perth, Ontario.

Charles Allan (1862–1882), and Georgina Clara (1864–1946). Their fifth child, William John Grier, would become the father of William Milton Grier, Sr.

Eliza Patterson Grier died at age fifty-nine on October 14, 1884; she was buried in St. John's Episcopal Cemetery in Iroquois. Her husband died eight years later on May 11, 1892 while in Toronto and was buried next to Eliza and his son Charles Allan, who had died of tuberculosis at twenty.

Anne Merrigold Patterson, c. 1866,
Perth, Ontario, Canada

26

LANNON

PATRICK JOSEPH LANNON (1868–1946)

Patrick Lannon, Elo Grier's father, was born on April 13, 1868, the fourth of five children born to Thomas Patrick ("T.P.") Lannon and Mary Elo Owens in Strokestown, Roscommon, Ireland. [1] His four siblings were: Thomas D'Arcy, John A., Theresa Mary ("Tess," b. 1866), and Matilda Ellen ("Nellie," b. May 7, 1869).

His father T.P. owned and operated a fourteen-acre farm in Strokestown, and it was from him that young Patrick learned to cultivate the land—an avocation he later pursued with great joy.

Patrick emigrated to America in the mid-1880s when he was in his teens, staying briefly with his brother John in New York City before settling in Sacramento. He received his U.S. citizenship on June 4, 1894.

Two years earlier, on October 3, 1892, Patrick Lannon was married to his Irish girlfriend, Julia Mary McDermott, in Sacramento's Cathedral of the Blessed Sacrament at 1017 11th Street. Reverend Thomas Grace officiated, and Bernardo Lavelle and Patrick's youngest sister Nellie served as witnesses.[2]

JULIA MARY MCDERMOTT LANNON (1866–1944)

Born in Strokestown, Roscommon, Ireland on August 26, 1866, Julia was one of nine children. Two of the McDermott children died as infants; surviving were: Winifred, Margaret, Mary Ann, Roderick ("Roger") J., Julia, James, and John.

Julia emigrated to the United States in the late 1880s, living at first with her older sister Margaret and brother-in-law James O'Rourke in Provi-

---

1. Elo Lannon Grier was named after her paternal grandmother, Mary Elo Owens Lannon, who died following the birth of her fifth child, Matilda Ellen ("Nellie"). T.P. later married Mary Jacoba Farrell.

2. During their married life, Patrick and Julia lived in three homes in Sacramento: 408 N Street (1892-1894), 2523 I Street (1894–1927), and 5314 J Street (1927-mid-1940s).

dence, Rhode Island.[3] She received her citizenship there before moving to Sacramento and marrying Patrick Lannon in 1892.

Patrick and Julia had nine children, two of whom—Thomas McDermott and Annie—died in infancy and were buried together at East Lawn Cemetery in Sacramento, where their headstone reads: "Lannon Babies, 1905–1907." The Lannons' surviving children were: Mary Elizabeth (1893–1965), Elo Theresa (1895–1987), Julia Margaret (1897–1970), Joseph Martin (1899–1955), Norma Winifred (1902–1964), Ferdinand Henrietta (1909–1989), and Raymond James (1911–1945).

CHILDREN

Mary Elizabeth ("Marie") Lannon
1893–1965

Marie, Patrick and Julia's first-born, graduated from the John Marshall School (17th and G Streets) and from Sacramento High School. From 1910 to 1913, Marie worked for Weinstock Lubin Company, a department store in downtown Sacramento. She then was a bookkeeper for the Goodyear Coat Company, where she continued to work after her marriage to William T. Henn, a bookkeeper at the National Bank D.O. Mills & Company, during World War I. The Henns had one daughter, Wilma Marie, born in 1916.

The couple divorced in 1920. Later in that decade, Marie married Walter George Hall, who operated Sacramento Used Car Market.[4] In the early 1930s, Walter became an optometrist, opening an office first in Sacramento and later at Weinstein's department store in downtown San Francisco. He died of a heart attack shortly before World War II. The Halls had no children.

In the 1940s, Marie remarried her first husband, William Henn. In addition to their primary residence, an apartment in downtown San Francisco, they maintained a second home in Santa Cruz, California. William died in the 1950s.

_____

3. Before and after World War I, Julia and Patrick made several trips by train to visit Julia's sister Margaret O'Rourke and Patrick's older brother John and his family in New York City. Five of the Lannons' children—Marie, Elo, Julia, Joe, and Norma—accompanied them on one of the trips east.

4. Marie and Walter's residences in Sacramento included: 815 17th Street (in the 1920s), 901 26th Street (in the early 1930s), and 2023 I Street (in the mid-1930s). They then moved to San Francisco, where they lived at 610 Leavenworth Street.

As a widow, Marie continued to live in her San Francisco apartment at 610 Leavenworth Street, off Geary. She worked for Southern Pacific Railroad Company in San Francisco and was active in civic organizations, including the Native Daughters of the Golden West.

Marie's daughter Wilma, an alumna of the University of California at Berkeley, became a teacher at the Johnson School in North Sacramento. She married Jack Tamblyn, a pharmacist, and lived in Carmichael, California, a Sacramento suburb. Jack died in 1986. Their son Michael Hall Tamblyn holds a Bachelor of Arts in English from the University of San Francisco (1972), where he also completed a year of post-graduate study in English between 1972 and 1973.

Elo Theresa Lannon
September 26, 1895–July 16, 1987

Patrick and Julia's second daughter, Elo, was educated in Sacramento's public and parochial schools.

In 1923, while working as a secretary in the Sacramento offices of the Southern Pacific Railroad Company, she met William Milton Grier, a prominent railroad and civil contractor. They were married on November 9, 1927 in Reno, Nevada.

The couple was living in Piedmont, California when their two sons were born: William Milton Grier, Jr., on September 23, 1928, and Eloyd John Grier, on July 4, 1929.

In 1935, Elo's husband died of a heart attack at the age of fifty-seven. His wife, only forty at the time, raised their sons alone, never remarrying. She continued to work in San Francisco until retiring at seventy-three in 1968. She then moved to her native city, Sacramento, where she died in her ninety-second year in 1987. (See Part One and Part Two)

Julia Margaret Lannon
September 3, 1897–October 21, 1970

Julia graduated from the John Marshall School, Mary Jane Watson Junior High School (16th and I Streets), and Sacramento High School. A lifelong spinster, she was a registered nurse and worked as the supervisor of nurses at Sacramento County Hospital until her retirement in 1962. Throughout her life, Julia lived in her mother and father's homes. She died of cancer at Sutter Hospital in 1970.

Joseph Martin Lannon
June 27, 1899–April 13, 1955

Tall (6'2") and blue-eyed with brown hair, Joseph graduated from the John Marshall School and Mary Jane Watson Junior High School; he also attended Christian Brothers Academy, a Jesuit preparatory school, and graduated on June 23, 1916 from Sacramento High School.

Following graduation, Joseph worked in Sacramento as an accountant with Southern Pacific Railroad Company. On November 5, 1917, having passed the civil service exam, he went to work in the Postal Savings Department of the U.S. Post Office in Sacramento. On July 25 of the following year, however, Joseph enlisted in the U.S. Navy in San Francisco and became an apprentice seaman at the Naval Air Station, North Island, San Diego. After his discharge on April 9, 1919, he returned to his job at the Sacramento post office, but remained in the Naval Reserve Forces until September 30, 1921.

On May 14, 1921, Joseph married Wilhelmina Gertrude ("Mina") O'Hara in a civil ceremony in Sacramento; the witnesses were Richard L. O'Hara and Julia Lannon. Mina, born on April 18, 1899 in Pleasant Grove, California, was the daughter of Richard L. O'Hara and Wilhelmina Meiss of Drytown, Amador County, California. Joseph and Mina lived at 820 41st Street in Sacramento, and on March 2, 1926, their son Gerald Joseph was born in Sacramento's Mater Misercordiae Hospital.

While working as a postal clerk, Joseph studied law and received his Juris Doctor degree in 1927 from the McGeorge School of Law in Sacramento (now part of the University of the Pacific). Ten years later, after retiring from the U.S. Post Office, he became a detective and special investigator for the County of Sacramento's district attorney's office, Room 201, Sacramento Courthouse.

Joseph and Mina were divorced in the mid-1940s. Following their divorce, Mina worked as an auditor for the State of California and lived at 2830 J Street. On March 1, 1946, at age forty-six, she drowned in the American River and was buried in Odd Fellows Lawn Cemetery.

After World War II, Joseph became a real estate investor in Sacramento, while continuing as a detective for the county district attorney.[5] Joseph died of a heart attack in his home as he prepared to go to his office

---

5. Joseph owned and occupied the following Sacramento homes: 820 41st Street (1925–1945), 4710 Del Rio Road (1948–1951), 2306 Granite Way (1951–1953), and 821 El Dorado Way (1953–1955).

on April 13, 1955; he was buried in the East Lawn Cemetery in Sacramento. A tribute to Lannon from the Senate of the State of California was introduced into the California Congressional Record by Senator Desmond on April 18, 1955.

SENATE CONCURRENT RESOLUTION NO. 60—
Relative to the passing of Joseph M. Lannon

WHEREAS, The Legislature has learned with regret of the death on April 13th of this year of Joseph M. Lannon, Sacramento County detective and special investigator for that county's district attorney's office; and

WHEREAS, Joe Lannon, a native Sacramentan, entered the service of the county in 1937 and in the course of his service became the intimate and valued friend of numerous judges and attorneys and others with whom he came in contact; and

WHEREAS, He was an active participant in the political and social life of his community, having served as president of the Fraternal Order of Eagles and the Sacramento parlor of the Native Sons of the Golden West and as a member of the Elks Lodge and the International Footprinters Association; and

WHEREAS, The Legislature shares the bereavement felt by Joe Lannon's family; now, therefore, be it

Resolved by the Senate of the State of California, the Assembly thereof concurring, That the Legislature extends to the surviving relatives of Joe Lannon its deepest sympathy; and, be it further

Resolved, That the Secretary of the Senate is directed to transmit a suitably prepared copy of this resolution to Gerald Lannon, son of Joe Lannon, and to his sisters, Julia Lannon and Mrs. Ferd Shaeffer.

Joe's son Gerald J. Lannon (March 2, 1926–) graduated in June 1944 from Sacramento High School, where he had been student body vice president. He received his Bachelor of Arts from St. Mary's College in Moraga, California and his Master of Arts from the University of San Francisco. A bachelor, Gerry lives and teaches literature and English at Hiram Johnson High School in Sacramento.

Norma Winifred Lannon
June 27, 1902–February 10, 1964

Norma Lannon, a graduate of the John Marshall School, Sutter Junior High School, and Sacramento High School, married Herbert Pope Langton on April 13, 1929 in a civil ceremony in Redwood City, California. Born Herbert Langerak on May 3, 1899 in Rotterdam, Holland, her husband had emigrated to the United States from Oslo, Norway, arriving in New York City on December 17, 1917.[6] He worked as an accountant for Oregon Washington Railroad and Navigation Company in Portland, Oregon until August 22, 1923, then became an accountant at Swayne and Hoyt in San Francisco.

Prior to her marriage, Norma worked as an accountant in Sacramento. Then, in the 1930s, she obtained her contractor's license and subsequently acquired land and built houses in the hills of Berkeley, California, where she and Herb lived in a white stucco, Spanish-style home at 1020 Miller Avenue. Shortly before World War II, the Langtons bought a Spanish Colonial estate at 617 Ansel Avenue in Hillsborough, California.

During this period, Norma owned and operated two women's clothing stores: Norma's Ladies' Apparel (at 1417 Burlingame Avenue in Burlingame, California) in the 1940s and Norma Langton's Women's Wear (at 86 East 3rd Avenue in San Mateo, California) in the early 1950s.

After World War II, she also returned to contracting and developed homes in Los Altos, California; she and Herb lived in two of these, first at 301 and then at 261 Langton Avenue. In the early fifties, they divided their time between their Los Altos home and a second residence in Guadalajara, Mexico.

Norma and Herb founded and operated Langton Bookkeeping Services in 1954, located at 131 University Avenue in Palo Alto. Their clients included individuals, corporations, partnerships, and trade associations.

Herb died of cancer on February 6, 1963; one year and four days later, Norma died, also from cancer, in Palo Alto. They were buried in Portland, Oregon. The Langtons had no children.

Ferdinand Henrietta ("Ferd") Lannon
February 6, 1909–May 4, 1989

Like her brothers and sisters, Ferd graduated from Sacramento schools: John Marshall, Mary Jane Watson Junior High, and St. Joseph Academy (9th and G Streets) in June of 1927, where she had won honors and the top prize for an essay on Abraham Lincoln.

Ferd received her General Education Teaching Credential from San Jose State College in June of 1930. (Her tuition, room, and board were paid by her brother-in-law Milt Grier.) Over the next twelve years, she would

---

6. Herbert was the son of Johannes Langerak, who lived on Rosenburgstraat in Rotterdam. His brother O. Langerak lived in Portland, Oregon, at 1126 Lincoln Street. Herbert changed his surname to Langton on August 27, 1923 while in Oregon.

acquire both classroom and administrative experience—four-and-a-half years in teaching and six months as a substitute principal— in schools with many foreign students.

While teaching in a San Luis Obispo elementary school from 1930 to 1932, she met Fred A. Shaeffer, a native of Arizona and a successful attorney in Santa Maria, California. Ferd and Fred were married first in a civil ceremony on April 29, 1935 in Wasco, Kern County, California, and then in Mission Santa Barbara. They had no children. (Fred, however, had two children, Marie and Freddie, from a previous marriage.)

In June 1940, Ferd earned her Bachelor of Arts in education, as well as her General Junior High School Teaching Credential from Santa Barbara State College, and completed cadet training in social studies and visual education at La Cumbre Junior High School in Santa Barbara.

During the summer of 1941, she studied children's literature, creative music, and arts and crafts at San Francisco State College. The following academic year, she taught third, fourth, and fifth grades at Columbine School in Delano, Tulare County, California.

The Shaeffers separated during World War II and were divorced in the early 1950s. Returning to Sacramento, Ferd did graduate work toward a Master of Arts in education at Sacramento State College and taught third grade at Ethel Phillips School, where she remained until her retirement in 1972 after thirty-two years as a public school teacher. Neither Ferd nor Fred remarried, and they remained good friends after their divorce until Fred died of a heart attack on August 31, 1956. Ferd died in Sacramento on May 4, 1989.

Raymond James Lannon
August 16, 1911–May 3, 1945

Raymond, who graduated from the John Marshall School and attended Christian Brothers Academy in Sacramento, became a licensed machinist and mechanical contractor and also worked for the City of Sacramento Parks Department. He and his wife Clara G. Lannon lived in Sacramento at 1026 22nd Street.

During World War II, Raymond served as a machinist in the Air Corps, Detachment "A" of the 36th Mobile R & R Squadron in England, France, Luxembourg, Belgium, and Germany. On May 3, 1945, Staff Sergeant Raymond J. Lannon died at the age of thirty-four in an Army hospital in Germany and was buried in Sacramento's East Lawn Cemetery. The cause of death was acute poisoning from an alcoholic beverage ingested at a Displaced Persons Camp of friendly Allies. He died three days after hospitalization.

Raymond's commanding officer, 2nd Lt. Robert D. Ross, described the youngest Lannon in his letter of condolence:

(Raymond was) a valuable man. The skill he learned in civil life as a machinist enabled him to complete repairs on airplanes entrusted to his care in good time. He became adept at improvising under difficult conditions in the field (and) came to undertake more than his share of work. His skill as a machinist contributed materially towards making his Mobile Unit the most outstanding in the Detachment.

As his commanding officer, I learned to place the greatest confidence in him....His interest in his work soon earned him two promotions after he joined this organization in England.

In any construction work around the Squadron he generally took charge. He built showers and many other things. Most notable was a steam table for the mess, which enabled the mess personnel to serve hot food at all times. This table brought many favorable comments from inspecting officers.

He has been with us since England and through Normandy, Northern France, Luxembourg, Belgium and Germany. He was awarded the Good Conduct Medal, the European, African, Middle-East Campaign ribbon with three bronze service stars for the campaigns, "Normandy," "Northern France" and "Germany." He is also eligible for battle participation bronze stars for the campaigns, "Rhineland" and "Central Europe" when such credits are authorized....All of the men and officers of the Squadron wish to extend to you and your family our deepest sympathies, for we feel that your loss is also in a great measure our own....

Respectfully,
Robert D. Ross
2nd Lt., Air Corps
Commanding

PATRICK AND JULIA LANNON
IN LATER YEARS

Patrick was over six feet tall and lean, with a ruddy complexion, blue eyes, and gray, short-trimmed hair. A mild and genial man, he wore gold-rimmed glasses, suspenders, and white straw hats with black bands.

At age sixty-five, in 1933, he retired from his position as foreman in Southern Pacific Railroad's shops and in his retirement years led an active life. With his seven children—two sons and five daughters—married or independent, his time was spent cultivating his land, managing the rental of his second Victorian home at 2523 I Street, and, with his wife, visiting his children and their families in California (in Piedmont, Berkeley, San Francisco, and Santa Maria). He also spent time with his two married sisters—Tess (Mrs. Edward J. Flanagan) and Nell (Mrs. James Knapp)—and their families in Sacramento. He smoked pipes and liked to walk about the city—downtown, to parks, and along the levees of the Sacramento and American Rivers.

At his home in Sacramento, Patrick tended his flowerbeds, shrubbery, and lawn; his trees—plane, poplar, and fruit; and his vegetable crops and chickens. In the late afternoon, while irrigating his crops, he liked to sit in the shade on one of his wood benches, to smoke his pipe and view the results of his labor, to savor the solitude and the sounds of nature.

A quiet, thoughtful, and jovial man, he enjoyed being with his four grandchildren—Bill and Eloyd Grier, Gerry Lannon, and Wilma Henn. On hot summer afternoons, he would set up sprinklers on the lawn so they could frolic and cool themselves; he played ball with them, took them on hikes, and treated them to soft drinks and popsicles.

Julia Lannon was of medium height, stout, blue-eyed, and fair, with long white hair which she usually wore pinned high on her head. She was animated and quick-tempered, gregarious and a gifted raconteur. She was also unfailingly kind and compassionate. (During the Depression, she frequently shared her family's food with the itinerant hobos who came to her door—men short on hope and luck who rode freight cars from town to town in search of work, often carrying their possessions in worn knapsacks.)

As mistress of her home, Julia kept the family's Victorian house tidy, did the marketing and food preparation herself. In the fall, she and Patrick canned some of the fruits and vegetables grown in their garden each summer, and together they managed their Victorian rental property, at 25th and I Streets.

Julia paid the bills, kept the books, and was the family correspondent. She also planned their train trips to visit relatives in the East and California. In her leisure, she read and entertained friends, played her piano and sang popular, folk, and Irish ballads.

Both Patrick and Julia died in their seventy-eighth year—he in 1946 and she in 1944. They are buried together in Sacramento's East Lawn Cemetery.

PATRICK LANNON'S SIBLINGS

Thomas D'Arcy Lannon and
John A. Lannon

When Patrick's older brother Thomas was sent to England to study agriculture, his father mailed him ten pounds each month for expenses.

However, unbeknownst to his family in Ireland, Thomas quit school, married an English actress named Maybell Lowe, and became the assistant manager of a Liverpool theatre. He fathered four children who would grow up around the stage. His son John, at twenty-four, stole 134 theatre tickets and sold them, was arrested and served three years in prison. When released, he changed his name to Lennon to escape the stigma of a prison record. He then married Nancy Pell, a nightclub entertainer, and had four children— one of whom was John Lennon, the Beatle, born in Liverpool on October 9, 1940 and assassinated in New York City forty years later.[7]

Patrick and his two sisters—Tess and Nellie—emigrated to America in the late 1880s and settled in Sacramento, while their brother John A. remained in New York City.

Theresa Mary ("Tess") Lannon (1866–1940)
(Mrs. Edward J. Flanagan)

Tess was married in Sacramento to Edward J. Flanagan (1866–1937), a native of Kings County, Ireland. She bore three children: Edwin James (1893–1975), Helen Lavina (1897–1965), and Frank Thomas (1898–1963). In the 1890s and 1900s, the family lived at 1118 I Street and 2307 I Street; later, they moved to 2213 N Street. Edward died in Sacramento on May 17, 1937; Tess died there of cancer on November 10, 1940. Both are buried at St. Mary's Lawn in Sacramento.

Edwin James Flanagan
(1893–1975)

The Flanagans' eldest child, Edwin, lived with his wife Alta (1898 –1971) in the ground floor flat of his family's Victorian house at 2213 N Street in Sacramento, where he managed the McLaughlin Draying Company. Their first child, Edwin Wallace (1923–), married Nora McCabe (1930–) and had four children: Francis McCabe (1953–), Maureen (1955–), Peggy Ann (1957–), and Timothy Edward (1962–). Francis, now married to Lynn Larkin (1953–), is the father of Michael McCabe (1981–), Patrick Larkin (1986–), and Laura Larkin (1988–). Peggy Ann Flanagan married Blair Sprague (1955–) and has three children: Sean Jeffrey (1981–), Molly Clare (1984–), and Caleigh Flanagan (1986–). Timothy Flanagan is married to Lisa Bergfeld (1966–). Edwin and Alta Flanagan also had a daughter, Beverly Ann (1927–), who married William Derheim and had two children.

---

7. The details on Thomas Lannon were provided by James M. Knapp, Patrick's nephew and his sister Nellie's son, in a letter written to Bill Grier in November 1983. James was the only grandchild to visit his grandfather and see the family farm in Ireland.

Helen Lavina Flanagan
(1897–1965)

Tess and Edward's daughter Helen married Albert Henry Becker
(1894–1986), who later became executive director of the Sacramento City
and County Housing Authority. They lived at 1715 M Street in Sacramento
and had one child, Constance ("Connie") Frances (1918–1975). On December 17, 1936, in Sacramento, Connie married William Pierce Wright
(1911–1978), a partner in Wright and Kimbrough, the Sacramento residential real estate and insurance firm started in the 1870s by William's grandfather Charles E. Wright.

Connie and William lived at 1448 45th Street and had two daughters, Rita Ann (b. 1938) and Margaret Elizabeth ("Meg") (b. 1941). Rita was
first married to Royal Robert Bush 3d, then to Frederick P. Brousse, and has
two sons—Stephen Michael Brousse, who is married to Heidi Smith, and
Gregory Patrick Brousse (b. March 17, 1968). Meg, now divorced from Alan
Hill Gallaway, has two sons and a daughter—Wallace Alan (b. April 14,
1967), Rita Lynne (b. February 7, 1969), and Russel Wright (b. January 1,
1971). Meg's father-in-law, A. Russel Gallaway, Jr., acquired her father's
company in the early 1960s. His sons, Alan Hill and Robert ("Rob") Russel
Gallaway, later joined him in this business, specializing in insurance and
real estate respectively. By the mid-seventies, the sons received their
father's interest in the firm, and in 1978 Rob formed Gallaway & Company,
a real estate brokerage, while Alan retained the Wright & Kimbrough
insurance business. In 1984, he sold this to Don Deebles, but kept both the
Aviation Insurance and Werthof Aviation Insurance companies.

Frank Thomas Flanagan
(1898–1963)

Frank, Tess's youngest child, began a forty-five-year career with
Standard Oil Company (now Chevron) at their Sacramento offices in 1918.
He transferred to the firm's San Francisco office in 1927 and, while working
during the days, studied in the evenings at the University of San Francisco
School of Law. In 1931, he earned a Certificate in Law, the equivalent of an
L.L.B., under USF's program tailored to "special situation students." Prior
to his 1963 retirement from Standard Oil, Frank was manager of employee
relations for the company's Western Operations Incorporated in San Francisco. He lived with his wife Lucille in San Francisco's Marina district, at
3789 Fillmore Street, in the 1930s; then, later, at 1040 Monterey Boulevard.
They had no children.

Matilda Ellen ("Nellie") Lannon (1869–1955)
(Mrs. James E. Knapp)

Nellie was the last family member to emigrate to the United States. Her brother Patrick and sister Tess, who had preceded her to America, sent $50 to pay her steamer passage across the Atlantic in the 1880s.

She lived in New York City with her Farrell relatives before moving to Sacramento. San Francisco's chief of police Lawrence Farrell, the brother of T.P. Lannon's second wife, later accompanied Nellie on her move to the West.

Nellie Lannon was married to James Edward Knapp (1869–1934) on Easter Sunday 1895 at Sacramento's Cathedral of the Blessed Sacrament. James, born in Sacramento on April 16, 1869, was a carpenter for the Southern Pacific Railroad Company and later became a security officer at the State Capitol building. He died in Sacramento on August 15, 1934, as did Nellie, on September 24, 1955.

During their married life, they lived at 918 Q Street and had three children, all born in Sacramento: Edwena Mary (b. March 18, 1896), James Morrison (b. February 27, 1901), and Lucille Deirdrie (b. May 30, 1903).

Edwena Mary Knapp
(1896–)

Edwena, a graduate of Chico State College, taught in Sacramento and San Francisco primary schools before marrying Spence John Dickson (1889–1969) of Santa Rosa, California on July 31, 1920 in her hometown and settling in San Francisco. An alumnus of St. Mary's College, Spence was a construction engineer on the Golden Gate Bridge from the beginning of construction, then became maintenance engineer until his retirement in 1958. He was also a director of Exchange Bank, Santa Rosa, and trustee of St. Mary's College, Moraga, California. Spence died March 5, 1969. Their only child, Deirdrellen Dickson (b. March 29, 1922), is a University of California at Berkeley alumna, Class of 1944, with a year of graduate study. She taught elementary school in San Francisco for one year after college. She and her husband Carrell A. Peterson, M.D., retired, have two daughters and two sons and now live at 6801 Estates Drive, Oakland, California.

The Petersons' eldest child, Karin Ellen (b. July 16, 1948), received her B.A. from the University of California at Berkeley and her M.B.A. from UCLA. Married to Dennis D. Clark, she is the manager of market planning for the water division of McKesson Corporation in San Francisco. The Petersons' second daughter, Kathleen Ann, was born on October 13, 1949. She

269

attended Connecticut College and received her B.A. from the University of California at Berkeley, as well as a master's degree in art history, Asian studies, and English from Columbia University. A managing editor with Warren, Gorham & Lamont in New York City, she lives in Princeton, New Jersey with her husband Peter Trafford Hahn, daughter Julia Trafford (b. September 25, 1984), and son Peter Dickson (b. October 24, 1988).

The Petersons' third child, son J. Dickson Peterson, was born on November 9, 1954. He, too, is a graduate of the University of California at Berkeley (B.A. degree) and is the joint owner of Rock Transport Company of Oakland and Rite Away Ready Mix. He is married to Barbara Edelston. His brother Blair William Peterson (b. March 10, 1961) received his bachelor's degree from the University of California at Davis and is now the manager of maintenance and repair for North America, Triton International in San Francisco.

James Morrison Knapp

(1901–1987)

Nellie's son James pursued careers in geology, mining engineering, and construction in Mexico, China, Burma, and the Middle East.

Following his graduation from Sacramento High School in 1917, James served with the U.S. Army in England during World War I, flying open cockpit planes on patrol in France. (While stationed in England, he visited his grandfather T.P. Lannon at his farm in Ireland in 1918, '19, and '20.) After the war, he earned a Bachelor of Science degree at Case School of Applied Science in Cleveland, and on January 1, 1936, he married Esperanza Araquistain in Managua, Nicaragua, where he was working as a mining engineer for Bechtel Corporation.

James and Esperanza had four children: Lorenzo Charles, a cabinetmaker in Santa Fe, New Mexico; Deirdrie Louisa Marie del Carmine, a lieutenant colonel and administrator of the Nurses Division of the U.S. Air Force; Petra Esperanza, a graduate of Fullerton University, who became a nurse and is now a retired U.S. Army major living in Tustin, California; and Yvonne, who resides in Mexico.

Lucille Deirdrie Knapp

(1903–1976)

Nellie's youngest child, Lucille Deirdrie Knapp, was an alumna of San Francisco State College, taught music for thirty years in the Sacramento public schools (including Lincoln School at Fourth and O Streets), and played violin in the Sacramento Symphony Orchestra. She married her Irish third cousin, Michael Berrigan, and lived at 6660 Greenhaven Drive in

Sacramento.

Berrigan's emigration to the United States was sponsored by Deirdrie's mother Nellie. With their encouragement and Deirdrie's financial support, Michael received a bachelor's degree and a Master of Arts in education. After serving in the U.S. Army, teaching, and being a substitute principal for several years in various Sacramento public schools, he was assigned to an administrative position in the Sacramento City Unified School District.

The Berrigans owned a second home—"Ocean Marin"—in Dillon's Beach, Sonoma County, Lots 19, 20, and 22. After a brief illness, Deirdrie died of cancer on August 28, 1976 and is buried in St. Mary's Cemetery in Sacramento.

JULIA MCDERMOTT LANNON'S SIBLINGS

Winifred and Margaret McDermott

Julia's eldest sister Winifred stayed in Ireland, married Thomas McGreevey, and bore four children—Elizabeth (b. 1898), Winifred, Patrick, and John (who died at a young age). Winifred let her younger, childless sister Margaret (Mrs. James O'Rourke) raise Elizabeth in her home in America.

After graduating from Rhode Island College of Education with a teaching degree, Elizabeth married James Connolly, settled in Providence, and gave birth to one child, Maureen, in 1934. Widowed on April 24, 1974, Elizabeth lives in West Warwick, Rhode Island.

Her daughter Maureen graduated from Pembroke College (Brown University) in 1956 with a classics major. She received a master's degree in education in the early 1970s from Framingham State and taught in the Newton (MA) public schools until her death in 1988.

Maureen's husband, Travis Merritt, was raised in Plattsburgh, New York, where his father was superintendent of the public schools. Travis graduated from Williams College and received a Ph.D. in English from the University of Chicago. Today, he is Dean of Student Affairs and a professor of English literature at the Massachusetts Institute of Technology.

Maureen and Travis had four daughters. Grace Elizabeth (b.1958) graduated from Hobart and William Smith College in 1980 and worked for the *New Haven* (CT) *Register*. Currently a reporter for the *Hartford* (CT) *Courant*, she married Peter Celella in 1986. Lisa Clare Merritt (b.1960) is a 1984 graduate of Hamilton College and received an M.B.A. from Simmons College two years later. Today, she is a financial consultant with Digital Equipment Corporation. Amy Victoria Merritt (b.1964) graduated from

271

Lafayette College in 1986 and now works for the Tennis Industry Council at the United States Tennis Association in Princeton, New Jersey. The Merritts' youngest child, Susannah Connolly (b.1968), is currently a junior at Vassar College, majoring in English.

Roderick J. ("Roger") McDermott (1879–1960)

According to Elizabeth McGreevey Connolly, Julia Lannon's younger brother Roger was "a rascal" who emigrated to America to seek his fortune. He was born August 15, 1879 and baptized in the Diocese of Elphin, Parish of Iarmonbarry and Scramoque, Longford, Ireland. When he sailed for America, he left behind a wife and two daughters and never saw them again. He worked a number of years for the Southern Pacific Railroad Company in San Francisco and Sacramento, where he died in 1960 and was buried in East Lawn Cemetery.

James, John, and Mary McDermott

Julia's younger brother James made enough money in America to return to his homeland and buy a business. Another brother, John, remained in Ireland and helped sister Winifred operate the family farm. Elizabeth Connolly adds that Julia's older sister Mary Ann "married well, lived in Dublin, and had a boy."

Patrick Joseph Lannon in San
Francisco in the late 1880s

Mary Elo Owens Lannon
(Courtesy of James M. Knapp)

273

Elo Theresa Lannon

Julia, Patrick, and firstborn Marie, c. 1894

Julia Margaret Lannon

Joseph Martin Lannon

Ferdinand Henrietta
Lannon

Norma Winifred Lannon

276

Raymond James Lannon

Patrick and Julia in San Francisco, c. 1938

Tess Lannon Flanagan
and Edward J. Flanagan,
September 18, 1937
*(Courtesy of Edwin Wallace
Flanagan)*

Nellie Lannon Knapp
and Francis McCabe
Flanagan, July 1953
*(Courtesy of Edwin Wallace
Flanagan)*

Albert and Helen Becker with
daughter Connie, c. 1919
(Courtesy of Margaret Wright
Gallaway)

Connie Becker Wright in Sacramento, c. 1940s
(Courtesy of Margaret Wright Gallaway)

Frank Thomas Flanagan
(Courtesy of Margaret Wright Gallaway)

Maureen Connolly Merritt and Bill Grier in a Cambridge, Massachusetts cafe, May 6, 1988

THE LANNON FAMILY
Genealogical Tree of Elo Lannon Grier's Paternal Branch

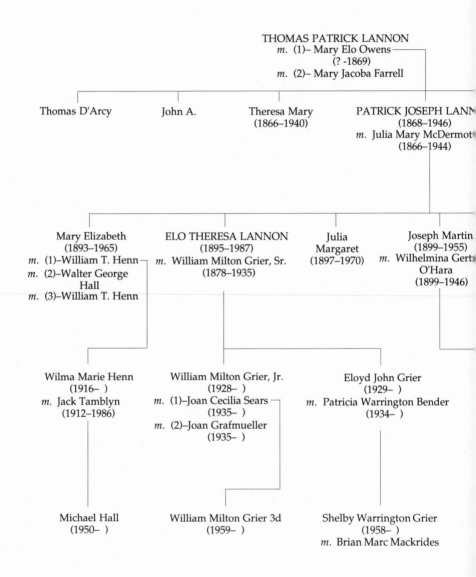

THOMAS PATRICK LANNON
m. (1)– Mary Elo Owens
(? -1869)
m. (2)– Mary Jacoba Farrell

Thomas D'Arcy   John A.   Theresa Mary   PATRICK JOSEPH LANN
(1866–1940)   (1868–1946)
m. Julia Mary McDermot
(1866–1944)

Mary Elizabeth   ELO THERESA LANNON   Julia   Joseph Martin
(1893–1965)   (1895–1987)   Margaret   (1899–1955)
m. (1)–William T. Henn   *m.* William Milton Grier, Sr.   (1897–1970)   *m.* Wilhelmina Gert
m. (2)–Walter George   (1878–1935)   O'Hara
Hall   (1899–1946)
m. (3)–William T. Henn

Wilma Marie Henn   William Milton Grier, Jr.   Eloyd John Grier
(1916–)   (1928–)   (1929–)
m. Jack Tamblyn   *m.* (1)–Joan Cecilia Sears   *m.* Patricia Warrington Bender
(1912–1986)   (1935–)   (1934–)
m. (2)–Joan Grafmueller
(1935–)

Michael Hall   William Milton Grier 3d   Shelby Warrington Grier
(1950–)   (1959–)   (1958–)
m. Brian Marc Mackrides

---

* *Died in infancy.*
** *Name changed from Langerak to Langton in 1923.*

Matilda Ellen
(1869–1955)

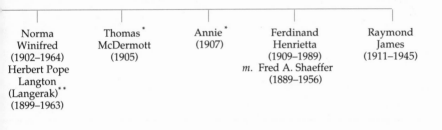

Norma	Thomas*	Annie*	Ferdinand	Raymond
Winifred	McDermott	(1907)	Henrietta	James
(1902–1964)	(1905)		(1909–1989)	(1911–1945)
Herbert Pope			*m.* Fred A. Shaeffer	
Langton			(1889–1956)	
(Langerak)**				
(1899–1963)				

Gerald Joseph
(1926–)

THE MCDERMOTT FAMILY
Genealogical Tree of Elo Lannon Grier's Maternal Branch

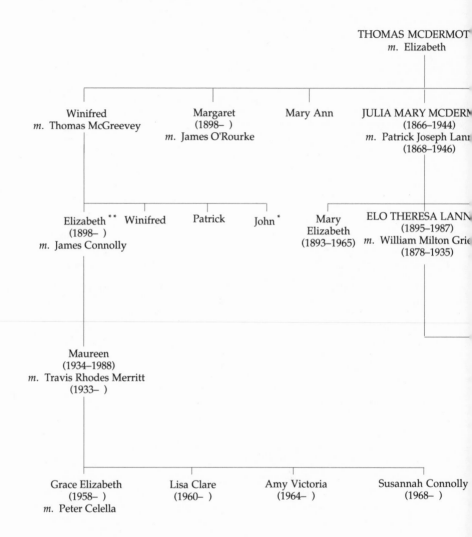

THOMAS MCDERMOT
m. Elizabeth

Winifred
m. Thomas McGreevey

Margaret
(1898–)
m. James O'Rourke

Mary Ann

JULIA MARY MCDERM
(1866–1944)
m. Patrick Joseph Lann
(1868–1946)

Elizabeth** Winifred
(1898–)
m. James Connolly

Patrick

John*

Mary
Elizabeth
(1893–1965)

ELO THERESA LANN
(1895–1987)
m. William Milton Grie
(1878–1935)

Maureen
(1934–1988)
m. Travis Rhodes Merritt
(1933–)

Grace Elizabeth
(1958–)
m. Peter Celella

Lisa Clare
(1960–)

Amy Victoria
(1964–)

Susannah Connolly
(1968–)

* *Died in infancy.*
** *Raised by her mother's sister and brother-in-law,*
Margaret McDermott and James O'Rourke, in Providence, Rhode Island.

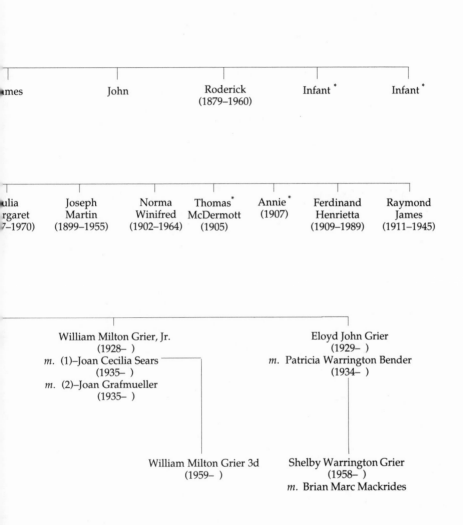

┌─────────┬──────────────┬─────────────┬────────────┬────────────┐
| ımes | John | Roderick | Infant * | Infant * |
| | | (1879–1960) | | |

ulia	Joseph	Norma	Thomas*	Annie *	Ferdinand	Raymond
rgaret	Martin	Winifred	McDermott	(1907)	Henrietta	James
7–1970)	(1899–1955)	(1902–1964)	(1905)		(1909–1989)	(1911–1945)

William Milton Grier, Jr.
(1928–)
m. (1)–Joan Cecilia Sears
(1935–)
m. (2)–Joan Grafmueller
(1935–)

Eloyd John Grier
(1929–)
m. Patricia Warrington Bender
(1934–)

William Milton Grier 3d
(1959–)

Shelby Warrington Grier
(1958–)
m. Brian Marc Mackrides

THE LANNON AND FLANAGAN FAMILIES

Genealogical Trees of Thomas D'Arcy Lannon and
Theresa M. Lannon (Mrs. Edward J. Flanagan)

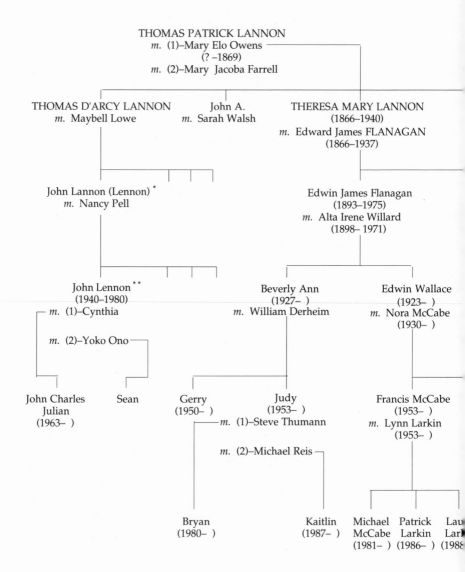

THOMAS PATRICK LANNON
m. (1)–Mary Elo Owens
(? –1869)
m. (2)–Mary Jacoba Farrell

THOMAS D'ARCY LANNON   John A.   THERESA MARY LANNON
m. Maybell Lowe   *m.* Sarah Walsh   (1866–1940)
m. Edward James FLANAGAN
(1866–1937)

John Lannon (Lennon) *
m. Nancy Pell

Edwin James Flanagan
(1893–1975)
m. Alta Irene Willard
(1898– 1971)

John Lennon **
(1940–1980)
m. (1)–Cynthia

Beverly Ann
(1927–)
m. William Derheim

Edwin Wallace
(1923–)
m. Nora McCabe
(1930–)

m. (2)–Yoko Ono

John Charles   Sean
Julian
(1963–)

Gerry
(1950–)

Judy
(1953–)
m. (1)–Steve Thumann

m. (2)–Michael Reis

Francis McCabe
(1953–)
m. Lynn Larkin
(1953–)

Bryan
(1980–)

Kaitlin
(1987–)

Michael   Patrick   Lau
McCabe   Larkin   Lar
(1981–)   (1986–)   (1988

---

* *Name changed from Lannon to Lennon in Liverpool, England (See Allied Family: Lannon)*
** *Member of the Beatles (See Allied Family: Lannon)*
*** *Adopted by Frederick P. Brousse*

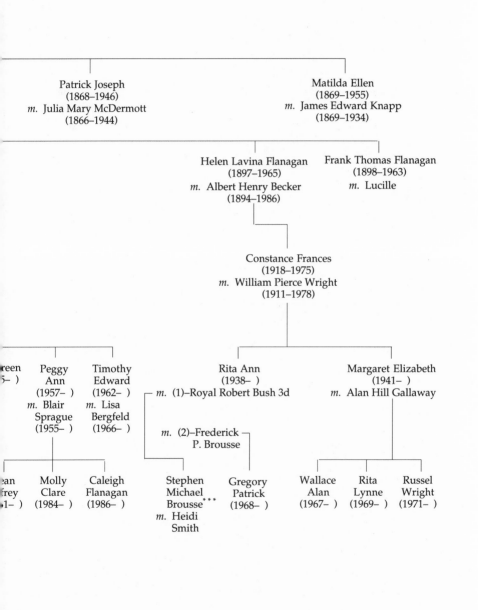

Patrick Joseph
(1868–1946)
m. Julia Mary McDermott
(1866–1944)

Matilda Ellen
(1869–1955)
m. James Edward Knapp
(1869–1934)

Helen Lavina Flanagan
(1897–1965)
m. Albert Henry Becker
(1894–1986)

Frank Thomas Flanagan
(1898–1963)
m. Lucille

Constance Frances
(1918–1975)
m. William Pierce Wright
(1911–1978)

een
5–)
m. Blair
Sprague
(1955–)

Peggy
Ann
(1957–)

Timothy
Edward
(1962–)
m. Lisa
Bergfeld
(1966–)

Rita Ann
(1938–)
m. (1)–Royal Robert Bush 3d

m. (2)–Frederick
P. Brousse

Margaret Elizabeth
(1941–)
m. Alan Hill Gallaway

an
frey
1–)

Molly
Clare
(1984–)

Caleigh
Flanagan
(1986–)

Stephen
Michael
Brousse***
m. Heidi
Smith

Gregory
Patrick
(1968–)

Wallace
Alan
(1967–)

Rita
Lynne
(1969–)

Russel
Wright
(1971–)

THE LANNON AND KNAPP FAMILIES
Genealogical Tree of Matilda Ellen Lannon
(Mrs. James E. Knapp)

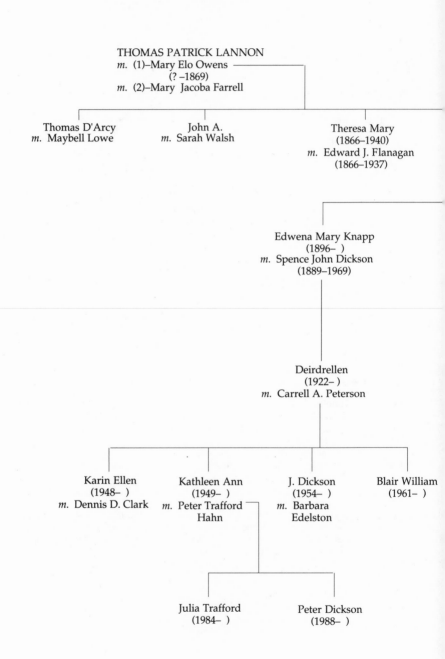

THOMAS PATRICK LANNON
m. (1)–Mary Elo Owens
(? –1869)
m. (2)–Mary Jacoba Farrell

Thomas D'Arcy
m. Maybell Lowe

John A.
m. Sarah Walsh

Theresa Mary
(1866–1940)
m. Edward J. Flanagan
(1866–1937)

Edwena Mary Knapp
(1896–)
m. Spence John Dickson
(1889–1969)

Deirdrellen
(1922–)
m. Carrell A. Peterson

Karin Ellen
(1948–)
m. Dennis D. Clark

Kathleen Ann
(1949–)
m. Peter Trafford
Hahn

J. Dickson
(1954–)
m. Barbara
Edelston

Blair William
(1961–)

Julia Trafford
(1984–)

Peter Dickson
(1988–)

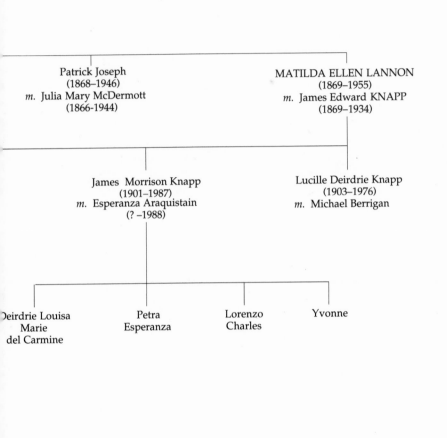

Patrick Joseph
(1868–1946)
m. Julia Mary McDermott
(1866-1944)

MATILDA ELLEN LANNON
(1869–1955)
m. James Edward KNAPP
(1869–1934)

James Morrison Knapp
(1901–1987)
m. Esperanza Araquistain
(? –1988)

Lucille Deirdrie Knapp
(1903–1976)
m. Michael Berrigan

Deirdrie Louisa
Marie
del Carmine

Petra
Esperanza

Lorenzo
Charles

Yvonne

27

GRAFMUELLER/BROWNLEE
DE RHAM/GLAZEBROOK

CHARLES EDWARD GRAFMUELLER (1902–1983)

Charles Edward ("Ed") Grafmueller—the father of William Milton Grier, Jr.'s second wife, Joan—was born in Manhattan in 1902. He grew up in Rutherford, New Jersey, and summered with his family in West Redding, Connecticut.[1]

Ed graduated in 1921 from Blair Academy, where he played tennis and was a pitcher on the baseball team. At the University of Pennsylvania, Ed was editor-in-chief of the *Red and Blue*, a monthly illustrated magazine, and started a pictorial rotogravure section for the *Daily Pennsylvanian* which featured Penn athletic events and players. A member of Sphinx Senior Society and Phi Delta Theta fraternity, he received his Bachelor of Science in economics from the Wharton School in 1925.

He began his career as a salesman for his father's firm, H. Boker & Company, in Manhattan. Within a year, however, he was lured to Wall Street, where he spent over fifty years and became managing partner and vice president of Riter, Pyne, Kendall and Hollister. He retired in the late 1970s.

Lean and handsome—over six-feet-four-inches tall—he was married three times, twice remarried after becoming a widower. He and his family resided in Greenwich, Connecticut for forty-three years and main-

---

1. Charles Edward Grafmueller's younger brother, Albert M. ("Fife"), also an alumnus of Blair Academy and the University of Pennsylvania, received a Bachelor of Science degree in economics from the Wharton School. He was a member of the Phi Delta Theta fraternity, an assistant editor of the *Daily Pennsylvanian* newspaper and the *Red and Blue* magazine, and a member of the tennis team. After graduating in 1928, he worked for eight years at R.H. Macy & Company in New York City, the last four as a merchandise buyer. He later established his own business in Manhattan as a manufacturer's representative serving retailers nationally. He retired in 1975.

Twice married, Fife has two daughters by his first wife: Patricia, a Wheaton College graduate who married Paul Buddenhagen and lives in Boston with her daughters Caroline and Eliza, and Rev. Mary Anne, an Episcopal minister at Grace Church, Broad Brook, Connecticut, who received a B.A. in psychology from Bennington College, a B.S. in nursing from the University of Massachusetts, and a Master of Divinity from Trinity Episcopal School for Ministry.

tained a winter home in St. Croix, Virgin Islands.

His father Edward (1864–1945) was with the firm of H. Boker & Company for fifty years until his retirement; he became vice president, general manager, and partner of this Newark, New Jersey firm, which manufactured and imported (from Solingen, Germany) cutlery and hardware.

Ed's mother was Katharine Margaret Plump (1877–1931), born in Old Harlem, as it was known then, in New York City. She and her husband are buried in the Grafmueller plot at Hillside Cemetery in Rutherford, New Jersey.

Katharine Plump had two sisters, Henrietta (known as Aunt Etta) and Anna (who never married and lived with the Grafmueller family). Her brother Charles Plump lived most of his life in Redding, Connecticut, just below the Grafmueller acreage.

Aunt Etta married John Zahn of Rutherford and persuaded the Grafmuellers to move there, as well. Her husband was president of the Rutherford National Bank and partner of Zahn and Bowlie, a glass business. His son J. Kenneth Zahn is still living in the family home in Rutherford, at age eighty-eight.

Katharine Plump's father was born in Germany, came to America at an early age, and ran a successful business manufacturing celluloid piano keys in Harlem; he died at seventy-five. Her mother Sophia Chord Plump lived with the Grafmuellers at 12 West 126th Street until she sold the brownstone residence and moved to Rutherford. She died in her ninetieth year, in 1929.

BARBARA ROSE BROWNLEE (1903–1939)

Ed Grafmueller's first wife, Barbara Rose Brownlee, was born in 1903, the eldest daughter of Dr. Harris Fenton Brownlee and Adelaide Dennis.[2] A second daughter, Janet, was born March 4, 1907 and died six years later of pernicious anemia. Their third daughter, named Adelaide, was born on June 8, 1917 and died in May of 1988.

A practicing physician in Danbury, Connecticut for thirty-seven years,[3] Dr. Brownlee had been born September 14, 1866 in Lawyersville,

---

2. Dr. Brownlee had three brothers: Eugene from Tryon, South Carolina; Clarence from Vancouver, British Columbia; and Clayton from Birmingham, Alabama.

3. In the early 1930s, Dr. Brownlee performed an appendectomy on a student at Connecticut's Choate School who, three decades later, became America's thirty-fifth president—John F. Kennedy.

New York; his wife was born June 8, 1880 in Newark, New Jersey. Her Dennis ancestors were among the first settlers of Newark and became prominent in banking, commercial, and professional circles in New Jersey. The family later donated the Dennis Library in Newton.

Barbara graduated from Miss Porter's School in Farmington, Connecticut and Finch College in New York City. She and Ed had met in Danbury, Connecticut and were married there in 1926 at St. James Episcopal Church.

Their only child, Joan, was born in New York City on September 21, 1935 and was three-and-a-half years old when Barbara died of a brain tumor on August 28, 1939. Barbara was buried with her own family in Wooster Cemetery in Danbury, Connecticut.

EDITH COLBY DE RHAM (1905–1973)

Edith ("Edie") Colby de Rham was Ed Grafmueller's second wife. Her father Everett Colby was a New Jersey state senator for three terms and the grandson of the founder of Colby College in Maine. He graduated from Brown University, where he roomed with John D. Rockefeller, Jr.

Edith attended day school in West Orange, New Jersey and graduated from Foxcroft School in 1923. Her sister Ann married William Vanderbilt, former governor of Rhode Island and, in retirement, lived in Williamstown, Massachusetts.

Edith's first husband was Henry Longfellow de Rham, a relative of poet Henry Wadsworth Longfellow. The de Rhams had two children. Son Charles, born in January 1929, graduated from Kent School in 1947 and Harvard University in 1956 and served in the Marines. Their daughter Edith ("Edie"), born in September of 1933, is an alumna of Vassar College, Class of '55.

Edith and Ed Grafmueller were married in 1942 at her mother's home in Llewellyn Park, New Jersey. Some thirty years later, in 1973, Edith died of cancer, leaving Ed a widower for a second time.

EMILY GLAZEBROOK PIERSON (1913–1986)

Ed married his third wife, Emily Glazebrook Pierson, widow of Morton Norris ("Norrie") Pierson, on May 18, 1974 in St. Luke's Parish, Darien, Connecticut.

Born in Elizabeth, New Jersey, Emily was educated at Kent Place School for Girls in Summit, New Jersey and at Stuart Hall in Staunton, Virginia. Her mother was Emily Holmes Robinson; her father, Haslett

McKim Glazebrook. She had three brothers—Francis Page, Haslett McKim, and Thomas Spotwood—and a sister, Louise Robinson (Mrs. Nason).

Emily married her first husband on March 14, 1936 in Basking Ridge, New Jersey. Norrie was head of personnel of refinery operations in Australia, South Africa, and Greece for Standard Vacuum Oil Company; he died on January 11, 1972.

After marrying Ed Grafmueller two years later and moving to Greenwich, Connecticut, Emily was active in the community, particularly at the Nathaniel Witherell Hospital.

Less than nine years after Ed and Emily were married, he suffered a fatal heart attack while in St. Croix on March 29, 1983. His ashes were placed in the family plot in Hillside Cemetery, Rutherford, New Jersey. Three years later, on August 22, 1986, Emily died of cancer in Greenwich; her ashes are in St. Luke's Parish, Darien, Connecticut.

Barbara Rose Brownlee
(Courtesy of Joan Grafmueller Grier)

Charles Edward Grafmueller, c. 1940
(Courtesy of Joan Grafmueller Grier)

Ed Grafmueller in Redding,
Connecticut, c. 1921
(Courtesy of Joan Grafmueller Grier)

Joan Grafmueller, 1936
(Courtesy of Joan Grafmueller Grier)

Joan in Danbury, Connecticut, 1940
(Courtesy of Joan Grafmueller Grier)

296

At the wedding of Joan Grier's cousin William Bingham Bolton to Katherine Howard, May 7, 1988, Marblehead, Massachusetts. *From left*, Joan Grier, Nicholas and Polly Lampshire; David R. Williams, Jr.; Kenyon C. Bolton 3d; Bill Grier (*Photo by Julie Dempsey Cox*)

28

SEARS

Joan Cecilia Sears, William Milton Grier, Jr.'s first wife, was the granddaughter of Nathan and Rose Sesarsky, Russian Jews who emigrated to New York City in the 1890s. The Sesarskys later moved to Hartford, Connecticut, where their two sons, David M. (Joan's father) and Nathan E. ("Ned"), were born on November 30, 1896 and December 24, 1899, respectively.

David Sesarsky graduated from the Columbia University School of Pharmacy on May 16, 1918, while Ned attended Fordham University's School of Pharmacy from 1923 to 1925. Both men eventually changed their surnames to Sears—David on October 19, 1923 in the State of Connecticut Superior Court in Bridgeport (Docket #19631) and Nathan on September 19, 1924 in the same court (Docket #21128). Judge Francis D. Haines presided in both cases, and David and Nathan were represented by Edward J. Lang.

David Sears and his wife Edna Cotter had one child, Joan Cecilia, born on July 3, 1935 in Bridgeport, Connecticut. Ned remained a bachelor. The Sears brothers were partners, owners, and operators of two drug stores in Devon and Stratford, Connecticut. After his retirement, Ned built a home in Milford, Connecticut, where he died in his eighties.

BIBLIOGRAPHY

The author's documents, photographs, and memorabilia and a computer disk of this text are available in the William Milton Grier Collection at The Bancroft Library, University of California at Berkeley.

BOOKS

Bancroft, Hubert H. *A History of California*. San Francisco: History Co., 1886–1890.

A Brief Historical Sketch of the California Heavy Artillery, U.S.V., and the Operations of Batteries A and D in the Philippine Islands. San Francisco: Patriotic Publishing Co., 1898.

Bronson, William. *The Earth Shook —The Sky Burned*. New York: Doubleday & Co., 1959.

Brown, John Henry. *Reminiscences and Incidents of the Early Days of San Francisco*. San Francisco: Grabhorn Press, 1933.

Burgess, Gelett. *Bayside Bohemia*. San Francisco: Book Club of California, 1954.

Burlingame, San Mateo, Hillsborough, and Millbrae City Directories. San Mateo, California: Coast Directory Co., 1946–1947.

California's Tribute to the Nation. San Francisco: Patriotic Publishing Co., 1898.

De Russailh, Albert Benard. *Last Adventure*. San Francisco: The Westgate Press, 1931.

Faust, Karl Irving. *Campaigning in the Philippines*. San Francisco: Hicks-Judd Co., 1899.

First to the Front: First California U.S. Volunteers. San Francisco: Patriotic Publishing Co., 1898.

Flight of the Eagle. San Francisco: Patriotic Publishing Co., 1898.

Hittell, John S. *A History of San Francisco*. San Francisco: A.L. Bancroft & Co., 1878.

Husted's Oakland, Berkeley and Alameda Directories. Oakland, California: Polk-Husted Directory Co., 1908–1934.

Irwin, Will. *The City That Was*. New York: W.B. Huebsch, 1906.

James, Marquis and Bessie R. *Biography of a Bank : The Story of Bank of America N.T. & S.A.* New York: Harper Bros., 1954.

Kipling, Rudyard. *Rudyard Kipling's Letters from San Francisco*. San Francisco: Colt Press, 1949.

Langley's San Francisco Directories. San Francisco: Directory Publishing Co., 1878–1888, 1899–1929.

Levison, J.B. *Memories for My Family*. San Francisco: privately printed, 1933.

Lewis, Oscar and Hall, Carroll D. *Bonanza Inn, America's First Luxury Hotel*. New York: Alfred A. Knopf, 1939.

Maybeck, Bernard R. *Palace of Fine Arts and Lagoon*. San Francisco: Paul Elder & Co., 1915.

Osbourne, Katharine D. *Robert Louis Stevenson in California*. Chicago: A.C. McClurg & Co., 1911.

Portland City Directories. Portland, Oregon: R.L. Polk & Co., 1906–1921.

Prieto, Guillermo. *San Francisco in the Seventies*. San Francisco: John Henry Nash, 1938.

Reedy, William Marion. *The City That Has Fallen*. San Francisco: Book Club of California, 1933.

Sacramento City and County Directories. San Francisco: McKenney Directory Co., 1888–1935.

Shapiro, Nat, ed. *Popular Music, 1930–1939: An Annotated Index of American Popular Songs*. New York: Adrian Press, 1964–1973.

Stetson, James B. *San Francisco During the Eventful Days of April, 1906.* San Francisco: privately printed, 1906.

Stevens, John Grier. *The Descendants of John Grier with Histories of Allied Families: A Biographical and Genealogical Record.* Baltimore, 1964.

Writers' Program of the Work Projects Administration in Northern California. *San Francisco: The Bay and Its Cities.* 2d rev. ed. New York: Hastings House Publishers, 1947.

MAGAZINES

Dana, Marshall N. "The Celilo Canal—Its Origin—Its Building and Meaning." *Oregon Historical Society Quarterly,* June 1915.

DeNeffe, Frederick M. "The Mysterious Shoe-String Railroad." *Oregon Historical Society Quarterly,* September 1956.

Dope Bucket: The Spokane, Portland and Seattle's Golden Jubilee Issue (a publication of the Spokane, Portland and Seattle Railroad Company), March 1958.

Dope Bucket: The Spokane, Portland and Seattle's Gold Spike Issue (a publication of the Spokane, Portland and Seattle Railroad Company), 1961.

George, M.C. "Address Delivered at Dedication of Grand Ronde Military Block House at Dayton City Park, Oregon, Aug. 23, 1912." *Oregon Historical Society Quarterly,* March 1914.

McCall, E. Kimbark. "The Growth of a City." *Oregon Historical Society Quarterly* (n.d.).

Mills, Randall V. "Prineville's Municipal Railroad in Central Oregon." *Oregon Historical Society Quarterly,* September 1941.

Official Journal of the British North America Philatelic Society, September 1965.

Rutherford, Frank. "Palermo Chronicles." *The Palermo Progress,* October 17, 1890. Reprinted in Butte County (California) Historical Society's *Diggin's,* Fall 1974.

303

Stindt, Fred A. "Peninsular Service: The Story of the Southern Pacific Commuter Trains." *Western Railroader* 20 (1957).

Teal, Joseph N. "Address of Joseph N. Teal." *Oregon Historical Society Quarterly*, June 1915.

NEWSPAPERS

Bathurst (Ontario) *Courier*. October 29, 1852; July 25, 1862; May 17, 1867.

Brockville (Ontario) *Times*. *May 11, 1892; April 11, 1908*.

CalReport: A Newspaper for Selected Alumni and Friends of the University of California in Berkeley, November 1987.

Lead (South Dakota) *Daily Call*. September 23, 25, 26, and 28, 1914; September 28, 1916.

Montreal Daily Standard. September 28, 1925.

Montreal Gazette. November 26, 1946.

Montreal Standard. May 6, 1911.

New York World-Telegram and Sun. March 17, 1956.

Oakland (California) *Post Enquirer*. November 26, 1926.

San Francisco Call. April 18, 1906.

San Francisco Chronicle. August 25, 26, and 27, 1899; April 18, 1906.

San Francisco Daily News. April 18, 1906.

San Francisco Examiner. April 19, 1906.

NAME INDEX

INDIVIDUALS ARE CROSS-REFERENCED UNDER NAMES IN PARENTHESES;
PRINCIPAL ENTRIES ARE INDICATED BY ITALICS. REFERENCES TO
ILLUSTRATIONS ARE PRINTED IN BOLDFACE TYPE.

311

314

315

SUBJECT INDEX

318

319

188845